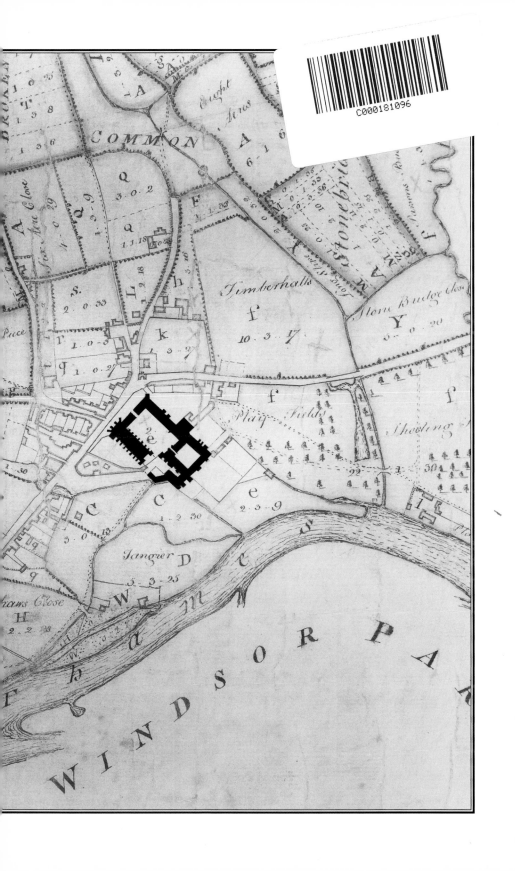

Eton Established

By the same author
Eton Renewed: A History from 1860 to the Present Day

Eton Established

A History
from 1440 to 1860

Tim Card

JOHN MURRAY
Albemarle Street, London

Endpapers: Details from a map of Eton
by Richard Burfield, 1797

© Tim Card 2001

First published in 2001
by John Murray (Publishers) Ltd,
50 Albemarle Street, London W1S 4BD

A catalogue record for this book is available from the British Library.

ISBN 0-7195-6052 7

Typeset in 11/13 Garamond by Servis Filmsetting Ltd, Manchester

Printed and bound in Great Britain by Butler & Tanner Ltd,
Frome and London

For Jenny and Antony Acland

Contents

Illustrations

Preface and Acknowledgements

IN 1984 THE Provost and Fellows authorized David Macindoe, the Vice-Provost, and Archie Nicholson, a retired Housemaster, to write an official history of Eton College up to 1963, the year in which Robert Birley retired as Head Master. The intention was to emphasize the more recent period, since an authoritative Victorian history of Eton College had been written by Sir Henry Maxwell-Lyte. Sadly both men died before their time, and it fell to me, their successor as Vice-Provost, to take up their task. With intimations of mortality before me, I determined to write a history from 1860 on to 1990: *Eton Renewed*. The year 1860 was a natural starting point, on the eve of the Royal Commission examining the Public Schools. It was also where Maxwell-Lyte's work became more sketchy.

When *Eton Renewed* was published in 1994, it sold well enough to encourage me to go back in time and to cover Eton's origin in 1440 and development to a school of some 800 boys in 1860. There was enough new scholarly work on the reign of Henry VI to make it desirable to reassess the history of the foundation. In later centuries rather more material has accumulated to permit a fuller picture to be painted of boys' lives. Also there has inevitably been some change in educational perspectives. Consequently I am hoping that even those who have read Maxwell-Lyte will find what I have to say new, stimulating and accessible. Naturally enough, Eton developed with considerable changes over the years, but even in 1860, it was a very different place from Eton of 2000. In a final chapter I have tried to put some of these developments into a modern perspective, but throughout the narrative the reader will have glimpses of what Eton was to become. Those who are beginning at the beginning – unlike the author – should be encouraged to read *Eton Renewed* to see how the School that seemed so established in 1860 was yet able to change, without losing its position, to what it is today.

The reader will observe that Eton is referred to as the School and its teachers as Masters, using capital letters, whereas other schools have masters. This is not Etonian arrogance: it is rather to help the reader know what is under discussion. I have been less consistent in imposing uniformity where the titles of the same position changed, and this may require reference to the Glossary which follows the main text. I have also sometimes preserved the spelling of an original letter to give a period flavour, or an impression of a young and hasty author; at other times I have modernized for ease of reading.

The Provost and Fellows trusted me to use the Eton archives, and I was much helped in this task by Penny Hatfield, the College Archivist. I am also most grateful to Michael Meredith, the College Librarian, and his assistants, first Linda Fowler, then Nick Baker. Sir John Smith provided me with a copy of the recollections of Oswald Augustus Smith. My sister, Petronella Macnaghten, found in the nick of time some letters owned by her late husband, Robin Macnaghten. Roger Hudson, David Evans, Robert Franklin and Tim Connor read all or parts of the draft and offered advice, most of which I gratefully accepted, but they should not be blamed for shortcomings that remain. I am particularly grateful to Professor Euan Cameron who looked over the history of the first two hundred years, and saved me from several errors, while at the same time giving me the confidence to write about the historical background of the College's foundation; he too should not be faulted for my judgements. Finally my thanks to Pippa McCullough and Irene Watling, who struggled to reduce my unruly script and many erasures to an acceptable typescript.

CHAPTER ONE

King Henry VI and the Foundation of Eton

KING HENRY VI has for many years been regarded as probably the most inept King that ever ruled England. 'A saintly muff' was a characteristic verdict, suggesting a mixture of fool and monk unsuited to his rough times.[1] His foundations of Eton and King's College, Cambridge, were seen as golden aberrations from a story of general incompetence. Surely historians would find a case for a more favourable revision? But no – since 1981, when biographies by Griffiths and Wolffe appeared, the King's character has been seen in even harsher light; and Watts, the latest historian to write of his reign, regards it not so much like that of a weak housemaster unable to control self-seeking and undisciplined prefects, as like that of a housemaster whose prefects, aware that their authority derives from him, contrive for as long as possible to cover up for his inadequacies until they are driven into almost inevitable dispute. The King's educational foundations are seen as little more than chance survivors of grandiose and unrealistic schemes developed by a capricious monarch, or even possibly as the work of men in the King's household who managed to associate the King with what were essentially their own projects.

Certainly the King's character is something of an enigma, its true nature obscured by the idealistic memoir of him, composed by John Blakman, who may have been his Chaplain, from which the Provost piously reads to Etonians on Founder's Day. It is also hard to see how Henry evolved into someone so different from his exceptionally successful father.

Henry was born at Windsor to Queen Catherine of Valois, whom Henry V had married, establishing himself thereby as Regent and heir to the kingdom of France. The date, St Nicholas's Day, 6 December 1421, may have been significant, for St Nicholas is the patron saint of children (as well as of sailors, thieves and town clerks). A precious relic, Our Lord's foreskin, was brought across from France to assist at the birth. The happy news of an heir was conveyed to the King in France, but the King was never in fact to see his child. Within nine months he was dead of dysentery. Two months later Charles VI of France, the boy's grandfather, died, and thus before his first birthday Henry VI was King of both England and France.

A contemporary copy of King Henry V's Will, together with codicils added when he knew he was mortally ill, was discovered in Eton College Library in 1978;[2] until then the contents had been uncertain. By the codicils, Humphrey, Duke of Gloucester, his younger brother, was made the Warden of England and guardian to the child. John, Duke of Bedford, the elder brother, was entrusted at the deathbed with maintaining the French dominions. One other relative, Henry Beaufort, Bishop of Winchester and later Cardinal, the second of three illegitimate sons of John of Gaunt and thus the child's great-uncle, was only an executor to the Will, but he was also to play a significant role.

These arrangements did not in fact last long. Bedford asserted his right as an elder brother to be Regent of England as well as of France. Beaufort became in practice the most powerful figure of the Council established to rule during the young King's minority. Gloucester was left disaffected, recurrently feuding with Beaufort, his influence as a scholarly patron of learning only spasmodically available to the child.

Queen Catherine had been in France with her husband when he died, but returned with his corpse, and was in charge of the boy until he was seven. But shortly before he reached that age, she secretly married Owen Tudor, a Welsh gentleman, and any influence she might have had on her son was lost. He had been given a governess, Lady Alice Butler, to train him ('with license to chastise Us reasonably from time to time') and some companions, other noble orphans. In 1428 she was succeeded by the highly regarded Richard Beauchamp, Earl of Warwick, whose job was to make the King literate and a competent linguist. He was also allowed to punish the

King for any disobedience or other misbehaviour. He appears to have had the help of a tutor, John Somerset, who was also the royal physician and a well-educated man by the standards of the times.

At the end of 1429 Henry was crowned at Westminster Abbey, and the next year he was also crowned at Notre Dame in Paris, in an attempt to shore up the English position in France which was under attack from Joan of Arc and Charles VII, recently and more properly crowned at Rheims. The King bore the physical ordeal of these two exhausting ceremonies remarkably well: he was apparently a tough schoolboy.

By Henry's eleventh birthday, the Earl of Warwick was finding him hard to control and had to secure extra powers from the Council. The Council meanwhile was struggling with financial difficulties, in particular the expense of defending the French kingdom. Financial stringency, a problem which would remain with Henry, did indeed cause the Court to save money by spending the beginning of 1434 at the monastery of Bury St Edmunds. Later that year Bedford and Gloucester were again at odds and the 12-year-old Henry found himself required to reconcile them. He appears to have been eager to take up an active role, and when Bedford died in 1435 he became more or less continuously involved in questions of government. In November 1437, when he was still not quite 16, his initiation into the affairs of state was completed, and his personal rule began.

Up to this point he might have been regarded as a promising boy, but soon psychological problems became evident. Various visitors to the Court spoke of his immaturity, and the history of his reign supports them. It is sometimes hard for a boy to grow up without an adult male model; it is also sometimes difficult for a son to have a very successful father. Henry suffered in both ways. He may have looked for support to his very orthodox Catholicism, as the young nowadays may look to fundamentalism in religion as a guide. Henry was also orthodox in his hostility to Lollardy. He was not a man of simple faith, eschewing ceremony, as is sometimes supposed; a Portuguese visitor has left a record of impressive rituals. He was entirely of his time in holding the view that salvation could be acquired along with ownership of holy relics, or by means of masses continued after one's death.

The foundation of Eton, together with the foundation of King's, was to be described in a document of 1448 called the King's 'will' (or intention) as 'the primer notable work purposed by me after that I took unto myself the rule of my said Realms'.[3] This work was very much religious in inspiration. In a Charter addressed to the parishioners of Eton in 1446,[4] Henry described his intention to pay especial honour to the Blessed Virgin and to establish a church dedicated to the glorious festival of the Assumption.* His eyes had fallen (quite literally, from his favourite home, Windsor) on the church at Eton, because, although it was very poor and humble, it was dedicated 'under the name of the Assumption of the Most Blessed Virgin, to which feast we are very much attached'. An additional attraction may have been that its chantry was dedicated to St Nicholas.†

By 1439, the King had acquired the advowson of Eton and installed his own man as Rector, and on 11 October 1440 he issued the Charter by which he founded Eton College. Two days later Commissioners of the Bishop of Lincoln, whose diocese extended south to Eton, 'raised, transformed and converted' the parish church into 'the Collegiate Church of the Blessed Mary of Eton next to Windsor'.

There was nothing unusual in the foundation of colleges by rich men at this time. The church would be under the charge of a corporate body rather than a priest, and thus able to hold property and raise its own revenue. The main purpose of a college would be to offer prayers and masses for the founder and anyone else he might name. Attached to the church might commonly be a choir, a grammar school, an almshouse. Education was now regarded as a good work for the laity; it had long ceased to be a monastic preserve. The most elementary schools taught reading and singing, perhaps under local priests. Grammar schools gave training in Latin language, and provided the essential basis for continuing to study Law or Theology. There were also 'business schools' which taught letter-writing, together with Accountancy and Law, and some French. Some further education was also carried on in schools attached to cathedrals or religious orders. Eton was to be a grammar school.

---

* The doctrine of the Assumption, that Mary did not die but was bodily received into heaven, originated in the Eastern Church in the eighth century, and had been generally adopted in the West by the twelfth century.

† This was probably founded in 1375 by the widow of a London fishmonger who had dealt in dried cod. Masses would have been sung for the souls of the two of them.

Typically there were five to ten such schools open to boys in a county.[5]

The King's original Charter is quite conventional,[6] though the College was designed to be more substantial than most. There were a Provost, ten Fellows, four Clerks, six choristers, a Schoolmaster with twenty-five poor and indigent scholars, and twenty-five poor and infirm men. Masses and prayers were to be said for the King and his father and mother (who had died at the beginning of 1437). A Provost, Henry Sever, was inducted and appointed Rector of Eton, the temporary incumbent of the parish soon becoming a Fellow. Envoys were dispatched to secure the Pope's approval. From 1441, property was transferred to the College, mainly from what were known as the alien priories, subordinate cells in England of abbeys in France, which had been effectively nationalized during the reign of Henry V. There was no distinction between the King's wealth and what would now be thought of as the State's. Henry V had used some of this wealth to finance religious foundations at Sheen and Syon, and there was some perceived obligation to continue to use it charitably.

It is certainly possible that there was a school serving local boys attached to the old chantry. This would have been quite normal. Two scholars are named in the 1440 Charter, and other boys could have made use of the free schooling provided as day boys. Be that as it may, in 1444 two rooms and a house were erected at one end of the church for the school.

During the 1440s, however, Henry's plans developed dramatically in two directions. The more remarkable, but ultimately less important, conception was that Eton should become a centre of pilgrimage, second, if at all, only to Canterbury. Sir Robert Birley believed it possible that the Blessed Virgin of Eton was venerated even before the foundation of the College.[7] Certainly Thomas Bekynton, Archdeacon of Buckingham and Secretary to the King, finding himself becalmed in the Bay of Biscay in July 1441, vowed to make an offering to the Blessed Virgin of Eton, and persuaded his fellow-travellers to join him in an antiphon in her honour: after this, a favourable wind sprang up. Bekynton was one of a team who were helping Henry develop his plans, and might therefore have been thinking of the future rather than of a pre-existing veneration. Before July 1441, the King had decided that a new church would be needed for the pilgrims, and already the foundation stone had been laid – probably on 5 June, since that date was referred to subsequently as 'Dedicacion day', on which the workmen on the church had a paid holiday. Pilgrims had to be attracted, of course, and by the end of May the King had also secured from the Pope a bull granting indulgences to penitents who visited the Church of the Blessed Mary of Eton on the Feast of the Assumption (15 August). An ordinary indulgence replaced the penances which a penitent's confessor had imposed for sins committed: when the penitent died he would reach heaven after a shorter period in Purgatory. In 1442 the Pope made the indulgences plenary, which would secure those who died with their sins confessed immediate entry to heaven (though many theologians at the time questioned this). The licence to grant plenary indulgences was limited to the King's lifetime; in return three-quarters of the offerings of the pilgrims was to go to finance the defence of Christendom against the Turks, with the rest helping the building of the College. In 1443, Henry dispatched Dr Vincent Clement to Rome to ask for yet more, that the indulgences should be made perpetual, so that Eton could become a permanent centre for pilgrimages. The ambassador had to work hard and long, and spend a good deal; Henry grew impatient: 'When shall we hear news of Master Vincent?' he asked daily, according to Bekynton. In 1444 the required bull reached England, making the indulgences perpetual. Henry was so delighted that he spared the life of Thomas Carver of Reading, who had rashly criticized Henry's lack of martial prowess – but not before Carver had undergone part of the ritual of a traitor's death. A further bull in 1447 conferred some powers to grant absolution to visitors at other times than the Feast of the Assumption.

Meanwhile Henry acquired an astonishing collection of relics and plate for the College. Two lists survive, compiled in 1445 and in 1465.[8] Besides fragments of the True Cross,* of the Crown of Thorns, of nails, scourge and spear, there was a silver ampulla full of Our Lord's blood, a piece of Our Lady's thumb, and relics of many other saints. The splendour of all these treasures can only be guessed at; the reliquary in the shape of the Virgin under a tabernacle weighed 64 lbs. Some must have been beautiful in themselves, as for

---

* The College was offered a fragment of the True Cross in the 1970s. This was declined.

instance the image of the Virgin sitting in a vineyard, made of gold, but with eighty clusters of white pearls to represent the grapes. A letter from a French sculptor survives, asking £15 for 2,000 leaves of fine gold for an image of the Virgin of the Assumption; he needed the money quickly if the statue was to be ready for the next Feast, when crowds would come wanting to see it.[9]

Crowds did indeed come, even though the College Audit Rolls show that receipts from the pilgrims were disappointing. Perhaps fewer came than were expected, or they were less generous. Expenditure on wafer bread, however, increased. In 1445, the College needed to hire thirty extra beds for confessors at the Feast. Difficulties were inevitably caused for the townspeople, who had to lodge workmen and builders as well as the pilgrims. The 1446 Charter to the town of Eton accordingly allowed the townspeople of Eton two annual fairs, one at the beginning of Lent and the other on the days following the Feast of the Assumption, and the field now known as Upper Club was purchased as a suitable location. Merrymaking no doubt went on at the fairs, and in 1448 an inquest tells of a drunk falling into the Thames. Other evidence has been turned up only recently: metal detectors have brought to light from Thames mud in London badges to be worn by the pilgrims.

The College not only needed more land; it needed a bigger staff, for example more singers to take the male voices in the Choir; and then it needed a bigger church. Thus Henry set in hand the building of a new church and, as a temporary measure, extended the parish church – which cannot have been all that small, since Bekynton was consecrated Bishop of Bath and Wells there in October 1443 (and two other consecrations were to follow). In fact, up to 1460 more money was spent on repairing the old church than on building the new. Henry's first plan for his new church was simple, but the pilgrims needed more confessors, and therefore more altars, as well as more space altogether. To this requirement was added Henry's desire to exceed any rival so far built, evidenced by workmen sent out to make comparative measurements of other buildings. Consequently the architectural history of the Church, or College Chapel as we now know it, is extraordinarily complex.

Eton was not in any case an easy site on which to build. It was a Saxon town on an island, straddling a road which ran from the Windsor Bridge to Baldwin's Bridge, across what is now known as Barnes Pool, then a substantial arm of the Thames.* North of Baldwin's Bridge there were further buildings in what is now the heart of the College. That was where the Church stood, and just beyond it was the site of the College. This part also would be at times an island and was certainly swampy. Thus a first task was to 'enhance' or raise the level of the ground on which the College was to be built, and then further to raise the level of the new church. Whereas brick would suffice for most of the College buildings, the Church had to be of stone, at first brought from Caen by boat to Fellow's Eyot. But losses of territory in France soon stopped that source, and the stone came instead from Yorkshire and Taynton on the Oxfordshire–Gloucestershire border. It was nearing completion as a simple chancel when, by the King's 'will' of 1448,[10] a choir and nave were planned. But almost at once the King wished to build bigger, and thus required the destruction of what had already been built. Then in January 1449, the Clerk of Works was sent to measure the cathedrals of Winchester and Salisbury, with the result that a fourth and final plan, known as 'the kynges owne avyse', was produced. One can imagine a few Anglo-Saxon expressions from those who had worked on the first structure. This fourth, cathedral-sized building was never completed, and the existing College Chapel is only its choir. Some of the foundations could be retained, and stonework could be reused, most evidently in the arch of the present east window, which does not fit into the available space since, a decade or so later, the builders tried to adapt recycled straight stones to a curved frame. Although some historians have reckoned that the rebuilding can be explained by problems with the foundations, or by a change in the accepted architectural style, it is more probable that a megalomaniac streak in the King was responsible, justified in part by the success up to this point of his schemes for attracting pilgrims; why else should he have been concerned to outdo rival churches? Such shifts of plan, together with the lack of practical sense, are also found in his other policies.†

---

* The rather stagnant water was covered over in the nineteenth century, some time after a boy drowned in it (1822). The name Baldwin's Shore, still used for a house that accommodates bachelor Masters, indicates Baldwin's sewer, rather than a riverside pleasance.

† The various changes of plan have troubled historians. Willis and Clark assumed that the Chapel begun in 1441 was described in the first of various documents of 1448/9. The chancel is there said to be 103 feet long and 32 feet

The King's ambitions for the School within the College grew also. In August 1441 he visited Winchester for the first time, and realized that what he had so far envisaged was far short of what existed there. Winchester had seventy scholars, Eton only twenty-five. Winchester was linked to and fed New College, Oxford; King's was founded a year later than Eton, but probably only linked to Eton after a change of plan in 1443. (In February 1441 the King had granted lands of the alien priory at Ogbourne to support five Etonians at Oxford.) Some men, such as Bekynton and the Earl of Suffolk, appeared in both the teams of trustees that implemented King Henry's foundations, but others did not. The dominant figure at Cambridge, John Langton, was not part of the Eton team. One can only guess that Bekynton, who had been educated at Winchester and who was undoubtedly ardent for education (his diocese was later especially noted for the high standard of its priests), urged Henry to visit Winchester. This led to the King's changing his College to something closer to Winchester, but a little grander, and to his establishing a tie between Eton and King's, as William of Wykeham had done between Winchester and New College. Furthermore he was so impressed by William Waynflete, the headmaster of Winchester, that he attracted him to be Provost, to Eton's great advantage. Henry Sever went back to Oxford and became Warden of Merton College. At this point the links between Eton and Winchester were so close that in 1444 an alliance known as the '*Amicabilis Concordia*' was established between Winchester and New College on the one hand, and Eton and King's on the other. There is no doubt that Eton benefited from Winchester, and that Eton fed King's. In fact Millington, Provost of King's, disliked the

---

wide. Possibly, however, this was merely the first of many revised plans, and the original church was distinctly smaller. The King's various enlargements may simply have been characteristic of the medieval wish to outdo others in piety. Nevertheless, there is clearly a possibility that the first building failed because of inadequate foundations on damp ground. The 'avyse' lays down specific directions for the new lower courses, perhaps to guard against further failure. There is also no provision for a stone roof: possibly this would not have stood up, particularly because of its low pitch and relative width. It is also possible that the plainer style of English Gothic evident in Oxford building since 1440 appealed to the King. Roger Keys, Warden of All Souls, was appointed 'Master of the Works' in 1448. The King's 'will' urges the avoidance of 'curiouse werkes of entaille and besy moldying'. These possibilities are discussed in the *History of the King's Works* by R.A. Brown and H.M. Colvin (1963).

provisions in the King's College Statutes that required him to take his scholars from Eton, and that gave the College independence from the jurisdiction of the Chancellor of Cambridge University. He showed remarkable foresight, but he was deprived of his job for his resistance.[11] Scholars of Eton went to King's, but there was to be little traffic back from King's to Eton until the eighteenth century. Eton was influenced more by Oxford than by Cambridge, perhaps quite simply because it was easier to reach Oxford. Certain Kingsmen who have been appalled to think that their College was harnessed at its birth to Eton may be comforted to think that the link was rather less strong than is generally supposed.

In 1443 the School at Eton grew. Eton's school buildings were of brick brought from le Sloo, as Slough was then usually known. They are one of the first large ranges of brick buildings in the country, and some of the brickwork appeared unnecessarily massive – until the bomb fell in 1940. More than 1.5 million bricks were delivered between 1442 and 1445; up to 140 bricklayers and 70 stonemasons were employed.* The north side of School Yard, with the schoolroom and dormitory above, the north and east sides of the Cloisters, and the Hall on the south side with its kitchen and pantry were all nearing completion in 1447. An almshouse, which has vanished, had also been built. In 1449 John Utynam, a Fleming, was granted the first-ever patent in England, for stained glass for Eton, probably initially for College Hall and then for the Church.

The aggrandizement of the Church by Henry's 'will' was matched in 1448 by the intention to build much larger cloisters and school yard. Only the Hall would have been undisturbed. On the west flank there was to be an amazing bell tower, 140 feet high. The road would, of course, have had to be diverted to accommodate the plans for the Church, and the entrance of the College would have been on the north side, with another tower. This unrealistic and abortive scheme did not have such a drastic effect as the earlier change of plans had had on the Church, for nothing substantial was pulled down.

The Statutes of the 1443 College have not survived but they were presumably not very different from what the College accepted as its

* Some of the stonemasons were pressed men. Twelve were released from All Souls College, Oxford, on condition that the rest should not be touched. The College Audit Rolls are one of the principal sources of information on wages and conditions of employment in fifteenth-century England.

governing document, the *Liber originalis* compiled in 1452–3.[12] These Statutes were to remain in force until 1869, with minor adjustments at the end of Henry's reign. There is an interesting but incomplete version, apparently originating between 1444 and 1446, which lay in St John's College, Cambridge, until it was given recently to Eton College Library.[13] This much emended document has the feel of a working model. Just as the King's ideas for his buildings changed, so too did his views on the regulation of his College; no doubt too, more of Waynflete's experience was incorporated: for example, of the need for the Vice-Provost to act as delegate for the Provost.

The Royal College of the Blessed Mary of Eton near Windsor, 'commonly known as the Kynges College of our Ladye of Eton beside Wyndsore', was to consist of a Provost; ten Fellows who were to be priests and members or former members of either of the foundations at Eton and Cambridge, one of whom was to be chosen as Vice-Provost and two as Bursars; ten Chaplains and ten Clerks of various sorts, one of whom was to be organist and to instruct the choristers, sixteen boys under the age of 12; a Schoolmaster and an Usher in charge of seventy poor and indigent scholars; and thirteen poor weak almsmen.

The Provost was to be over the age of 30, one of the few requirements that still persists, and a priest. He was to be Rector of the parish of Eton. His power and influence in the College was very substantial, and his stipend (£50 p.a.) and perks reflected this. Nevertheless, he could be removed by the Fellows for gross negligence, for incurable disease or for substantial crime, such as homicide, the matter to be reported to the Bishop of Lincoln, who, as Visitor to the College, was then, as now, ultimately responsible for the College's operating within its Statutes. The Provost was normally required to be resident, though he was expected to inspect the College property throughout the country.

The very large clerical and musical establishment reflected the primacy of Henry's religious aims. The Chaplains were paid £5 a year, and given their food in Hall, but they could be dismissed. Choirboys would have received the sort of education offered fairly widely in reading or song schools round the country in order to equip boys to play their part in church services; training the memory was also regarded as important when books were rare.

Both the Schoolmaster and the Usher were to be unmarried, and in practice seem normally to have been young men. They seldom held their posts long, either because they could be dismissed or because they obtained a better job. Their pay was modest, 24 marks (£16) and 10 marks p.a., but with benefits in kind. This was ahead of other schoolmasters, however, who might typically earn £10. Schoolmasters' status was also low before John Somerset and William Waynflete. For at least 250 years the Schoolmaster was an insignificant figure compared with the Provost.

The seventy scholars normally entered between the ages of 8 and 12, but they could be allowed in at a higher standard up to their seventeenth birthday, providing they would be scholastically qualified to go on to King's at 18. They had to be of good character, well able to read and to sing plainsong, and they must know their Donatus, the rather elementary Latin Grammar then standard. (Donatus was a fourth-century author, and his twelve pages gave some account of parts of speech; it was added to and modified and in the fifteenth century was translated into English.) The boys had to be English. Choristers of Eton and King's were particularly favoured, then boys from parishes where the two Colleges owned property, and then boys from Buckinghamshire (at that time Eton's county) or Cambridgeshire. In practice early scholars came from every county in England except Northumberland, but there were none from Wales. One wonders how boys from Yorkshire and Westmoreland among the first arrivals knew of the opportunity of being an Eton scholar. No boy could be admitted if he was a villein or a bastard, nor could he be diseased or physically imperfect, for that would render him ineligible to take orders.* There were few who were technically 'villeins' left after the Black Death, but Hugh Thompson, son of Thomas Chapman, from Piddlehinton, a College estate in Dorset, was given his freedom and entered the College as late as 1469.[14] A scholar's own personal property had to be worth less than 5 marks a year income. In view of the exclusion of the lowest class of society (the villeins) and this generous upper limit for the boys' income, let alone their parents', how seriously should we take the description of scholars as poor and indigent? Perhaps the adjectives rather describe the attitudes to life that the scholars were expected to adopt, eschewing luxury. Certainly some of the early

---

* It is good to know that for more than fifty years boys with major physical handicaps have occasionally been admitted as Eton scholars.

names suggest that Eton scholars were well born, though not sons of nobles. For example, Sir Thomas Rotherham from Yorkshire had two sons, the younger of whom almost certainly was a scholar at Eton before 1448; the elder may have been accepted as an Etonian in order to qualify for King's, which would be a very early instance of the establishment looking after its own: the boy ended as Archbishop of York, and a benefactor of Cambridge and of Lincoln College, Oxford, though not of Eton. The most arbitrary requirement was the knowledge of Donatus; this must have depended upon the chance of an educated priest in the parish, or of a good song school. In most of Eton's history the need for a start on classical education before school was to be the most powerful barrier to there being a social mix of Collegers, and this was probably the case even in the first days. Interestingly more boys were elected than were admitted, eighty in 1453, the largest number in a surviving electoral roll: an indication of strong demand.

The King made provision for the sons of the rich to go to Eton, but the names of few survive from the early days. Non-scholars could attend lessons freely, but they were expected to pay for boarding. Up to twenty were sons of noblemen and friends of the College who were treated generously, dining at the second table in College Hall, and known as Commensals ('table companions'), whereas others had to eat with the scholars and choristers. There were thirteen poor lads who helped with the waiting and only ate after the rest: they were not part of the School, but they might hope to take orders or become transcribers of books. They were the true poor in Henry's foundation.

Quite how many there were in each category in the early years is hard to say – harder still to determine the names of non-scholars. The accounts showing expenditure in Hall give some idea, for the expenditure on different classes varied from the Provost, allowed 36d. a week (more in times of scarcity and high prices), down to the scholars and choristers and lesser clerks, allowed only 10d. In 1447–8 the tally of seventy scholars and sixteen choristers seems to have been complete, but how many of the 120 or so eating in Hall were Commensals, and how many servants, can only be guessed. There were also almost certainly from the beginning boys living in the town and taking advantage of the free lessons, but they did not eat in Hall and were not part of the foundation. In 1446 the King gave Eton a monopoly over education within a 10-mile radius;[15]

many local boys must thus have attended Eton. All the non-foundationers became what we now know as Oppidans. They would probably have paid something like 8*d*. a week for board and lodging; tuition fees, which all would have escaped, would have been something like 8*d*. a quarter at a typical school.

The Statutes do not just deal with the membership of the College: they regulate thoroughly the behaviour of its members. The adults are expected to obey the Provost; sanctions included loss of pay, or loss of commons (their free food), or for graver indiscipline, such as whispering against authority, loss of their jobs. It is somewhat shaming to see what it was thought necessary to forbid those (the Fellows and the Schoolmaster) who lived on the first floor of the Cloisters: they were told they must not cause fluid to descend on the lower rooms by urinating, by washing or by spilling drink.

Regulations about behaviour in Chapel and Hall presumably affected old and young alike. There were rules for dress, and Fellows were expected to wear hoods in Chapel as they still do on high days. There were fines for absence. There were to be seven services daily, which reflects the religious character of the foundation. The services must usually have been attended by the choristers, but not by the scholars, who were expected to make their devotions while they were rising and retiring, or going about their school business. In College Hall, the seating and service was laid down. There were to be readings from the Bible or the lives of the Fathers of the Church during meals, which the company were enjoined to listen to silently; the iron reading-desk still exists in College Hall and constitutes a hazard to those who attempt to serve the high table. There was to be a grace, either an antiphon for Mary or the psalm *De Profundis*, or prayers for Henry's parents, to be replaced after his death by one for himself. After dinner a loving-cup might be passed around the company. After feasts or councils, or when there was a fire in winter, there could be singing, reading of poetry or something else suitable. There was to be no jumping, wrestling, throwing of balls or stones, or other disorderly sports; this was presumably aimed against the young, and applied equally in the Hall, Cloisters or Church; but as the sanction was payment for damage and sharp punishment by withdrawal of commons, one must wonder whether there were not also light-hearted adults in the community. The boys would surely have qualified for the moderate chastisement the

Schoolmaster was allowed to inflict, and which they resisted on pain of being reported to the Provost or Vice-Provost.

The boys were not treated liberally. Their holidays were no more than six weeks a year; and much of that might be taken in travel between School and home. There were holidays related to the feasts of the Church in term-time of which we know since the College spent money on them. Boys required leave to go into Eton beyond Baldwin's Bridge, and into Windsor. Their hair was regulated, and a College barber was employed; the need for tonsures has recurred from time to time even in the twentieth century. Clothes could not be too exotic – for instance, no red, green or white hose, or painted shoes. The boys were forbidden taverns, not allowed hunting dogs, or girls. Indeed the establishment was almost all-male; there might be laundresses if male launderers could not be found, but they had to be elderly. The younger boys had also to accept the authority of the older boys. They also (to the age of 14) had to be prepared to share beds.

To remove any doubt about the acceptance of these Statutes, the Collegers were required on the completion of their fifteenth year (when they might have been becoming restive) to swear their allegiance to the College and their acceptance of the Statutes and of the punishments implicit in them. At the same time they were expected to reaffirm that they did not have the income to allow them to spend more than 5 marks a year. The average length of stay was six years.

On the positive side they would certainly have been educated in grammar, which would enable them to read, write, speak and understand Latin.* In the first place this would prepare them for a career in the Church, but it would also give them the ability to pursue a civil service career, as we would see it, either at home or as envoys. Furthermore, accurate command of grammar was seen as a tool of precise thought, and therefore as a necessity for study of the Law or Theology. In the Statutes there was provision for a disputation between the top scholars on St Thomas Becket's Day. There was also a library to encourage scholarship, which suggests that the College really was intended to have academic aspirations.

These Statutes very closely followed the Winchester model,

---

* Hopton, the Schoolmaster from 1448 to 1453, left the first gloomy Eton Masters' note, a Latin couplet that can be construed: 'It was painful labour to teach; he sweated to work the minds of his sons on to good grammatical lines.'

although Henry ensured that Eton was richer and could pay its officers better; the cloth which was part of the payment in kind was of higher quality. Among minor divergences was a provision for the Founder's kin to be educated freely at Winchester, which was not matched at Eton. On the other hand Eton did provide for thirteen old and poor men to be housed, and there was temporary accommodation for poor pilgrims. The animals not welcomed at Winchester were supplemented by a ban at Eton on a whole menagerie: monkeys, bears, foxes, deer, badgers. It is also fair to say that the Eton Statutes were more specifically directed towards training scholars for the Church. The prohibitions on gaudy clothes and hunting dogs were typical of rules laid down in religious establishments elsewhere, which seldom proved to be enforceable.

Not all scholars obtained places at King's, which – despite the splendour of its buildings – was a small College of Provost and seventy scholars, with sometimes a few non-Etonian commoners, until the second half of the nineteenth century. In late summer, the Provost and two Fellows of King's rode over to Eton to choose Etonians to fill vacancies. This process, known as Election, was done by nomination rather than examination. Then boys were chosen to fill the vacancies created at Eton. The unsuccessful Etonians could at first go to King's Hall, but from 1462 the Provosts of Eton and King's lost the control they had of King's Hall.

A high proportion of Kingsmen at this time did become priests as Henry wished, sometimes combining their vocation with some other job. For example, John Argentine, at Eton in the 1450s, became physician to Henry VII's son Arthur, Prince of Wales, as well as being Provost of King's, and he was indeed a benefactor of Eton as well as King's.* It is also possible to find early scholars who became lawyers or civil servants. For instance, John Dogget, a well-connected Colleger, who was admitted to King's in 1451, was used by Edward IV as an ambassador to the Pope and to the King of Denmark. These figures, however, were exceptions to the generality, who became parish priests; the idea that Henry planned a meritocracy of poor boys to provide the administration of the country is really a Victorian fancy with little foundation, but it is clear

---

* The Argentine family came from Argentan in Normandy. Years later another member, Cyril Argentine Alington, became Head Master. More recently still Argy Taylor was in the Eton Cricket XI.

that the door to public life was not closed. It was increasingly common for administrators to be laymen in the fifteenth century, 'gentlemen-bureaucrats', and some of these were doubtless Etonians.

Up to the end of the 1440s, Eton seems to have made progress, even if uncertainly at times, towards fulfilling the King's vision of a great religious and scholastic centre. In the country, however, problems were accumulating, and these were to engulf the College. Historians dispute how far responsibility was with the King, how far with his advisers. At the time the advisers would be blamed, and indeed could pay for failure with their lives; but that was because to blame the King was treason. Yet in that period sovereignty was vested in the King, once he had assumed his personal rule; without the King his advisers could do little. It was not, as his apologists used to claim, that the King's work was the royal foundations and the rest was that of his ministers. All was of a piece.

The greatest problem was the position in France. Arguably, without another great general, the English possessions could never have been maintained, and the best that could be achieved was to hold them as other vassals of the French King did. Henry VI wanted peace, but was a crowned King of France and would not be a vassal. He hoped that appeasement could buy peace for some of his dominions at the expense of others. Financial stringency argued against war, though popular sentiment was to fight, and men were even ready to pay something toward the cost. Moves towards peace from 1440, interrupted by further bouts of conflict, culminated in 1445 with the King's marriage to Margaret of Anjou, niece of Charles VII's wife. For this he was prepared to surrender Maine and any claims to the French throne. Although she was only 15, she proved to be tough, and well-disposed towards education.* The marriage and the peace policy which she naturally supported were not, however, popular. At this time a French envoy described Henry as standing around in a variety of opulent costumes, grinning and crying 'Saint Jehan, grant mercis!' when Charles VII was mentioned by name. But envoys do not always tell the truth.[16]

In 1447 Gloucester, always outspoken against the peace policy, and whose wife had earlier been imprisoned, was arrested and almost immediately died in prison – though he was probably not

---

* She figures briefly in the Statutes: Statute 31 provides for exequies for 'our dearest consort' on the anniversary of her death.

murdered. Some of his servants were, however, indicted for treason, dragged to Tyburn, hanged, and stripped ready to be quartered – when the news of the Pope's latest increase to the indulgences at Eton saved them, as in Thomas Carver's case. The harsh treatment of the Gloucesters does not support the Blakman picture of a 'kind and merciful' king.* In the end, the peace policy did not prevail; the marriage truce was broken, by the English in 1449, which led to the French overrunning Normandy within the year. It was an ignominious defeat.

If Henry had failed in one primary duty of a medieval king, to protect his people, he had done no better in the other, to maintain justice. After he took over rule, power was transferred to his Court. This was not in itself wrong, but unfortunately there were some very acquisitive men present, notably Cardinal Beaufort and his family, and William de la Pole, Earl of Suffolk. The latter, however he may be judged in a wider context, was indeed a real benefactor of Eton, not only by practical help, but by the gift of £666 – even though he had his own educational foundation at Ewelme.† In the 'St John's' Statutes, he and Waynflete are the two men outside the royal family for whom prayers were to be offered. Suffolk, rather than Beaufort, should perhaps lead the list of Eton's benefactors read on Founder's Day, but the resonance of Henry Cardinal Beaufort's name was too tempting. Blakman says that the Cardinal left the King £2,000, which the King refused, saying that it should go to Eton and King's; but in fact the Cardinal did leave £1,000 each to Eton and King's, money that the King owed to him; the Colleges were to provide a daily collect and a yearly service for the Cardinal. These men helped Eton, but perhaps at some cost to the royal reputation for securing justice.

Beaufort's death in 1447 caused Henry to move with unexpected speed, and he instantly ordered the Chapter at Winchester to elect Waynflete Bishop in his stead. The decision was a good one for this richest bishopric. Eton lost a notable Provost, but kept a powerful friend. After the very brief reign of the Vice-Provost, John Clerk,

---

* The Provost and Fellows of Eton and King's tried to get hold of Gloucester's notable collection of books, which had been bequeathed to Oxford, for their own libraries. Eton was unsuccessful; Waynflete, as an Oxford man, may have had scruples. King's was luckier.

† There are reminiscences of Ewelme in the architecture of Eton backing on the Slough Road.

who soon died, William Westbury, a Wykehamist who was already headmaster, became Provost. Again this was to prove extraordinarily good fortune for the College.

Another weakness of the King's was his foolish generosity to supplicants, many of them at Court, to whom he gave away lands. In favouring a few, inevitably he damaged the exchequer, adding to the problems of sustaining his forces in France and indirectly hurting those who were the more taxed. By his favouritism he encouraged factions. The national interest may have suffered, but Eton itself gained very substantially from the King's generosity. The leper hospital of St James, together with its supporting lands, was granted as a town house for the Provost in 1449. These 184 acres on the edge of London around the present St James's Palace were potentially very valuable, and this was the richest endowment that Eton ever received. When in 1449 Parliaments were twice called to provide finance, the King's ministers were attacked and Suffolk impeached. Henry protected Suffolk, who had certainly been his loyal servant, by allowing him to escape trial and go abroad, but he was murdered as he crossed the Channel. Parliament also urged the King to rescind his many grants, though they did exempt Eton from these 'resumptions'.

In the summer of 1450, a popular rising, known as Cade's rebellion, erupted in Kent. Many respectable people were involved, who shared and supported the position of Parliament. When the King took the field against them, they at first showed signs of collapsing, but a setback caused the King to compromise, and he failed in courage and determination, retreating towards his ancestral Lancastrian domains. It was after this renewed display of ineptitude that Richard, Duke of York (like Henry V, a great-grandson of Edward III), returned from Ireland where he was Governor, and began to be seen as an alternative king. York took the same line as Parliament, which reconvened in the winter of 1450, in once again petitioning for the resumption of the King's grants – this time including those to Eton and King's, whose endowments were described as 'over chargefull and noyus'. The King decided on concession: leases were to be given to those who were prepared to pay most, not to favourites. With this concession the royal finances were partly restored, while in practice the royal family and the Colleges were largely untouched. There was a brief period of effective rule, in which Henry travelled round England re-establishing confidence in his government in the traditional manner of medieval monarchs. This enabled him to convene a co-operative Parliament and to frustrate any Yorkist designs on the throne.

Just as a continuing Royalist revival seemed likely, assisted by the conception of a son, Henry VI lost his senses. The decline of the English position in France had continued and Gascony was being conquered. Now in 1453 occurred the final defeat of the Hundred Years War, the Battle of Castillon. It seems probable that the awareness of the total disaster of his French policies may have led to profound depression which lasted for eighteen months. Possibly there was an inheritance of psychotic disorder from his maternal grandfather, Charles VI of France, who was also certainly deranged. At any rate, Henry plainly ceased to be capable of ruling. A Council was established to carry on the functions of government, and in this York established himself as pre-eminent. During 1454 he became Captain of Calais, the last English possession, and Protector of the realm. At the end of 1454 Henry recovered, though he remembered nothing of the eighteen months of his illness. That there was a lovable side to the childish monarch is illustrated by a contemporary letter of Edmund Clere to his cousin John Paston.

> Blessed be God, the King is wel amended, and hath ben syn Cristemseday . . . And . . . the Queen came to him, and brought my Lord Prynce with her. And then he askid what the Prince's name was, and the Queen told him Edward; and than he hild up his hands and thankid God thereof . . . And my Lord of Wynchestr (Waynflete) and my Lord of Seint Jones were with him on the morow after Tweltheday, and he speke to hem as well as ever he did; and when thei came out thei wept for joye.[17]

Henry may have recovered at least temporarily from depression, but he had not become wiser. An assembly was called at Leicester. Perhaps York, no longer Protector, feared that he was going to be treated like Gloucester. At any rate, with a small force he met Henry, also with a small force, at St Albans, en route to Leicester. Negotiations took place but failed, and a short, sharp battle followed: the start of the Wars of the Roses. Henry's principal Beaufort supporter, the Duke of Somerset, was killed, while Henry himself was wounded and captured. York and Richard Neville, Earl of Warwick and son-in-law of the King's old tutor, were minded to manage him in the same fashion as had been attempted by Suffolk and the Beauforts, rather than to replace him. The King suffered periodic though less severe relapses; and a hostile Parliament was also convened, which would in the autumn again try to disendow Eton and King's.

Before then, Henry had replaced the existing Statute 61, which had laid down a reduced scale of operations for the College, should stringent financial times come about. Civil disruption had already reduced the number of pupils and revenues. Now difficulties seemed only too likely, at least if Henry died. His new Statute 64 provided for the continuance of services according to the Sarum rite (in use at Salisbury Cathedral from the eleventh century to the Reformation), and stressed the duty to carry on building the Church. The School could cease. This decision, taken *in extremis*, suggests again that, in Henry's mind, the foundation of the School was always secondary to the religious objects of the College. There was no altogether similar Statute for King's, an indication that Eton was the dearer to Henry.

In July 1455, the King issued letters patent to the Bishops of Winchester and Lincoln authorizing them to emend the Statutes further. He must have realized his own incapacity, or have been persuaded by Waynflete. The alterations made were relaxations to allow the Provost and Fellows to accept benefices which would provide them with extra income, and to excuse other breaches of Statute which could be attributed to loss of revenue.

The period from 1455 to 1461 was to see further fluctuations in the government of the country. York was embarrassed by his sworn allegiance to Henry, and when it appeared that he was about to overthrow Henry, his support diminished. When he was killed at Wakefield in 1460, his son Edward, Earl of March, was less compromised. The Lancastrian cause, now led by the Queen, won a last victory at the second battle of St Albans, but failed to use it to seize London. (Michael Palmer, the first known Etonian to die in battle, was fighting in her army.) Edward and Warwick forestalled the Queen, and in 1460 the balance of advantage clearly swung to them. On Palm Sunday 1461 the Yorkists won the conclusive battle of Towton in a snowstorm. Henry was deposed, and Edward of York became Edward IV.

The rest of Henry's life was of no great significance. He escaped, and with the Queen resisted in the North of England for a time; then she and the Prince fled to France. Henry was captured in 1465, and imprisoned, but apparently not too harshly, in the Tower of London. Then in September 1470 he was briefly restored after a rift between Edward IV and Warwick, his most powerful supporter. Aided by Louis XI of France, Warwick occupied London and released Henry. That Christmas Henry appears to have sent a message of goodwill to Eton. Efforts by Warwick to bring the Queen and Prince Edward from France failed to get them back in time. Edward IV was able to reoccupy London and recapture Henry, who apparently was not sorry to return to custody. Edward then defeated Warwick on Easter Day, the same day that Margaret and the Prince landed at Weymouth. On 4 May, Edward IV defeated their forces at Tewkesbury. The Prince was slain, and as soon as the news of his death reached London, Henry was murdered in the Tower, 21 May 1471: plainly the King's life had been preserved only for fear that his son might prove a more attractive legitimate King.

There followed an extraordinary coda. Within ten years of Henry's death, he became popular and revered as a miracle worker. As early as 1473 an image of him in York Minster was being venerated. The King's body, at Chertsey Abbey, began to attract pilgrims, until Richard III felt that it would be better placed in St George's Chapel at Windsor. No doubt Henry himself would have preferred to rest at Eton. Pilgrim badges were once again made, this time for those going to the King rather than to the great Church that he had planned. Many miracles were recorded.[18]* Ordinary people forgot the disasters of his rule, and in any case their lives had not been conspicuously improved since he was deposed; what they did realize was that he had suffered something like a martyrdom.

This belated popularity was to prove helpful to Eton in the reign of Richard III. Later his Lancastrian successor, Henry Tudor, son of Henry VI's half-brother Edmund Tudor and of Margaret Beaufort, was anxious to promote the canonization of his uncle for the

---

* There are no fewer than 172 listed in manuscripts in the British Museum, some even documenting the curing of distressed farm animals. (Etonians should perhaps remember that he cured a rupture caused by a kick in a football match.) According to Roger Ascham, early sixteenth-century Etonians in their Latin Grammar had to translate 'King Henry doth many divers miracles'. The hymn 'Rex Henricus sis amicus nobis in angustia' ('King Henry, be our friend in times of trouble') is still sung in College. At evensong in St George's on the eve of the King's obit and birth, lilies and roses are laid on Henry's grave. The Henry VI Society works for the canonization of the King.

political advantages that it would bring to the uncertainly grounded Tudor dynasty. It was in that context that John Blakman wrote his memoir,* of which no actual manuscript survives. Blakman became a Fellow of Merton College, Oxford, in 1436, possibly a royal Chaplain and certainly a Fellow of Eton, and Precentor from 1447 to 1452, when he left to be Master of King's Hall, Cambridge, one of the constituent elements of Trinity College; later still, he became a Carthusian monk. Quite when the memoir was actually written is unclear. It speaks of the miracles, which really began after the King's body was moved to Windsor in 1484, so it cannot have been written until the early years of Henry VII's reign, and even then it was not printed until 1510. Clearly it was written in very old age, and it may have been doctored. Its purpose is shown in its first paragraph, where the King is placed in the register of saints: it is a collection of anecdotes to illustrate his saintliness, rather than a biography – it does not even mention his mental illness.

Blakman's picture of the King has influenced Etonians, particularly since M.R. James made an English translation available in 1919, written in more distinguished English than the original low-grade Latin. The Founder's Prayer, '*Domine, Jesu Christe, qui me creasti, redemisti, et preordinasti ad quod nunc sum . . .*' ('O Lord Jesus Christ, who didst create me, redeem me, and foreordain me unto that which now I am: Thou knowest what Thou wilt do with me: deal with me according to Thy most compassionate will'), which is drawn from it, has moved generations, sung as it habitually is at the end of memorial services. Perhaps Blakman is more to be trusted (though he is certainly not always correct) when he writes about the King at Eton. Henry may well have said that he would rather the priests were somewhat weak in music than defective in knowledge of the Scriptures; he may have wished his young lambs to be brought up in virtue as well as in learning, and warned them against the corrupt deeds of courtiers. Perhaps when he did meet Etonians he would give them money and urge them, 'Be you good boys, gentle and teachable, and servants of the Lord.' (This is the basis of the form of admission used for new Collegers in recent times which

---

* Blakman was not the only author among the first Fellows. William Weye, who went to Santiago and twice to Jerusalem, was the first of a large number of Etonian travel-writers. Blakman was a book collector, and his copy of Higden's *Polychronicon*, with a drawing probably by himself, is in College Library.

begins with the injunction to be a good boy, teachable and truthful.) Blakman's picture of Henry is important to the history of Eton, but it does not tell us what sort of man Henry was; sadly, it seems there was less in him to admire.

In 1971, 500 years after his death, the College asked John Saltmarsh, Fellow and historian of King's College, to give a commemorative lecture at Eton. They asked him some questions, and the first was: what sort of man was the real Henry VI? He took a more charitable view, accepting much of Blakman's memoir. The second question was: 'How was it that in spite of King Henry's lack of success in politics, the foundation of Eton and King's seems to have been very efficiently managed?' When we consider the changes of plan, particularly over the buildings, we may question the use of the word 'efficiently'. Yet the Colleges have proved to be the only durable achievements of Henry's reign. Saltmarsh's answer was that the King took advice from a good team of administrators; that when Henry says in his 'will' of Eton Chapel, 'I have devised that the breadth of the church shall be of such a width,' he really means that his chief mason, Robert Westerley, had drawn up the plan, and that he had approved it. Saltmarsh also attributed much to the Royal Commissions mentioned at various times. There are other foundations attributed to Henry VI, for example the universities at Caen and Bordeaux, but nobody supposes that he did more than give his name to these. Some historians now argue that Suffolk and others in the royal household were anxious to strengthen their political hold, and that they saw Eton and King's as improving the image of royalty.[19] The attraction of pilgrims was little more than a convenient way of publicizing the foundations. Bekynton, and then Waynflete, had the real care for education, Suffolk perhaps the drive to carry forward the building, which certainly slowed down after his death. The Commensals, too, might have created links between important families and the royal foundation. The differences between the Statutes of the two Colleges may reflect the differences between the two teams of advisers: for example, the existence of Commensals at Eton but not at King's, and the greater emphasis on public service at King's. Certainly the Commissioners were important; yet the King was the main inspiration of the religious establishment, if not of the School. So much in the history of the foundations mirrors the execution of Henry's other policies: the changes of plan, the lack of realism, the devotion to the religious purposes of the Church, the prayers to be said there for himself and his family. Henry's was the vision that founded Eton, but others, notably Suffolk, Waynflete and, later, Westbury, deserve much of the credit for the ultimate success.

A third question asked of Saltmarsh was: how far did the subsequent history of Eton and King's reflect or conflict with the Founder's intentions? Saltmarsh admitted that he had found Eton closer to Henry's intentions than he had expected, but very reasonably argued that he would not have the time or knowledge to answer this question fully. Certainly Henry would not be happy with the present arrangements in College Chapel, but at least the Chapel is still an important part of Eton's life. He would find more boys being helped towards their education, but fewer being educated totally freely; but this would perhaps not worry him since the concept of paying schoolboys was always in the Statutes (possibly by another's engineering rather than his own).

I will try to answer a final question: what were the Founder's most valuable legacies to Eton? First of all, the site has proved to be a great source of strength. It was urban, not rural. Initially the river was valuable as a means of access. Eton proved to be convenient to London without the handicap of actually being in London. Proximity to Windsor, and thus to royalty, was undeniably useful over the years. This was a matter of chance: that the parish church at Eton happened to be dedicated to the Assumption. Yet there are plenty of business enterprises that succeeded because their sites, selected for no calculated reason, happened to have the right qualities. Secondly, because of the grandiose schemes for pilgrimages, Eton was bequeathed fine and substantial buildings, which were to allow the later expansion of the School. Thirdly, the College was more splendidly endowed than any other educational foundation up to that time. Finally, in providing a College structure, Henry also made it more possible for Eton to survive. Medieval schools vanished readily; in the fifty years up to 1439 over seventy grammar schools had perished. The College proved more durable.

CHAPTER TWO

Survival

WHEN QUEEN MARGARET and her forces retired to the North after the second battle of St Albans, Provost Westbury must have foreseen the final triumph of Edward IV, as the College sent two representatives to meet him before he even entered London. Edward, still young enough to be a pupil, and needing all the support he could get, took the College into his protection; the College still possesses the document affirming this, signed E. York, a rare example of his signature between his life as Earl of March and as crowned King.[1] On reflection, however, and once his confidence had grown, Edward became more hostile to his rival's foundations.

In the summer of 1461 Edward had taken the revenues of King's, and might well have seized Eton's revenues too, but for a timely gift from the Provost of 400 marks, which would have helped towards Edward's coronation expenses. In spite of his very different temperament, the new King was to prove as capricious as Henry. He was not hostile to education as such, just to Eton and King's. Thus he did not protect Eton when the Parliament of November declared that grants of the three Lancastrian kings were null and void; yet he did regrant some possessions in 1462. This, however, was a prelude to a sustained attack in 1463. Edward petitioned Pope Pius II successfully for a bull of union transferring the property of the College of Eton to St George's in Windsor. No doubt the Pope recognized that political power in England had shifted and was keen to attract the support of the new King. It is not quite certain that the School survived without temporary closure, but the College had a consecrated (even if incomplete) Chapel, and, as a college, it had a legal identity which it would have lacked had it merely been a school. Westbury made a courageous public protest in July 1465: he declared that he would never consent to this bull of union, and if he appeared to do so, it would only indicate that his courage had failed. He could not, however, prevent the transfer of Henry's lovingly collected treasures to St George's that September, the occasion of the inventory which enables us to know what they were. The eighty-seven choir books which went at that time indicate the contents of the services, though none survives to tell us of the music; there were anthems, processionals and organ music, among much else. The only furnishing extant today is the remarkable lectern in College Chapel.

By 1467 the King had relented. He petitioned the new Pope, Paul II, to revoke his predecessor's bull, and though the answer was three years in coming, and though even then a final decision was entrusted to the Archbishop of Canterbury and not delivered until 1476, it is clear that the signals given to Eton became more favourable. The audit book of 1466–7 showed Eton's income down to £320 from an average of £1,200 between 1440 and 1461, but this proved to be the nadir. Measures of economy taken were not reversed: the salaries of Schoolmaster and Usher were cut from £16 and £10 to £10 and £4 respectively. The Provost and Fellows had to forgo their own stipends in 1468; the number of Fellows was reduced to four, and when recovery came, it was only raised to seven. Expenditure on food in Hall was halved. The almsmen were abolished. Yet in 1467 forty-four scholars were admitted, an indication of how few there must have been before – probably only twenty-one in 1466.

In 1468 some of the alien priories were restored to Eton, and Westbury could confer with Waynflete on resuming the building of College Chapel. Gifts of salmon from the Thames were made to the King; and in 1470 St George's was told to restore the Church ornaments, but Eton never recovered them all. As Sir Robert Birley wrote, 'A present made by the College to the Dean of Windsor a few months after the restoration of the property of one trout and one pike . . . must have been a gift without much love behind it.'[2] The restoration did not revive Eton as a centre of pilgrimage; although in 1479 Pope Sixtus IV renewed some of the indulgences at Eton, there is no other indication of pilgrims, who were indeed more attracted to the tomb of Henry himself. That meant that even the

Choir of the Church was of an adequate size for the School and town. Waynflete provided the finance for the building to be completed by an antechapel in not very durable Headington stone, and a wooden roof was constructed over the building. (Timbers with the Sun of York symbol were found in the Chapel roof when it had to be replaced in 1957.) Sadly, even at this time when choral polyphony was developing in England, the musical establishment of the College was still reduced; Henry VI would not have felt that the School should have priority over the Church.

Despite Waynflete's great age and his own concern with the foundation of Magdalen College, Oxford (whose Statutes draw something from those of Eton), and of a school at Wainfleet in Lincolnshire, his birthplace, he saw the Church to structural completion and must have commissioned, or agreed to, the wall-paintings which were completed in the 1480s, with one William Baker apparently the principal artist. Almost certainly Waynflete himself began to pay for them, because the College only paid artists' bills after Waynflete died. These paintings, which depict, on one side, miracles of the Virgin, on the other, episodes in the life of a legendary Empress, both well known in medieval literature, are the most extensive in Britain. The two sides are fairly evidently by different artists, and possibly more than two were employed. The influence on them was from the Netherlands, and cultural contacts with the Netherlands were strong at Court. There were originally two rows of pictures on the north and south sides, but of the upper row a mere fragment now remains. It is possible to see that the paintings were lit from the west, and that therefore a screen divided the building, with the boys presumably at the east end, and the people of the town at the west, cut off from the main action but able to divert themselves by the enjoyment of the narrative painting. This screen apparently came from the old parish church, together with stalls; the last mention of the old church occurs in 1480, and it must have been pulled down about that time.[3]

There was a second crisis in 1474, when Edward again granted Eton lands to St George's, but this proved temporary. Just possibly this second reprieve, or even the first one, may have been achieved by the intervention of the celebrated courtesan Jane Shore.[4] Mistress Shore certainly existed, apparently by birth Elizabeth Lambert and married to a mercer, William Shore. She appears in Sir Thomas More's *History of King Richard III*, a production, like Blakman's, of the Tudor school of myth-making, but one that is destructive rather than hagiologic. It is suggested that she may have been the mother of Edward's children, which would have discredited Edward's line, and that she was made to do penance and ill-treated by Richard, which would have damaged him too. Richard is also said to have accused her of conspiring with the Queen to procure his deformity by sorcery, and this was used by Richard to bring down the Lord Chamberlain, Lord Hastings, who had brought Mistress Shore into his protection (and his bed) after Edward's death. After her public penance, however, when she won sympathy by her demure behaviour, she made a subsequent and successful second marriage, and did not die until 1526 or 1527, some years after More's *History* was written. Soon she became a literary figure of some celebrity, with her name changed from Elizabeth to Jane. A portrait of her is mentioned at the end of the sixteenth century, and in 1660 one certainly existed at King's. In the eighteenth century Horace Walpole mentions one of the two at Eton, both of which derive from the well-known portrait of Diane de Poitiers, mistress of Henry II of France. Presumably some time in the late sixteenth or early seventeenth century, she began to be credited with doing Eton and King's a great service. If indeed she saved Eton in 1467, she must have lived to about the age of 80, and it is more probable that her intervention, if it occurred, was in 1474. Tradition says that she had a confessor, Henry Bost, who was to become Provost in 1477, which conforms with the suggestion that her influence was at the later date. But Sir Thomas More says nothing of her helping Eton and King's, and perhaps Edward's Queen, Elizabeth, may have been a protecting angel, if one was needed. Certainly her brother Earl Rivers, the patron of Caxton, was a valuable ally of Eton; he gave some property and was rewarded by the prayers of the College.

The 1470s were much less difficult for Eton than the 1460s. Westbury was able to attend the funeral of Henry VI at Chertsey Abbey without adverse comment. The King began to take more interest in Eton and even ordered a boat to be kept there for his use. When Westbury died in March 1477, the College appeared to be secure. Thomas Barker, a former Vice-Provost, was chosen to succeed him on the vote of the Fellows, but he quickly perceived that the King would not wish this: 'The wrath of a king is as messengers of death; the wise man will pacify it.' So he stepped aside and the Fellows elected Henry Bost, a Yorkist, first giving him a

Fellowship, so that he would be statutorily qualified – if one over-looked his provostship of The Queen's College, Oxford and of King's Hall, Cambridge, jobs which he clung to for some time. He was to prove an expert politician, securing the generosity of the Queen and the goodwill of the various monarchs. Edward IV made several visits to Eton, the last just before his death. Then his coffin was stopped at Eton and censed by the Bishops of Lincoln and Ely and members of the College: one feels that Bost's colleagues must have performed these final rites with a certain relief.

The reign of Richard III did not present any real threat to the College. Indeed Provost Bost was at his coronation, and brought back to the College a portrait of the new King. Nevertheless the accession of Henry VII, a great-nephew of the Founder, proved to be a sign that early troubles were over. For some years it was even surmised that Henry VII might have been educated at Eton, but there is no evidence of such a connection.

One year after Henry's accession, Waynflete died. He had lived long enough to ensure that Eton was securely based. Though he was probably not educated at Winchester, his experience as headmaster there enabled him to learn what was requisite for a school. Yet it was Eton that captured his affection, and he recognized that his short period there as Provost laid the foundation of his own career. This bred in him a lasting interest in Eton, and while Henry VI founded the College, arguably Waynflete should be regarded as the true founder of Eton as a school. He was by vocation a school-master; and since he was essentially a royal servant, he could survive changing regimes without being regarded as a trimmer.

From this period we have the earliest surviving correspondence about an Eton schoolboy, William Paston, an Oppidan.[5] In 1477 his mother, a widow, wrote to Sir John Paston, William's eldest brother, about her inability to keep the boy in gowns and other gear; she needed John's help. (Sir John was a friend of Earl Rivers, who may have influenced him to send William to Eton.) In November 1478, William himself wrote to 'his worchepful brodyr, ohn Paston'. He had received a gold noble from a servant, Alwedyr; but his creanser (Tutor or guardian), one of the Fellows, Thomas Stevenson, was owed money for his commons which he would pay on to his land-lady (or Dame). Clothes were still a problem: he wanted bright hose cloth for holidays, coarse cloth for working days, a stomacher, two shirts and a pair of slippers. He ends by hoping that he might be allowed to come up to London by boat with Alwedyr to 'sporte me with you at London a day or ii thys terme time'. This letter is refreshingly normal.

There is a third letter, written in February 1479, when William would have turned 19. The letter is again very respectfully addressed to his 'Ryght reverent and worchepfull broder', whom he thanks for 13s. 4d. for his landlady, and for the promise of 12 lbs of figs and 8 lbs of raisins arriving (from Norfolk) on another barge. Then the letter turns to more serious matters: he may be in love with a Margaret Alborow, whom he met at a local wedding; could John find out how well off her family is, and look at her hands, which he has been told are thick? Then William turns to the possible time of leaving Eton. He feels he is competent in all but Latin verse. He gives a line which would seem to have been set as a task, and then adds three lines of his own which at least bear out the inadequacy of his Latin – unsurprisingly, since some surviving Fellows' epitaphs suggest that even the authorities were not great Latinists. One wonders what he was learning, other than grammar, in days when English spelling was not codified. As for the main matter of his letter, we should not be altogether surprised: girls have occupied boys' thoughts over the centuries, and in those days when life was often brief, early and rich marriages were advisable, in order to continue the family. (In the end, William did not marry Margaret Alborow but Lady Anne Beaufort.)

Another document of this time probably refers to Eton.[6] It is addressed in Latin to Commensals, and a manuscript addition says that it is written by the anchorite of Lynn for Eton scholars. Only Eton had Commensals, sons of the wealthy who boarded and ate in Hall, but who this anchorite was, and whether he ever taught at Eton, is quite unknown. It has much in common with the *Babees Book*, the best-known of medieval books on manners. Injunctions to wash hands before meals and to clean plate, knife and spoon with bread, are mingled with more specific injunctions not to criticize the Dame, to be up at dawn, not to speak English in school, to be quiet and to keep a notebook. The Commensals were intended to behave like proper gentlemen and to have a basic classical education.

CHAPTER THREE

Renaissance and Reformation

THE CORONATION OF Henry VII initiated a period of prosperity for Eton. The King's slender claims to be the legitimate sovereign derived from the Beaufort line, but his father was Henry VI's half-brother. Thus, while he was sensible enough to attempt accommodation with surviving Yorkists by marriage to Edward IV's daughter, he wanted to bolster Lancastrian achievements. The attempt to promote the Founder's canonization was part of this policy. In 1489 Provost Bost and the Provost of King's felt bold enough to petition for the restoration of their lost land, pleading that their Colleges were greatly decayed and impoverished. Some properties were indeed returned, but Eton still argued that it was not rich enough to restore a full complement of Fellows.

The College was, however, wealthy enough to spend money on the Church: for example, purchasing a new pair of silver shoes for the feet of an image of the Virgin. At this time the building must have looked fine with its fresh paintings, its glass, and a number of relics and representations of the Assumption. In 1497 two braces were made to support a large choirbook, and in 1507 a new and larger organ was installed. The large choirbooks which certainly existed mostly vanished at the Reformation, but one book of Marian antiphons, anthems in praise of the Virgin, has survived, though incomplete, and is kept in College Library.[1] Apparently someone in the College caused a fair copy to be made of pieces which were sung at Eton around this time, and this has become the principal source for knowledge of English music of the time. The music is not

at all easy to sing, and is now usually performed by adults.* The
difficulty leads some experts to suppose that the trebles were boys
of up to 15 or 16 years old, with voices breaking later than now
happens; but this is unlikely, since the Statutes laid down that
choristers should not be more than 12, and there are instances of
choristers becoming Collegers at that age. It seems more likely that
the boys were very intensively trained. Also former choristers with
unbroken voices may have been re-enlisted to sing anthems
with unusually large numbers of parts.[2] Some of the surviving compositions are by composers who had been educated at Eton. There
would also have been settings of the Mass, and of Propers, which
were services for particular days. In the fifty years before the
Reformation the services conformed closely to the Founder's wishes.
There were no pilgrims, certainly, but commemorative services
grew in number; for example Provost Bost, who died in 1504, left
furniture and property to the College, and funds for an extra
Chaplain to say masses for him and his family.

The educational standing of Eton grew. Richard Croke, who was
at Eton in the early years of the century, was the first Etonian to
obtain an international reputation for scholarship. In 1505 it was
laid down that a school founded at Cromer was to have a headmaster who should preferably have been educated at Eton or
Winchester. Then in 1528 the Master of Cuckfield Grammar School
was instructed to teach 'after the practice of Eton'. A document
exists, sent from Eton, to say what this practice was.[3] Similarly in
1530 the Headmaster of Saffron Walden School was expected to
follow the example of Eton or Winchester, and obtained accounts
from both schools of their educational systems.[4] The first text-
books, too, survive from this time. Such evidence makes it easier to
picture everyday life at Eton.

From both the accounts we learn that boys went into school at
6.00 a.m. chanting *Deus Misereatur* and a Collect. At 9.00 they
recited *De Profundis* and had quarter of an hour to eat breakfast.
They returned to school until 11.00, when dinner was served. At
1.00 they would be tested in grammar, and at 3.00 in construing
Latin. At 5.00 they had supper before an anthem, and again *De*

---

* In 1519 the Visitor complained that not enough clerks stayed after
Vespers, when the Marian antiphons were sung. Today the Eton boys' choir
occasionally sings pieces, and they have made one recording.

Profundis. They probably worked after supper until prayers and bedtime at 8.00. There appears to have been just one weekly 'remedy', apparently a half-holiday from 2.00, and that never on Friday. Saturday and Sunday were somewhat different. Work is prescribed for Sunday at Winchester, but not at Eton – though this may simply mean that the Eton Masters did not mention everything that occurred. The long hours are typical of schools in Tudor England.

All the instruction was in Latin. The Latin grammars in use were by Stanbridge and his pupil Whittington. Stanbridge, an Old Wykehamist, was Master of Magdalen College School in Oxford at the end of the fifteenth century, and made that school educationally fashionable. Later, Colet's foundation of St Paul's, in London, moved ahead of Eton by paying its High Master far more than any other school paid its headmaster – £34 in 1518.[5] Acknowledging that St Paul's had acquired better scholarship, between 1528 and 1530 Eton adopted the Grammar by Lily, the Master of St Paul's School, and this work, revised at Eton in the eighteenth century, was to be the basis of the somewhat impertinently named *Eton Latin Grammar*, used into the nineteenth century. Grammar was varied by 'Vulgares', sentences which were to be translated into Latin, almost by rote. A notable collection was Horman's *Vulgaria*, published in 1519 in an edition of 800 copies, but assembled earlier. Horman was the Schoolmaster at Eton from 1484 to 1495, and at Winchester from 1495 to 1501, when he returned to Eton as a Fellow until his death in 1535. (His funeral brass is incorrect in claiming that he was nearly 100, since he was a Winchester scholar in 1468, and thus must have been about 80.) His book, published in 1519 but written earlier, attempts to make Latin more interesting and informative by giving model sentences in English and then in Latin, relating for instance to natural history or everyday life. It also was traditional in the sense that it aimed to give pupils the Latin words that could be useful in adult life. Thus sections deal with politics, law, and the military life ('The power and dominion of the Turks recheth almost to Italy,'). Others deal with trade, the crafts, gardening, agriculture, cookery ('Let us have chickens in pike sauce,' – but can such food often have been served generally in College Hall?). Sections on crime are as lurid as today: 'He made his own mother to be drowned.' Sentences on women, marriage and childbirth show that Personal and Social Education, as it is now called, was not entirely neglected; but a male cynicism can be detected: 'It is convenient that a man have one several place in the house to himself from cumbrance of women. He that saw some women out of their array would have less courage to be enamoured of them,'; 'Women that be out of all beauty buy their husbands with riches,'; 'Some nuns keep their virginity but easily.' There is a warning, however: 'It becometh not clerks to haunt a nunnery nor early nor late.'

Other sentences are evocative of Eton the place – the Thames being frozen over, or in flood, for example. Yet other sentences capture Eton boys: 'I have laboured about nought all day,'; 'Lend my thy Terence for my brother,'; 'Young fellows have a pleasure in writhed and curled locks,'; 'Some children be well ruled for love: some for fear some not without beating or correction,'; 'A principal point of a schoolmaster is to discern the difference of wits in children, and to what thing every wit is best disposed.' The sentences about recreation are particularly attractive: 'Would God we might go play.' There are several references to tennis – both in relation to exercising all the joints, and to the risk of physical injury ('He hit me in the eye with a tennis ball,'); did Eton have a tennis court? A boy might cast off his gown, so that he should not be hindered in running. 'We will play with a ball of wind,' refers to handball rather than (unlawful) football. He should learn to swim with a cork. He might dance a variety of dances – most alluringly, 'a satyr's dance'. There is mention of fishing and hunting ('a plain recording of war'), of musical instruments, of chess. Dice and cards are not commended. Some sporting activities would now be thought very incorrect: 'my cock had the best in this fight,'; while some sentences show the debasement of English: 'he is a gay wrestler.'

Horman was aware of the new learning spreading through Europe: 'Men that be well learned in these days take up many things that were of antiquity,'; 'By reading of substantial authors thou shalt bring about or attain to speak elegant and substantial Latin,'; 'We have played a comedy of Latin,'; 'We have played a comedy of Greek'. Horman was not against studying Latin literature, yet he was criticized later by Ascham, the most widely known Tudor educationalist, because of his moderate Latin; good Latinists would have to unlearn it in order to follow classical models. Horman, after all, was a very old man, and his scholarship was of the previous century: Erasmus provided a more commonly used set of everyday dialogue pieces: his *Colloquies*. Eton cannot claim to have been in the forefront of the Renaissance in England, but it was undoubtedly influenced by the Renaissance and helped to carry it forward.

Certainly Robert Aldrich, who was the Schoolmaster from 1515 to 1521, appears to have introduced Greek, but it may not have been a permanent introduction, since it does not figure in the 1528 and 1530 descriptions. Aldrich, who had been educated at Eton and King's, had met Erasmus at Cambridge and secured his approbation as 'a young man of a certain winning eloquence'. He later became Provost, and may then have given a renewed impetus to Greek studies. Sir Thomas Pope, founder of Trinity College, Oxford, learned Greek at Eton in the early 1520s, but reported that by 1556 study of the language was much decayed. Nevertheless Latin clearly remained the staple of education.

The enforcement of order in the School was by praepostors (prefects). There is no evidence of more than two schoolmasters. So in 1530 there were two praepostors in each form to check that all were present, two who were to be in the body of the Church, and two to see that Latin was spoken in the Third Form (and presumably above). Praepostors had to ensure that heads were kempt, faces washed and clothes clean; praepostors were in the field when the boys played, to put a stop to 'fighting, rent-clothes, blue eyes or such like'. Monitors were to escort those who did not board in College back to their houses, and if a house held four or five boys, there would be a monitor in it 'for chiding and for Latin speaking'. Each form also had a 'custos', or dunce, who would be the first called to answer questions and was then expected to report other boys who lapsed into English during the testing. Avoiding this role was one incentive to work and good behaviour, presumably reinforced by some chastisement or other. The 1530 description also makes it clear that dullards could be sent away after a warning.

What of the boys who lived this hard life? At the beginning of the sixteenth century, College seems not always to have been complete to the tally of seventy, but Collegers who did not go on to King's would not have been recorded. There may also have been up to a hundred Oppidans, to judge from the 1530 account. Their names are rarely known. Lord Grey de Wilton, who died at Eton in 1521, and whose funeral brass is in the Antechapel, is an exception. He was in fact a second son, and there is not much evidence of the aristocracy sending eldest sons to school at all at this stage. Most of the Collegers pursued the same sorts of career as their predecessors, usually in holy orders, but occasionally also as public servants or lawyers. About 1540 a change took place.[6] Up to that point only ten Etonians can be identified as having entered the House of Commons, but in Elizabeth's time forty future Members of Parliament are known – and they were usually from established families. Frequently Etonians can be recognized going on to the Inns of Court. It would seem therefore that there was a new perception of the usefulness of an Eton education, which can no doubt be attributed to the spread of the Renaissance. Whereas in the first hundred years the value was thought to be for the clergy, well connected perhaps, but without likelihood of coming into a landed estate, during the sixteenth century academic education became something appropriate for all the upper classes. Winchester suffered an influx of wealthy Founder's Kin, claiming free places, at much the same time; at least at Eton the rich newcomers were paying for their lodging. We still do not know the names of Oppidans, except by chance; but two successful boys at Eton around 1550 were Sir Thomas Sutton, the founder of the Charterhouse school and hospital, and Sir Humphrey Gilbert, who set up the first English North American colony in Newfoundland in 1583.* In 1562 and 1563 Sir Francis Knollys, at one time Queen Elizabeth's Treasurer, had four sons together as Commensals, known as Knoles senior, junior, minor and minimus.

Turning now from the boys to the men who taught them, we begin to find schoolmasters with identifiable personalities. The headmaster was still known as the Schoolmaster and still paid only £10, so that young men with aspirations to advance their careers were appointed. William Horman is one who would be recognized by modern schoolmasters as a professional. His brief successor, Edward Powell, ended at the stake at Tyburn in 1540 when the Reformation began to claim its martyrs; an ally of Catherine of Aragon, he was executed as a traitor to the Royal Supremacy. Another more notable Schoolmaster, Richard Cox (1528–34), an Etonian, was to be on the other side, an exile from Mary's Catholic restoration, later Bishop of Ely. To his credit Cox, who faced an episcopal visitation when he was Master, complained that the boys were not adequately provided for in College Hall. He also thought

---

* His Eton education much later prompted the depiction of School Yard on a Newfoundland stamp.

it wrong that the Oppidans had to lodge in the town at their parents' expense.

Cox was succeeded by Nicholas Udall (1534–7 and 1538–41), possibly the most disgraceful of Eton headmasters. Thomas Tusser, an agriculturist and poet, wrote in his autobiography:

> From Paul's I went, to Eton sent
> To learn straightways the Latin phrase,
> When fifty three stripes given to me
>   at once I had
> For fault but small or none at all,
> It came to pass thus beat I was;
> See, Udall, see, the mercy of thee
>   to me poor lad!

There was, however, nothing unusual in severe schoolmasters in those days; Walter Haddon, a distinguished scholar and public servant, who had flourished at Eton under Cox, described Cox as 'the best schoolmaster and the greatest beater of our time'. Udall, who was educated at Winchester, became a humanist and an author, praised by an Oxford pupil (Parkhurst, Bishop of Norwich): 'You understand Greek and Latin letters and you teach them truthfully. The natural disposition of your talent, Udall, is to make them full of life.' His *Flowers for Latin Spekynge* anthology may have helped to secure his Eton job. He encouraged declamation and possibly drama. Yet he lived beyond his means and became financially severely embarrassed, despite having, in addition to his headmastership, the living of Braintree.

In 1541 two Etonians stole silver, and sold it to a London silversmith. He and the boys were examined by the Privy Council and taken into custody. (One boy, Cheney, must certainly have been a rich Oppidan, as his father had to find £100 surety for him.) The next day, Udall was interrogated and confessed 'that he did commit buggery sundry times', and he was sent to the Marshalsea. William Edgerton, the biographer of Udall, speculates that an error was made by the man taking the records of the Privy Council. Perhaps the word 'buggery' was written when 'burglary' should have been. We cannot now be sure whether Udall tampered with the College silver or the boys, but perhaps his financial troubles make the former more probable. Anyway, from prison he wrote a long and cringing letter to an unknown patron, confessing unspecified misdeeds and promising to change from vice to virtue. Somehow this secured his release, and he was able to extract from Eton arrears of salary. He then lived as an author and protestant controversialist, and contributed to a medical compendium. He became a Canon of Windsor, where oddly there had also been trouble with the silver, and early in 1553 he apparently wrote *Ralph Roister Doister*, the first English comedy, for Edward VI – though its many swear-words suggest it may originate from a less Puritan era. Some have claimed this was written for performance by Etonians, but it is more probable that choirboys of St George's would have taken part. Possibly it does give some idea of the sort of plays, heavily influenced by Terence and Plautus, that might have been acted at Eton.* His colourful career ended with his death in 1554, shortly after he had become headmaster of the school at Westminster.

Provosts served for longer. Henry Bost died early in 1504, bequeathing furniture at Eton and at St James's to the College. He is not a Provost who is often remembered, but he was a successful politician when political management was needed. On the other hand his successor, Roger Lupton, chosen by a majority of Fellows, is known to all Etonians because of his buildings, particularly the splendid tower that bears his name. Almost at once the audit book was recording 'a new children's chamber' and the rebuilding of the kitchen. By 1517 Lupton had started to reconstruct the west side of the Cloisters, to contain his own house, a library and a great gate. The Library is what is now known as Election Hall; the stained glass windows are thought to show the different subject matter of the books adjacent to them. The new gateway, which replaced an existing one, did not have a clock or the turrets that we now know, but it was decorated in its brickwork with Madonna lilies, and the statue of the Assumption whose height off the ground protected it from Reformation iconoclasts. This building, together with the fine Chantry Chapel that Lupton added to College Chapel at his own expense, indicates that almost on the eve of the Reformation, there was no decline in religious devotion, or in veneration of Our Lady. Lupton left a penny for each Colleger annually, and Robert Rede of Burnham left two pence, which bequests are still given to Collegers

---

* Collegers at Eton in the 1980s put on *Ralph Roister Doister*. It proved a very moderate entertainment.

each year on Threepenny Day. This has lost much value, but then the Collegers no longer celebrate masses for the souls of Lupton, Rede and his wife.

Lupton's long rule covered the early reign of Henry VIII. The King was a visitor in 1510, giving 13s. 4d. to the Church and £3. 6s. 8d. to the Schoolmaster and scholars; his entertainment had, however, cost the College £18, an imbalance that has been regarded as symptomatic of what was to follow. In 1531 Henry required the surrender of St James's Hospital and its surrounding lands (but fortunately not Wild's and Chalcots Estates, in what became north London). In exchange he gave some rural properties. But for this, Eton must have become the richest educational establishment in the world (though others might well have proved as covetous as Henry). Later, in July 1534, the Provost and Fellows acknowledged the Royal Supremacy, along with the great majority of Englishmen. The King would also have acquired the first-fruits and tithes of the College's properties, but for a Statute that exempted Eton and Winchester, along with the two universities, in exchange for solemn masses to be said twice a year.

Possibly Lupton may have disliked the turn of events. At any rate, in 1535 he resigned as Provost (dying in 1540), and the next day Aldrich, the former Schoolmaster, was elected Provost. He was the first properly qualified by the Statutes, having himself been at Eton and King's; but it was hardly in accord with the Statutes that in 1536 he became Bishop of Carlisle. He was indeed questioned by the Privy Council for his neglect of his diocesan duties; he was often in London, where the College now had to pay for him to rent an apartment.

In 1542 King Henry required another slice of Eton's property on the edge of London, and in 1545 a more alarming development occurred, when the King, who had already dissolved the monasteries, obtained from Parliament a grant of all chantries, free chapels, hospitals and colleges. Commissioners visited Eton in 1546, and found the revenues to be about £1,000 a year. This was not so different from the revenue at the beginning of the century, but was worth less because of the inflation Henry's policies had created. At the same time inventories were made of the ecclesiastical ornaments and the plate. There could hardly have been any other end but the extinction of the College – though probably it would have been subsequently refounded. But God in His mercy took King Henry to Himself. As the grand funeral procession passed through Eton on

15 February 1547, the Provost, robed as Bishop, and all the College must have mixed their *De Profundis* with other prayers of thanksgiving. It was reminiscent of the death of Edward IV, but on this occasion the danger to the College had been more urgent.

The Chantries Act of 1547 was still before Parliament, but again Eton was to be excused suppression. Aldrich, having seen the College survive, resigned as Provost, though he continued as Bishop of Carlisle. The Duke of Somerset, Protector of the young Edward VI, chose Dr Thomas Smith, an eminent man of affairs and a scholar who had once been a clergyman, but who was not at all qualified to be Provost. Somerset arranged a royal dispensation, which overruled the Statutes and allowed Smith to hold other jobs in plurality. At the end of 1547 Smith was elected Provost and, shortly afterwards, became Dean of Carlisle. A few months later he married, subsequently becoming a Secretary of State, and Sir Thomas Smith. It was a remarkable transformation, and a scandal to any who held Roman Catholic beliefs.

A number of other Fellows followed the example of their Provost, and also married, which effectively cemented their allegiance to the Protestant cause. The Schoolmaster, Barker, was allowed to retain his post despite his marriage. This breach of the Statutes meant that Fellows of Eton had an advantage over the celibate Fellows of Oxford and Cambridge. The arrival of wives led to Fellows' requiring more luxurious accommodation. With the religious changes, some of the lesser clergy became redundant and their departure allowed for some expansion of the Fellows' apartments. None, however, could match the aggrandizement of the Provost's Lodge, which extended across the west side of the Cloisters. The Library was ejected, but to what part of the College buildings is unclear. It probably did not have more than 500 books, of which at least a respectable proportion survive to this day. The Provost lived in the grandest style, and his total emoluments from the College were of the order of £300 rather than the £50 due to him by Statute. And he had other incomes.

The financial position of the Fellows was also improved. Their stipends were restored to the original levels set by the Founder, and various payments in kind for food and clothing were replaced by sums of money. The Schoolmaster also benefited by his salary being raised to its original level. At this time he was living at the western end of Long Chamber, having direct access to it and therefore some effective control of the Collegers. Below was his office, to this day known as the Head Master's Chambers. The Usher had a single room at the opposite end of the Long Chamber. He had no room to be married, and Barker can have had little space for his wife.

Reformation of religious practices accompanied these social changes. Soon after Smith became Provost, images were cleared from the Church. In 1551 the altar frontals were adapted to furnish the ladies' chambers. The Choir's robes seem to have been converted for use in acting. Organs went out of use in the Church, but a shawm and viol were purchased for the Chapel, which were probably used along with other stringed instruments (bought for the boys' dormitory), for chamber music or to accompany plays.[7] Some of the old festivals vanished from the Eton calendar, and new service books were ordered. The wall-paintings were whitewashed. Even the mention of Our Lady in the title 'The King's College of Our Lady of Eton' was under threat, but it did in fact survive.

All this upheaval brought its problems. Although most of England accepted Henry VIII's political changes and the subsequent religious changes under Edward VI and Mary with little difficulty, Eton was more prepared to argue. In 1552 Sir Thomas Smith had to appear before the Council to explain his perpetual contention with the Fellows of Eton. He was, however, enough of a politician to ensure that he overcame this challenge, though he had already undergone a spell in the Tower of London in 1549 when his patron Somerset was temporarily eclipsed. Good fortune, rather than cunning, probably helped him when Edward VI suddenly died and Queen Mary succeeded, bringing back the Catholic religion, for his wife died opportunely the day the Queen entered London. Three married Fellows were replaced in a single day in March 1554.

Meanwhile the high altar in the Church was repaired, and the old services were restored, which required the purchase of books, bells and chalices. In July 1554, Smith married a widow, and this did occasion his resignation – after he had sought advice from the Visitor, the Bishop of Lincoln. He had perhaps used Eton for his own advantage and comfort, but he was the most distinguished Provost up to that time, excepting possibly Waynflete, and important not least as author later of the *Discourse of the Common Weal*, a book of political theory.

The Fellows tried to secure a Provost of their own choice, but the Queen insisted on Henry Cole, a Wykehamist. He set out to restore the old ways, cleaning the painted-over walls of the Church, purchasing new vestments, and even accepting a new estate for the College, in return for an old-fashioned obit (an annual mass for the deceased).

Provost Cole preached what would now be called the party line at the execution of Thomas Cranmer. He was also sent to extirpate heresy in Ireland. There was an embarrassing occasion when his papers were stolen in Chester and a pack of cards with the knave uppermost substituted. His zeal only served to place him in an extremely poor position when the Queen and Cardinal Pole died in November 1558. Cole proved less astute than Sir Thomas Smith (who lived on until 1577). In March 1559 he defended the Roman Catholic position in a disputation at Westminster Abbey. His reward was to be deprived of his preferments, fined and committed to the Fleet prison.

A Royal Commission was appointed to visit Cambridge and Eton to secure oaths to the Queen as Supreme Governor. One of the commissioners, William Bill, found himself shortly promoted Provost, which office he held jointly with the Mastership of Trinity College, Cambridge, and the Deanery of Westminster. Not surprisingly he was seldom at Eton. Once more, however, a Protestant reformation was set in hand. At this point the murals in the Church were again obliterated with whitewash, by the College barber for 6s. 8d. Provost Bill died in 1561, bequeathing to the College some of his library, and to the Collegers a coverlet for each bed. The Fellows were minded to choose Richard Bruerne, an admirably qualified colleague – except that he had had to resign from the Regius Professorship of Hebrew at Oxford because of immorality, and that he was of Roman Catholic sympathy. A commission was dispatched to Eton headed by Archbishop Parker of Canterbury. Bruerne sensibly resigned, and Queen Elizabeth appointed William Day, a celibate who betrayed her by quickly marrying. With Day as Provost, the time of religious turmoil was ended: he finished the Protestant transformation of the Church. Quite what the boys made of it, we can only surmise. There were, however, four known Etonian Protestant martyrs and two Catholics.*

* They were John Frith, burnt at Smithfield in 1533, John Hullier, burnt at Cambridge in 1553, and Robert Glover and Laurence Saunders, both burnt at Coventry in 1555. The Blessed Ralph Sherwin, a Commensal, was hanged (with Robert Campion) at Tyburn in 1581, and the Blessed Thomas Aufield was hanged there in 1585.

It was, however, almost an end of what King Henry VI had envisaged. The religious purposes of the College had vanished, and it became essentially a school. The Chapel was to be staunchly Protestant until the end of the twentieth century. Then a Roman Catholic priest was appointed at Eton and Catholic ceremonies were performed in the Chapel occasionally in a more ecumenical spirit than the sixteenth century could have conceived.

CHAPTER FOUR

Eton in the Elizabethan Age

THE INSPECTION OF the College by Archbishop Parker inspired some of the same work that is generated by modern inspections of schools. For instance, in the summer of 1561, the Library was cleaned and repaired. At this time too the new Schoolmaster, William Malim,* wrote an account in Latin of how the School worked, providing first a list of festivals and other important days in the Eton year, and secondly an account of the daily routine. This, known as his *Consuetudinarium*,[1] was probably written as advice to Westminster School, which was refounded at the beginning of Elizabeth's reign. Provost Bill was also Dean of Westminster. It does seem to have influenced the Statutes of Westminster School, but it was evidently reused for Archbishop Parker's Commission, since it exists in his Library at Corpus Christi College, Cambridge.

The daily routine was not so very different from what it had been in 1530. The 5.00 a.m. start was enforced by one of the praepostors of the Bedchamber. The boys were expected to rise at once, say their prayers as they dressed, wash under the pump, which was probably then in Weston's Yard, and set the room in order. At 6.00 a.m. the Lower Master (who was responsible for the First, Second and Third Forms, and shared control of the Fourth Form with the Head

---

* Malim is sometimes said to have been Schoolmaster before 1561, but probably the Schoolmaster at that time was Thomas Valence. Malim, who had been at Eton in the 1540s, was a Fellow of King's from 1551 to 1561. He stayed at Eton until 1571, and subsequently became High Master of St Paul's.

Master) began formal prayers. He started to test boys' prepared learning, while praepostors checked which boys were present and inspected their face and hands – rather reminiscent of barrack-room discipline some centuries later. The Head Master arrived at 7.00 a.m. to hear over passages learnt by heart. At 8.00 a.m. he gave out to the older boys a passage, to be translated by the Fourth Form, to be 'varied' by the Fifth Form, and to be translated into verse by the Sixth and Seventh forms; meanwhile the younger boys were similarly exercised by the Lower Master. Different Latin authors were covered on different days by different forms – the First Form, however, learning from Vives, the Renaissance educationalist. At 9.00 a.m. there was an interval for breakfast, and at 10.00 a.m. further prayers. At 11.00 a.m. they went to the Hall for dinner. At noon the Fourth Form had repetition with the Lower Master, then between 1.00 and 3.00 p.m. further teaching, followed by testing of the boys' work by both Masters. Then there was a break to 4.00 p.m. After another hour in school, which might include Greek for the top two forms, supper was at 5.00 p.m., and thereafter teaching was in the hands of the praepostors, who were expected to control the boys both for learning and for improving their characters. At 7.00 p.m. there was further light refreshment, followed either by more study or by play, depending on the season of the year. At 8.00 p.m. they went to bed, saying their prayers. Friday was rather a special day, for wrongdoers received correction for their offences, but there were no lessons before dinner.* On Saturday, exercises were 'shown up' (handed in to the Master), and declamations and debates were held for the senior boys. Curiously, nothing is specified for Sunday, but there were services according to the Book of Common Prayer; these were allowed to be in Latin for the edification of the boys, though services in English were required for the Eton town parishioners. No doubt there would also have been sermons.

The eighteen praepostors must have been essential to the working of the programme. Four kept order in the schoolroom, one in Hall, two in the Church, four in the playing fields, four in the Bedchamber; two were responsible for the Oppidans, and one had to

---

* The threat of beatings in store must have been particularly unpleasant. In 1563 several boys are said to have run away for fear of flogging, which occasioned some debate in Cecil's rooms at Windsor Castle, the spur to Ascham's treatise on education, *The Schoolmaster*. Ascham opposed corporal punishment.

inspect boys for cleanliness. There was still a dunce in every form, picked out for speaking English, for bad writing or spelling, or for failures on tests. Doubtless the praepostors, if not the dunce, gained from their experiences.

Each year began with the boys at School at Eton, but enjoying a relaxed timetable: more play, friendly verses for good luck, small presents. After Epiphany, they returned to work in earnest, but religious festivals and the commemoration of benefactors could provide a holiday, and even cash distributions, for example tuppence on 13 January, William Waynflete's day. The Conversion of St Paul, on 25 January provided the occasion for an excursion 'ad Montem', to 'The Hill', presumably Salt Hill in Slough; this was when new boys underwent an initiation ceremony where they 'faced blows in manly and stout fashion'; verses and epigrams were recited about them, full of drollery, but 'devoid of indecent coarseness'. 'Finally they bedew their faces and cheeks with salt tears' (a quotation from Lucretius), and are admitted to the rites of veterans. 'Acclamations ensue and small triumphs, and they rejoice indeed, both for their travails past and for their admission to fellowship with such lively comrades.' All of this sounds deplorable to the more correct views of the twenty-first century, but it confirms the early existence of initiation ceremonies at schools, and testifies to the importance of the fellowship among boys, which must have been the saving grace of school life in those hard and disciplined days.

Lent brought Shrovetide verses to extol Dionysus and an unattractive pancake ceremony when missiles were thrown at a crow, attached together with a pancake to the schoolroom door. On Ash Wednesday, boys had been expected to confess to a Fellow or Chaplain, but the passage is erased in the manuscript, suggesting that the practice was stopped at the date of writing. On Maundy Thursday, boys could walk abroad after dinner, so long as they avoided taverns. Some boys would be permitted to take Communion, and there was a vigil on Easter Eve. After Easter there would be play out of doors in the evening, instead of work. The Feast of St John before the Latin Gate, on 6 May, was curiously relaxed, with the boys allowed a siesta: 'The Latin Gate affords us play, and sleep and ale to mark the day.'

Holidays lasted for roughly three weeks from Ascension Day, and boys were permitted to go home. They had to return on the Eve of the Feast of Corpus Christi, or they would be flogged. On St John Baptist's Day, midsummer was celebrated in the traditional way with a bonfire, and boys were allowed to sleep in an hour the next morning; it was also the custom to decorate their bedspaces with pictures. On 7 July, the anniversary of the transfer of the bones of St Thomas Becket to Canterbury, there was another bonfire. Shortly thereafter came the season of Election to King's, and selection of new boys for College, 'the fittest out of all Britain'. After 29 August, the day of St John Baptist's beheading, summer was at an end, and with it out of doors play in the evening. (This day would, of course, have fallen in September on the modern calendar.)

In September they had a day for nutting, chosen at the Head Master's discretion. All Saints' Day was a holiday, but All Souls' Day brought a morning of prayers, the boys in Church in surplices, and appropriate readings preceded an afternoon of play. As Christmas approached, a Boy Bishop was elected, and the festivity started with plays, possibly in English as well as in Latin. Malim correctly comments: 'The actor's art is a slight one, and yet, for a proper action in speaking and deportment and movement of the body, it does more than anything else.' Writing lessons were continued over Christmas, but apart from these, there was play. (In 1595 a long list of acting clothes was recorded, many of silk and apparently converted from old cassocks, but also including servants' clothes in cotton and coarse materials, and even beards of the longest and the shortest sort.[2] Possibly this acting wardrobe, found in the Provosts' Lodge, was no longer used, as the religiously earnest had turned against the theatre.)

It was not a soft life, and only slightly better conditions seem to have prevailed for Commensals. The bill survives for Henry and William Cavendish for their first year at School, beginning in 1560, when they were aged respectively 10 and 9. They had to wear gowns, too, but seem to have had doublets more fashionably sewn with silk buttons, and their expenditure on shoes was considerable. A pair of fur gloves must have been welcome. At first they, and their servant, boarded with a Richard Hill, and their room had a fire. Later they moved into the College for eating. They were still paying Hill 12s. 4d. a quarter, and the Bursar £3. 12s. for board; the Bursar also charged them 6d. a quarter for birch, broom and ink, presumably all necessities of school life. One occasion of cost was 3d. given to a man who showed a camel and bear-baiting in the College. The year's bill for the two boys was £26. 6s. 5d.[3] (Since no further bills survive, it is possible that the Cavendishes subsequently returned home: their boarding may have been occasioned by the remarriage of their widowed mother, Bess of Hardwick. The elder was a disappointment to his mother, but the younger became Earl of Devonshire.)

This is not the oldest Eton bill, since there survives from the reign of Mary a less detailed bill for a boy called Dethick, son of the Garter King of Arms, a Commensal, but one who sat at a lower table than the Cavendishes. The Lower Master was writing to the father to ask for money, and drawing his attention to a rise in food prices. The curious feature of this bill is the mention of a quarter's stipend, 6s. 8d. It sounds as though, contrary to the Statutes, a charge was made for teaching, but no such item occurs in the Cavendish bill. Perhaps the quarter's stipend was in fact a lodging charge, or perhaps the Lower Master was acquiring a dishonest income.[4]

It is possible to trace the Eton careers of Commensals through the Audit books. Only one, a boy called Day, sat at the first table; could he have been a relation of Provost Day and separated from his friends, unlucky fellow? Some were Commensals part of the time, and then became ordinary Oppidans, boarding out; perhaps they preferred a small measure of extra comfort and freedom. Many Commensals, for example the Cavendishes, bore names that recur in the Eton school lists, though it is seldom possible to be sure that a tradition of son succeeding father at Eton had been established, since the records of Oppidans continued to be very incomplete. One Commensal of the 1570s was Sir John Harington, a godson of the Queen. It is also worth noting that Thomas Hatcher compiled a register of men at King's, and therefore of Etonians, to 1572; the drawing up of such a list shows that Etonians saw themselves as worthy of memorial.

During this period there is evidence that academic standards continued to rise. A collection of Latin verse written to celebrate the accession of Elizabeth survives, in which forty-four boys contributed work of varying length, all loyal and complimentary – many hoping that she would find a suitable husband. The standard is much higher than that exhibited by William Paston in the previous century. Just possibly the Schoolmaster added polish, but there is some evidence of spontaneity – for example, from Osmund Lakes, who signed off after two lines: '*Vive, valeque simul*'. Later, in 1560,

Provost Bill submitted another collection, an indication that the first set had found favour with the highly educated Queen. This time, there are epigrams and acrostics, of a kind that appealed to Elizabethan taste. In 1563 yet another set of verses marked the Queen's retreat to Windsor at a time of plague, when some of the boys were themselves removed to nearby Cippenham. Its object was doubtless the same as that of previous collections, but more obviously made: the boys request her favour 'for our dearest master'. It is hard to believe in the sincerity of the word 'dearest', but the wish for Malim's promotion may have indeed been genuine.

In fact the Queen's favour was rather questionably shown by her government's choosing to hold the French Ambassador hostage at Eton in December 1563. His retinue proved restive guests: for example, they thrust spits up through the floorboards and spiked Etonians unawares above; they shot the birds, threw bricks at scholars and turned night into day. These visitors were unwelcome, but others were not; and Eton retained its place in public life.

More desirable still to the Fellows, no doubt, was a dispensation allowing each to hold a living worth up to 40 marks, contrary to Henry VI's Statutes. There was undoubtedly a shortage of learned clergy in the Elizabethan Church, but this licence to absenteeism was to be a long-running scandal. Another privilege was gained by an Act of Parliament in 1575, decreeing that the Colleges of Oxford and Cambridge, together with Winchester and Eton, should receive some rent in wheat and malt, a measure that protected them from the prevalent inflation.

Eton remained in Elizabeth's favour, and even towards the end of her life she continued to pay visits there. There is a quaint graffito on the panelling in College Hall (which had been installed in 1547): 'Queen Elizabethe ad nos gave October X 2 loves in a mes 1596'. Boys sitting in that corner did indeed for a time receive a double ration of bread at dinner. (On this particular occasion, the Queen may graciously have received no fewer than 4,000 Latin hexameters, but they have not survived.) By then Day was no longer Provost. Earlier offers of a diocese could not tempt him; as Provost of Eton and Dean of Windsor, with a few minor jobs, he was richer than the Bishop of Worcester; and he could not secure that major bishopric that he desired until he succeeded his brother-in-law as Bishop of Winchester in 1595, a position he enjoyed for only a few months. His death, if not his preferment, terminated his provostship.

The Earl of Essex, Elizabeth's favourite, was certainly keen on Day's move, since he wanted his protege, Henry Savile, the Warden of Merton College, Oxford, to be Provost of Eton. Although an anonymous document from Eton argued that there were devout men from Eton and King's who would provide pastoral care for the College and parish, Sir Robert Cecil, the Queen's Secretary of State, was firm that it was a royal appointment and that it should be Savile; he was just possibly influenced by an offer of 300 angels* from Savile. The Queen may have felt that she should not appoint a layman, but she gave way in May 1596, and the Fellows went through the formality of electing her nominee. Despite his lack of qualifications and his continuing as Warden of Merton, Savile was to prove a notable Provost. He set about recovering a silver bowl and payment for many goods and much produce which Day had abstracted. Day's executors refunded £100 over four years and returned the bowl. Savile took an immediate interest in the Library,[5] from which Day had quite possibly appropriated some of the fittings, and which had apparently been transformed into a hay store. Probably the books had been moved to School Yard under the Long Chamber, though some were lost. To be fair to Day, the Fellows were becoming more distinguished in his time, but Savile attracted other scholars by his own learning. There was a setback when Essex's rebellion failed, and he was executed in 1601. (His son was being educated at Eton before Essex's fall, and returned after the execution. Savile thus made some recompense for his preferment.) Savile was himself arrested, but he was not detained for long, and the Queen visited Eton in the autumn of that year. In 1602 four Russian youths came to Eton and Winchester, Oxford and Cambridge in order to learn English and Latin – another mark of official approval.† (Elizabeth's Ambassador to Moscow in 1588, Giles Fletcher, had been an Etonian, as was his son Phineas, the poet.) Clearly the College prospered and ended the Elizabethan age with a rising reputation.

* An angel was a gold coin, worth 10s. (50 pence) at this time.
† Now Russians come to Eton again for short exchanges with boys learning Russian at the School.

CHAPTER FIVE

The Age of Savile and Wotton

ETON IN THE seventeenth century before the Civil War was domi-
nated by two Provosts, Savile and Wotton, who count among the
most distinguished to have held the position. Both were men of
commanding appearance and fine minds, as can be judged from the
portraits the College owns of them. We also know so much more of
their personalities than of earlier Etonian characters, that by comparison they inevitably stand out for the historian.

Savile was not an easy man: 'It is his custom to kick all men who
are generally considered learned, and to treat them as asses on two
legs,' complained Isaac Casaubon, the celebrated scholar. He was
widely read, sufficiently learned in Theology to be known as 'the
lay bishop', but also interested in Mathematics and Astronomy.
Having taken steps to restore the Library, soon after Day's departure, he subsequently expanded it by purchasing books, rather than
relying on gifts. By the time of his death Eton boasted an institutional library of over a thousand volumes, even though it was only
for a society of six Fellows and the Provost; it was not for the boys.*

James I, who favoured learning even if he lacked common sense,
knighted Savile on the occasion of his first visit to Eton. He had heard
of Savile's reputation, and Savile was to be one of the translators of

---

* Maxwell-Lyte reports that in 1597 Savile sent one John Joyner, presumably a carpenter, to copy Bodley's Library at Oxford, but that did not exist.
Joyner presumably copied the Merton Library. Lady Savile was so disen-
chanted by her husband's absorption with books that she complained: 'I would
I were a book too, and then you would a little more respect me.'

the Authorized Version of the Bible. The same year that Savile was knighted, his 8-year-old only son died, probably recently enrolled in the School. Savile seems thereafter to have become even more determined to devote his time to scholarship. At Oxford he founded the Professorships of Geometry and Astronomy. At Eton he set up a printing press in what is now known as Savile House. The buildings there were rebuilt, probably retaining some of their old character, to include not only a press but dormitories for Chaplains, Clerks, Commensals and Oppidans. Savile was himself responsible for most of the works printed, notably a great edition of the writings of St John Chrysostom, which acquired a European reputation. Casaubon, attracted to England by the moderation of the Anglican religious settlement, was further encouraged to send his son Meric to Eton; the boy was elected to College in 1610, though he was not strictly qualified as he was born in Geneva. Meric remained an Englishman, becoming an author and a clergyman, deprived of his living during the Civil War, but surviving until 1671.

Savile attracted some distinguished Fellows. His Vice-Provost, Baldwin Collins, was famous for his good works, but was perhaps even more remarkable for the fact that he and his son held Fellowships for seventy-seven years between them, most of that time as Vice-Provosts. The Vice-Provost was arguably more important within Eton than the Provost when, as in Collins's time, the Provost had outside interests. Chamber founded Postmasterships at Merton College for Etonians who did not go to King's. Robyns bequeathed the funds for the College to acquire a beautiful Portuguese silver dish and ewer when he died in 1613. Two new Fellows elected that year were Montague, a leading Arminian who was to become Bishop of Chichester, and John Hales. Hales,[1] one of the most attractive figures in Eton history, attended the Synod of Dort in 1618, the occasion of dispute between the Calvinists and the Arminians, who rejected the doctrine of predestination; Hales found himself forced 'to bid John Calvin good-night', and he became a lifelong opponent of all religious dogmatism. Another Eton Fellow, William Charke, was an extreme Puritan who had earlier believed that Bishops were the invention of Satan. The Visitor complained to Savile, who was able to deal with such a problem.

The Visitor was also scandalized by the Schoolmaster, Richard Langley, who held two rich benefices. Such pluralism was 'an apostemated ulcer'.[2] Besides, as a Doctor of Divinity, he was over-qualified to be a mere schoolmaster. Savile attempted to retain Langley, but in the end could not. The Visitor was also encouraged by those at King's to press for more Kingsmen to be appointed to Eton. Savile, who had replaced Langley with a Merton man, soon appointed a new Schoolmaster from King's.

In general Savile was a stern disciplinarian; for instance, he once fined two College servants who were over-friendly to the boys. Nor did he encourage bright pupils: 'Give me the plodding student; if I would look for wits, I would go to Newgate; there be the wits.' Notwithstanding this attitude, the School flourished in Savile's time. In 1613 there were more than a hundred candidates for scholarships. Elections to College seem to have been advertised only at Eton, but many candidates came forward from outside the locality by nominations. The King might reward his servants (as, for example, in 1605 the Serjeant of the Pantry) by recommending their sons as Eton Scholars; they were usually described as 'hopeful' boys. Other friends of the Provost and Fellows, and of the electors who came from King's, might also press the claims of their promising sons. Sir Henry Wotton in 1629 wrote sorrowfully that at the Election, 'annually I make shift to lose four or five friends' by being unable to help all who made application. The boys did face a simple test reminiscent of GCSE French: *Quod est tibi nomen? Quot annos natus es? Quo oppido?* The test established a minimum capacity, but was also designed to see whether the boys fulfilled the statutory residential requirements. Clearly this was not a reliable system of selection by merit, but it may not have been wholly absurd: at least someone thought the boys promising.

Despite increases in fees for the Commensals, their number grew, and the table in College Hall had to be lengthened to accommodate them. Whether there were also more Oppidans is not clear. Some Commensals would also have brought servants with them. Con O'Neil, son the rebel Earl of Tyrone, who was lodged by the government at Eton in 1616 and 1617, seems to have come with two servants, and his bill was about £90 a year. The books he needed were not cheap, a Bible costing him 6s. 8d.[3] We know little of the life of the boys, except for the occasional complaint about the food. There was a tennis court at Eton at the beginning of the century, but whether the boys used it or not is uncertain.*

* Four hundred years on, there is some pressure for Eton once more to have a real tennis court.

The College finances were also in flourishing condition, and the Fellows could authorize a number of charitable grants. It seems, however, at this time that they began the practice of distributing any annual surplus among themselves. In 1617, for instance, they shared over £400. The fact that other institutions behaved in this way does not make this conduct acceptable. There was some expenditure in erecting a new organ loft in the Church and other small works, but the surplus revenue could certainly have been directed to other improvements.

Savile died in 1622 and was buried in College Chapel. His widow gave the College his noble portrait, which was, appropriately, hung in the Library. She herself was to bequeath two Elizabethan silver flagons for use in College Chapel. His memorial at Merton College, Oxford, includes a picture of Eton. His printing press could not be maintained without Savile's private wealth, and the Greek type was sold to Oxford University and then lent on to Cambridge.

Before Savile's death, scheming to determine his successor as Provost had already begun, but James I was determined to assert his prerogative and appoint his favourite. This was Thomas Murray, who was disqualified – as the Visitor pointed out – on three counts: as a Scotsman, a layman and not a graduate. He was also possibly a Puritan. Nevertheless the Fellows and the Visitor bowed to royal pressure, and Thomas Murray became one of the early examples of that recurrent phenomenon, the Scotsman coming south to rule the English. In fact he was soon mortally ill, and he acquired the largest tomb in College Chapel, in inverse relation to his achievements.

When the news of his illness spread, scheming resumed. This time one aspirant was the recently disgraced Lord Chancellor, Francis Bacon, who seemed to think that the provostship would serve for a pension. The King, however, would not choose without the advice of the Duke of Buckingham, who was in Spain looking for a Spanish match for the future King Charles. Buckingham found a new candidate, Sir Henry Wotton, who had recently returned from being Ambassador in Venice.* He was also in need of a pension, especially as he apparently was not paid fully for his work. He was keen to be Provost, and though as a Wykehamist and Oxford man (he was the

---

* Wotton is famous for his remark that an ambassador is 'one sent to lie abroad for his country'. In Latin, which Wotton used, there is no pun: the Ambassador is unambiguously untruthful. Wotton, however, also advised diplomats to tell the truth: they would never be believed.

most distinguished product of Winchester at a dim period in its history) he was not fully qualified, he did at least take deacon's orders. Since he was himself both a cultured and literary man and keen to encourage education, he was a very happy choice. Like Hales, he was anxious to avoid the religious conflicts of the time, and the two were close friends. A hospitable man, Wotton also shared with Izaak Walton, who wrote a short biography of him, a great love of fishing, 'saying often, he would rather live five May months, than forty Decembers'.

In 1634 the Fellows of King's again showed their jealousy of Eton. The King had ruled that the Vicar of Windsor should be ex officio a Fellow of Eton, thus increasing his income, but making it more difficult for Kingsmen to acquire a coveted Eton Fellowship. This led to a more general complaint that Eton fellowships were still only seven in number rather than ten, and that these often went to Oxford men, despite the College Statutes. The Fellows of King's also attempted to disguise their essentially selfish complaints by talking about the hardships they had suffered at Eton when scholars, from inadequate bedding, clothing and food. (Such complaints were probably justified, but the few who did become Fellows did little to help the boys.) They appealed not to the Visitor but to Archbishop Laud, who heard from both sides and made a sensible ruling. Despite the Statutes, the practice had certainly been to allow Fellows from Oxford as well as Cambridge; and the College did not have all the endowments the Founder intended. Accordingly, he laid down that there should still be seven Fellows, five of whom should be drawn from King's. As for the Vicar of Windsor, he should indeed be chosen from among the Fellows of Eton. This arrangement, however, had few practical consequences because of the Civil War, and Kingsmen did not secure control of Eton until the eighteenth century.

The society at Eton over which Wotton presided was very appealing. The 'ever-memorable' John Hales, as he was called in his lifetime, attracted scholars to consult him from all over Europe; Wotton described him as 'the walking library'. Some time in the 1630s at a disputation at Eton, Hales was the first to maintain successfully that Shakespeare was the greatest of all poets, greater even than those of antiquity. Another most attractive figure was John Harrison, Schoolmaster from 1630 to 1636, and then Fellow. Like Wotton he was an encourager of youth and an amateur of science. Remarkably, College Library possesses two first editions of Copernicus' *De Revolutionibus,* one from Savile, one from Harrison.

Harrison took a particular interest in Robert Boyle, the youngest son of the Earl of Cork who was sent to Eton in 1635 with the brother who was closest to him in age.[4]* Because many letters were preserved at the Earl of Cork's home at Lismore in Ireland and because Boyle himself wrote a brief autobiography, we know more about Robert Boyle, later so distinguished as a scientist, than about any other Etonians until Horace Walpole and Thomas Gray arrived in the eighteenth century. Robert was only 8 when he came to Eton, accompanied by a watchful servant. He was obviously bright, and when Harrison became a Fellow, Boyle probably lodged with him as a Commensal. In one book left by Harrison to College Library, there is inscribed in a childish hand, 'I Robert Boyle, do say Albert Morton is a brave boy', and in another: 'Albertus Morton is a most brave and rare boy, 1638.' Morton was a Commensal who became a Colleger, presumably through the patronage of Wotton, since Morton's uncle, also an Etonian, had been Wotton's secretary.† In his autobiography Boyle says of Wotton that he was 'not only a fine gentleman himself, but very well skilled in the art of making others so'. Wotton took steps to cure Boyle of his stutter. Of Harrison he wrote, 'He was careful to instruct him in such an affable, kind and gentle way, that he easily prevailed with him to consider studying not so much as a duty of obedience to his superiors, but as a way to purchase for himself a most delightsome and invaluable good.' Boyle was not a games player, but had occasional alarming falls when riding. His life was also nearly cut short by a ceiling falling in on his room, and by a mistaken dose from the apothecary: such were the hazards of Etonian life. Boyle could not have learnt all that much by the time he left Eton at the age of 11, but he had acquired the will

---

* Known as Boyle a and Boyle i, abbreviated from Boyle ma and Boyle mi; the latter terms would still be used as shorthand for Boyle major and minor.

† That Morton, an Etonian, and his wife are remembered because of Wotton's epitaph:

> He first deceased; she for a little tried
> To live without him; lik'd it not, and died.

Albert Morton was appointed Henry Wotton's executor, though still a boy in the School.

to learn, and curiosity about science. He also had a smattering of French, and had taken some lessons on the viol. In Wotton and Harrison we can clearly see the pastoral care for the individual boy that was to be the distinguishing feature of Eton at its best throughout its history. Yet despite them, the Earl removed his two youngest sons from Eton when his three older boys returned from a European trip with their tutor, and soon after sent them to Europe in their turn. Clearly he regarded Eton's education less highly than learning to know the world.*

A slightly earlier Etonian, Henry More, also learnt to think for himself. Brought up as a strict Calvinist, he went to Eton, aged 14, in 1628. At some moment in the playing fields, 'walking as my manner was, slowly, and with my head on one side, and kicking now and then the stones with my feet', he rejected the idea of predestination. He became a noted philosopher and poet at Cambridge, and in due course a Fellow, like Boyle, of the Royal Society.[5]

By the time Robert Boyle left Eton, Harrison had become a Fellow, and was succeeded by the more rigid Norris. Sir Henry Wotton was himself ailing, and at the end of 1639 he 'put off mortality with as much content and cheerfulness as human frailty is capable of; being then in great tranquillity of mind and in perfect peace with God and man'. So says Walton, who also translates the enigmatic inscription on his tomb in the Antechapel: 'Here lies the first Author of this Sentence: the Itch of Disputation will prove the Scab of the Church. Inquire his name elsewhere.' Certainly he died at the right moment, for the gathering political clouds distressed him. The single word, *'Philosophemur'*, 'Let us philosophize', is written on his portrait; his name is rightly preserved in present-day Eton, where Wotton's Society does discuss philosophy. His fine poem beginning, 'How happy is he born and taught, that serveth not another's will', is still sung in Chapel.†

---

* The cost to the Earl of Cork of the two boys' stay at Eton was £914. 3s. 9d. 'for diett, tutaradge and aparell': a very large sum. Sadly Carew, the servant whose letters say so much, was disgraced when he fell in love with the College underbaker's daughter.

† Wotton bequeathed the manuscripts he had acquired in Venice to the College, together with the great view of Venice by Fialetti.

CHAPTER SIX

The Great Rebellion

WOTTON WAS IMMEDIATELY succeeded by Richard Steward of All Souls College, who was Clerk of the King's Closet and Dean of Chichester. Charles I had made a responsible choice: Steward was honest, learned and devout, and an enemy of the Puritans. Yet he did not prove to have the political skills that might have served Eton in the troubled times to come.

From just before the Civil War, perhaps 1640, a list survives of a procession to Montem, with many quasi-military designations. One Colleger called Batten appears as a senator; yet he was refused election to King's because of the insufficiency of his learning and the scandalous quality of his life; he had to go to Trinity College instead. We must not assume that Eton, whatever its prosperity and high repute, was without its blemishes.

When the King raised his standard in 1642, the Provost immediately rallied to him, taking the College seal, and probably some of the silver (little early secular plate survives). Windsor was seized for Parliament by Colonel Venn; and the tide of war only once touched Eton, when, after Edgehill, Prince Rupert made an attempt on the Castle, setting up some artillery in the College grounds, where it was too remote to have any effect. Fifty-one former Etonians are known to have fought, thirty-five as Royalists, with four more changing to the King's side after starting with Parliament.

From Oxford a royal mandate was issued in 1643 to postpone the College Elections, but it was no use trying to rule from Oxford. In practice a number of scholars were chosen, and they tended to be boys with Puritan backgrounds. The use of surplices in the Church, which at this time came to be generally known as Chapel, was forbidden, and Colonel Venn was ordered to remove scandalous monuments.

Not surprisingly the Provost's income was sequestered, but the College's endowments were spared; it would seem, however, that revenues from the more disturbed parts of the country did not reach Eton. In February 1644, Provost Steward was judged to have neglected the government of the College, and dismissed by Parliamentary ordinance; he survived in exile with Charles II until 1651, but never revisited Eton. Francis Rous, a West Country gentleman who served in all the Parliaments of Charles I's reign, was appointed in his place.* He was the author of some metrical versions of the psalms, and of the form of prayer authorized by Parliament in 1644. Rous managed to retain his place in the Commons, and was able to safeguard the College's property from taxation. In 1645, regular Elections were held for King's, and for scholarships at Eton. (One of the candidates proved proficient in Hebrew; this was unprecedented and a sign of the times, but it is fair to point out that he had previously been at St Paul's School.) The number of Commensals, however, fell and by 1646 only two were left, probably the last ever. Their fathers tended to be Royalists, and it is fairly certain that a few Etonians left School to fight for their King. When the Restoration came, Commensals were not restored. The same type of boy became an ordinary Oppidan, eating with his landlady rather than in College Hall.

The Chaplains were renamed Conducts, signifying hired (and so removable) men, a title retained to this day. It would appear that the Choir survived, since Clerks and choristers are to be found on lists of those dining in College Hall. On the other hand, a practice was begun which was ultimately to end its independence: whereas the Statutes had forbidden members of the Choir from also singing at St George's, now the Clerks, who had received a bonus when the College had surplus revenue, needed a second income and sang in both choirs. The number of boy choristers was reduced, and there seem to have been an extra ten Scholars at this time.[1] The Choir may have led the singing of the Provost's metrical psalms, but the services

---

* There is currently at Eton a Rous Society, but unlike Wotton's Society it does not commemorate a Provost: its interests are equestrian.

were shorn of other sacred music. Thomas Weaver, a Fellow from Wotton's day, attempted to preserve the old standards by covertly assembling past choristers of Eton and St George's; when Colonel Venn challenged him with singing popish music, he replied that 'he humbly conceived God was as well pleased with being served in tune as out of tune'.*

Weaver was not the only Fellow to be in trouble. In 1649, the Fellows, Masters and scholars of Eton were required to sign an 'Engagement' that they would be true and faithful to the Commonwealth of England as it is now established'.† Hales would not sign and was ejected. After various vicissitudes he was to end his days with a truly admirable landlady in Eton. His books were sold, but not well, for the market for scholarly books was depressed. Such money as he had, he tended to give to those he felt to be in greater need. When he died, he was buried in the churchyard, where a substantial monument was placed over his grave by a former pupil. Nicholas Gray, the Schoolmaster, was also expelled, but was allowed to become the Master of Tonbridge School, replacing the man there chosen to be a Fellow at Eton.‡

The new Puritan Fellows were less sociable than their predecessors, and from 1646 the custom grew of Fellows' drawing payments when they no longer dined in Hall. That would have suited married Fellows, but it also seemed proper to those who regarded feasting together as sin. Unfortunately the Fellows' consciences still allowed them to share in the division of any surplus income. When capital expenditure was needed, the College did not use collective savings, but instead borrowed. Consequently by the time of the Restoration the College was distinctly in debt.

Although this must count against Provost Rous, he did safeguard Eton from outside attack and he was genuinely concerned with the good government of the College. In 1646 he issued instructions for the religious welfare of the scholars, which was certainly his business. They were to rise at 5.00 a.m. with a psalm and prayers, and

* Rather as now some conceive God can be as well worshipped in good English as in bad.
† Eton, Winchester and Westminster were specially selected for this oath, an indication that they were regarded as the prime schools.
‡ Gray was probably Schoolmaster at Eton from 1643 to 1648 by which time he was nearly sixty. He is an interesting example of a professional headmaster, having started at Charterhouse in 1614. Sir Robert Birley was the only other man to have been in charge of both Charterhouse and Eton.

then to sweep the Long Chamber, as was customary. At 8.00 p.m. they retired with another psalm and further prayers. They were to take notes of the Sunday sermons and show them up to their Masters: on the morning sermon after their dinner, and on the afternoon sermon, funded by the Provost's giving £50 of his own money, on Monday morning. On Sunday morning they were also required to go to schoolrooms for prayers and catechism. By the same instructions the praepostors were told to keep them in bounds when they were at play; and they needed permission from the Provost, or in his absence from the Vice-Provost and Schoolmaster, if they wanted a night away. It is plain that the Provost's role in the School continued to include much that would now be left to the Head Master.

The Puritan ethos is also demonstrated by one bracing letter from a father to a presumably not altogether satisfactory Oppidan son. The writer, Peter Sterry was one of Cromwell's Chaplains.

Son Peter,
Wn I came from you, I left you with much Greife for wt was past & fear for ye time to come . . . Learn now to hold fast ye praecepts & rules of Scripture of your ffather, or your Governours, and Elders . . . Keepe your Bed & Bedfellow, keepe ye Colledge, and go not into Towne. Keep with yourselfe & be with no company especially in all private places. Never be in company of any womankinde. Be very free to yr Mr. Speake often with him, acquaint him with all your temptations, & dangers & troubles; be perfectly advised, and governed by him. Go to your Mr for wt ever you want pens, Incke or any other thing for yourselfe or brother, he will supply you; write to mee on munday next without faile at large; & give mee an exact account how everything stands with you in your Spirit in all respects, your debts your company & brother . . . If you find ye temptations of yt place still to strong for you, I am resolved to remove you before ye Devill have prevailed to farre over you, & brought you into greater snares of shame and trouble.[2]

Alas, the letter cannot have been fully effective, because around 1657, the 13-year-old Peter had to be sent off to sea. (However, he was admitted to the Inner Temple soon after, and later enjoyed a successful career as a merchant and a civil servant.) Sterry was prepared to send his son to Eton, despite any reservations he may have felt about a royal foundation. Cromwell himself sent his ward William Dutton, with Andrew Marvell as a private tutor. Both boarded with John Oxenbridge, a Fellow who had been a Puritan minister exiled to Bermuda.*

A further indication that Eton remained in good standing was the appointment of Rous as Speaker of the Barebones Parliament in 1653. In the portrait the College possesses, he is depicted in Speaker's robes and holding the mace. Naturally enough the cavaliers did not admire him, but he did love Eton, and wished to be buried there, 'a place which hath my dear affection and prayers that it may be a flourishing nursery of piety and learning to the end of the world'. He founded three exhibitions at Pembroke College, Oxford, for Eton Scholars who failed to obtain places at King's. He is also believed to have planted many elms. Without doubt Eton should feel in his debt. Rous died in January 1659, four months after Oliver Cromwell, and the Fellows, who did not have much regard for Richard Cromwell, the successor to the Protectorate, chose Nicholas Lockyer to replace Rous. Another former Chaplain to Oliver Cromwell, Lockyer had been a Fellow since 1649. They wrote to tell Richard Cromwell, whom they regarded as Visitor in succession to the Bishop of Lincoln (there were no Bishops in the Commonwealth); but oddly, they referred to the College 'Beatae Mariae' as of old.

Lockyer's election as Provost was irregular, but it is hard to see how any Provost could have been properly chosen in the circumstances of the time. It mattered little. Among those who were working for the Restoration was a clergyman, Nicholas Monck. He enlisted the help of John Price, an Eton Colleger who left for King's in 1646 and who was Chaplain to Nicholas's brother General Monck. When the General committed himself and marched on

---

* Noel Blakiston, a devoted labourer in the Eton archives, surmised that Marvell wrote his poem 'Bermudas' at Eton; and rather more fancifully, he wondered if the lines

> Thus sang they in the English boat
> An holy and a cheerful note,
> And all the way to guide their chime
> With falling oars they kept the time

were inspired by walking with Oxenbridge on the towpath, watching an Eton eight.

London, and Charles II was proclaimed King, Lockyer sensibly resigned to live quietly on his private income. Nicholas Monck was rewarded by being appointed Provost. Four Puritan Fellows resigned, and one was sacked; the other two clung on – one indeed, Nathaniel Ingelo, against evidence that he was an aggressive Puritan. John Price became a Fellow, and his brother William the Lower Master. Two Fellows who had been excluded because of their loyalty to Charles I returned, as did Nicholas Gray, who was briefly a Fellow before he died in 1660. The Puritan Schoolmaster was dismissed and the Royalist Lower Master Mountague, who had somehow clung to his position, was promoted. Thus Eton, perhaps surprisingly, emerged from the Great Rebellion comparatively unscathed.

CHAPTER SEVEN

Eton during the Reigns of the Later Stuarts

AN IMMEDIATE CONSEQUENCE of the Restoration was a return of life at Eton to what was remembered of the past. Surplices were again worn in Chapel, and the Book of Common Prayer adopted; a new organ was installed. School plays, which had not been permitted by the Puritans, were resumed; on one occasion a band of musicians was hired for £1. Possibly the mood of relaxation went too far, for soon the Provost and Fellows were tightening up on discipline. The Schoolmaster was to grant only one weekly half-holiday for play, and that only if there was no other holiday during that week. The Schoolmaster and Usher (Lower Master) were to occupy their rooms at either end of Long Chamber where the Scholars slept, in order to forestall disorder; they were also to be punctually in school, the Schoolmaster at 7.00 a.m. and 1.00 p.m., the Usher soon after 6.00 a.m. and at midday; and they were to be sure that the boys were kept busy. A 1670 curriculum shows no great changes from Malim's account of 1561.

When Monck died in 1661, soon after he had become Bishop of Hereford, Meredith, one of the Fellows excluded by the Puritans, became Provost, holding the post jointly with that of Warden of All Souls College, Oxford. (The Fellows had managed to resist the King's first choice, who was of doubtful religious orthodoxy.) Meredith also determined to tighten discipline. The School and the Long Chamber were to be locked in the evening, and a tariff of punishments laid down. Not long afterwards two boys were admonished and whipped 'for going to the Datchet alehouses and beating the fishermen in their way home, to the great scandal of the College'. One, Curwen, a second-time offender, must have been 18, since he went up to King's later that same year. There may be rather more sympathy for a boy called Tom Rogers, who was never whipped so much in his life as he was one morning for *not* smoking: smoking was believed to be a preservative against the plague.

Meredith died in 1665, and the King offered the provostship to Robert Boyle, who was certainly the most distinguished Etonian alive. Boyle was more scrupulous than others, and felt that he was disqualified by being a laymen. He cared for Theology, and might have followed Sir Henry Wotton into deacon's orders, but he believed that his theological writings carried more weight coming from a layman, and he did not want to sacrifice time from the study of Philosophy to the Provost's duties. No such scruples deterred Edmund Waller, the disreputable Cavalier poet and an Etonian, from applying to be Provost, but fortunately the Lord Chancellor, Clarendon, was too scrupulous for him and refused to affix the Great Seal to the document of appointment. (Waller was to take revenge soon after by pursuing Clarendon actively at the time of his fall from office.) Eton, having in turn nearly fallen to embodiments of the virtuous and the unprincipled, was thus entrusted to Dr Allestree in an act of farce – if one is to believe a quite conceivably mythical story. Charles II is said to have challenged a group of his courtiers to find a man uglier than his minister, the Earl of Lauderdale. Lord Rochester returned shortly with Allestree, and amid peals of laughter, it was agreed that the King had lost his bet. Allestree sensibly did not take offence, but obtained a promise of promotion, which the King honoured when he made Allestree Provost. All of this, however, is the undergrowth of history: Allestree was certainly extremely ugly, as the portrait in the Provost's Lodge shows, but he had been rewarded by promotions before Eton, and he was also the Regius Professor of Divinity at Oxford.*

Allestree was not an Etonian, but he was in other ways qualified to be Provost. Dr Richard Rawlinson, who began a history of Eton in 1717, says of him:

---

* No early biography of him, however, mentions the story, which is to be found in Jesse's *Favourite Haunts* of 1847.

The School he found in a low condition, but by his prudence in the choice of a learned, discreet and diligent master, and by his interest in bringing young gentlemen and persons of quality thither, and by his general kindness to them when there, and taking care for the building fit accommodation for their reception within the precincts of the College, in a few years the school grew into that great reputation and credit which it yet retains.[1]

His administration saw the College back to financial health, and when he was in residence, he made the College a warm community. Unfortunately he was usually in Oxford, which meant that the Vice-Provost, the Puritan Dr Ingelo, was left in charge. Ingelo fell out with one of the Conducts, and was also seen as tyrannical by the boys, who appealed to the Visitor against the Vice-Provost's unfair treatment of the offspring of old Cavaliers. The son of a Mr Hill, a watchmaker, was expelled for little fault (so they said), and the son of Harrison, Esquire, was threatened similarly. Young Hill had gone to Oxford without leave, which must have offered Ingelo some cause, though it was said that the Provost had been prepared to pardon the boy. What is interesting to us now is that the story shows Eton as socially diverse, but aware of social gradations.[2] It would, indeed, seem that the School flourished at this time, without attracting the number of sons of grandees that it had done before the Civil War. The earliest surviving school list, from 1678, shows about 200 boys, with only one peer, and a few sons of baronets.* Westminster, under the famous Dr Busby, was probably the most sought-after school of the time.

One who provided evidence of the School's prosperity was Samuel Pepys, who visited on 26 February 1666, the day before Shrove Tuesday:

At Eton I left my wife in the coach, and [Dr Child, the Windsor organist] and I to the College, and there find all mighty fine. The school good, and the custom pretty of boys cutting their names in the struts of the window when they go to Cambridge. . . . To the Hall, and there find the boys verses, 'De Peste', it being their custom to make verses at Shrove-tide. I read several, and very

* The list appears to have been written down from memory a year or two later. The Sixth Form is now top of the School; the Seventh Form has vanished.

good ones they were, and better I think than I ever made when I was a boy, and in rolls as long and longer than the whole hall, by much. . . . * Thence to the porter's, in the absence of the butler, and did drink of the College beer, which is very good; and went into the back fields to see the scholars play. And so to the Chappell . . .[3]†

As Provost, Allestree was assisted by an effective Schoolmaster, Rosewell, whose reputation is, however, darkened by the allegation that he once flogged a boy so severely that the boy died – causing Rosewell to fall into a state of melancholy, and to resign. If this doubtful story is true, it seems to have made little difference, except to the unfortunate boy, since within a few months of ceasing to be Schoolmaster he became a Fellow, and the school numbers were not adversely affected. Rosewell was succeeded by Roderick, who became Provost of King's when the Fellows there resisted the royal nomination of Sir Isaac Newton.

Already a new schoolroom had been built at Allestree's expense to accommodate growing numbers. The building was not well constructed, and had to be replaced in 1689 by the present Upper School, which indeed resembles the earlier building. Allestree was also responsible for the north door of College Chapel, with its steps down to School Yard. Whatever the circumstances of his appointment, Eton has strong reasons to be grateful to him.

When Allestree died in 1681, Waller made another move to secure the provostship, but Charles II had by now established some principles for the appointment, and he promoted one of the Fellows,

---

* The habit of writing verses in praise of Dionysus, 'Bacchus verses', at Shrovetide was mentioned by Malim. In 1666, the boys wrote about the Plague rather than Dionysus.

† The College's beer was also supplied at this time to the Castle, and thus was presumably admired by royalty as well as by Pepys. It was brewed from hops grown in the two-acre Hopgarden west of the Slough Road. On the north side of the garden there was a wall, buttressed against winter floods, which was turned into a terrace on which hops were dried, and this terrace seems to have been carried on an arch over the Slough Road and across College Field, presumably for ease of transport to the Brewhouse, east of the Chapel. At the other end of the terrace, there is an elegant seventeenth-century building, into which hops were presumably shovelled in the event of rain, with an oven below. This is a curious piece of industrial archaeology at Eton, and the building, converted into a music room in the eighteenth century, is arguably the most interesting west of the Slough Road.

Zachary Cradock, who was in orders and thus fully qualified. Cradock's elder brother was a non-conforming minister and local squire, another brother was a grocer: evidence that Eton was not a closed society at this time. Zachary Cradock himself was a distinguished preacher and a friend of the diarist John Evelyn, who in 1680 recorded an instance of a boy making a Latin declamation, an early example of what became known as Speeches.

When it was discovered that Allestree's new schoolroom was unsafe, £2,300 had to be raised to replace it. The College still could not afford to do so from its own funds, but some distinguished men, including the Lord Chief Justice, were induced to support an appeal, which was successful largely through the efforts of Old Etonians. Interestingly, around this time an annual Eton College Feast, preceded by a sermon, was held in the City of London. There must have been some of the nostalgia more normally associated with the period 200 years later.

Upper School would have been used by more than one Master, and by this period there were definitely Assistants to the Schoolmaster and Usher. In 1698, from which year a second school list has survived, there were seven 'Ushers', but it is not easy to tell exactly when they were first appointed. Clearly Fellows like Hales had at times tutored boys in whom they took a particular interest. Possibly some tutors who arrived in charge of aristocratic boys had been pressed into service. Certainly John Newborough, who became Head Master in 1689, had previously been Lower Master, and before that an assistant Usher.

Newborough, who served as Head Master for twenty-two years, was described by Dr Richard Rawlinson as 'Chief Master'. 'He was of graceful Person and comely Aspect; had a presence fit to awe the numerous Tribe over which he presided; Grave was he in his Behaviour, and irreproachable in his Life; very pathetical were his Reproofs, and dispassionate his Corrections; and when any Hopes of Amendment appeared, he declined severe Remedies.' Rawlinson, who clearly knew Newborough well, went on to praise his qualifications as Head Master. He cared for the boys' health; out of some 400 boys over a three-year period there was only one death. His teaching was lively, illuminating the classical period in 'bright and beautiful Colours', and 'drawing lessons for present government'; so that boys subsequently joined different parties or the Church by their own independent judgement. He was generous in helping poorer boys with their books, and he set up the first School Library. Evidently it had become the custom for those boys who could afford it to give a leaving present to the Head Master: 'To all young Gentlemen, who took their Leave of him handsomely, it was his custom to present some Book, wherein he accurately remark'd the Bent of the Receiver; but whatever the Value of the Present was, it was of no Worth, in Comparison of the Advice he gave with it, which was certainly delivered in the most engaging Manner imaginable.'[4]*

Under Newborough the School flourished and more of the aristocracy were once again attracted to send their sons. The 1698 list shows 196 boys in the Upper School and 149 in the Lower School, boys who would not now be regarded as old enough to come to Eton. Collegers might come as early as 9 years old – for example, a boy called Errington who had been baptized as a Roman Catholic (but who was now presumably content to be an Anglican, his father having died). Nor would ages necessarily be reported accurately: Robert Walpole who was admitted as a Scholar in 1690, was reported by his parents to be 12, though he was actually 13, and they cheated again to secure his admission to King's. (In fact when his elder brother died while he was at Cambridge, it was no longer necessary for Robert to think of taking orders, and he was able to cease his education. Clearly the gentry still distinguished to some extent between first and subsequent sons.) The Colleger Whig, Walpole, was balanced by the Oppidan Tory, Henry St John, Viscount Bolingbroke, who even at Eton had some reputation as an orator. A number of other contemporaries became politicians.

The 1698 list suggests that boys in the Lower School were subdivided according to their ability on arrival into six groups, ranging from Upper Greek to Lag Remove. Such a division would not have been possible without the Lower Master having his Assistants, and

---

* Richard Rawlinson first thought of writing a history of Winchester and Eton in 1712, but lacked enough material for a history of Winchester. Subsequently he advertised for subscribers to 'The History and Antiquities of the Famous College of Eton'. The passage about Newborough (who died in 1712) was included as a sample in the advertisement. Little else survives of the history, but manuscripts collected by Rawlinson remain in the Bodleian Library. Newborough may have cared for the boys' health, but in fact thirteen died during the whole period of his headmastership, which was not exceptional in those days.

without the additional teaching space created by the new Upper School.

One of the boys listed in the Fourth Form, Richard Barrett, lives in letters home.[5]* He arrived in 1692 from Dublin and boarded with a Mrs Detton, who was soon writing to his father, by the evidently unreliable post: 'Sr I love your little Son uery well and shall take as much care for him as you shall desior.' As for the boy, 'he Groes and Larnes Extremly well so much that the mrs. of this Colidg are uery proud of him'. In the spring of 1693, the boy was writing, 'Deare father It is so long since I heard from you that I cannot be satisfied till you make me happy with A line or two from your own hands which I heartily beg.' He goes on to praise Mrs Detton, and ask for her to be paid, and ends: 'I hope to be A Good Scholar for this is the best Schoole in England and so with my most humble duty to my mother and to your self I shall ever remain your dutifull Son: Richard Barrett.' No doubt the letters of both son and Dame were framed to impress their reader, but nevertheless there is much to admire. By the summer of 1693, Mrs Detton reports: 'I have writ many letters to you since I had your pretty Son who has bin like to dye with the meazels but I praise God he's a pon recovery.' The boy was still pleased with his brave school, with the best teaching in the world. By 1697 father Barrett was in Essex and seeing more of the boy: Richard's clothes were not as clean as they should be, but venison could be sent to him by river. At Christmas boys could now go home for a holiday, but Richard was worried at the end of November that he had not yet had a letter about it; the year was evidently divided into two halves, with the original holiday period at Whitsuntide remaining. It seems that holidays could only be taken by boys if their parents so requested; the school business ceased during the holiday period, and what happened if any boys could not go home is unclear. Even in autumn 1700, when Richard was near leaving, we find him writing repeatedly to Essex for his letter. But by then he was more a man of the world, relating gossip to his father, finding a source of melon seeds, and taking an interest in his father's affairs. He had ceased to study Aristophanes, but was reading Euripides, and he wanted his father to acquire an edition of

---

* Barrett (or Barret as he seems more commonly to have called himself) was the son of Dacre Barrett and Lady Jane Chichester, daughter of the Earl of Donegall. He married a cousin, Lady Jane Lennard, but died of smallpox, leaving his widow pregnant with a son.

Euripides for him. The correspondence is agreeably free of rancour and reflects credit on the School and on Mrs Detton.

Quite a number of school bills survive from this period, and it is clear that Oppidans were by now expected to pay for their teaching. Some record charges of 10s., perhaps for a half; the aristocracy paid more heavily. William Russell, a grandson of the first Duke of Bedford, who was at Eton from 1687 to 1690, was charged £3. 4s. 6d. in 1688 by Mr Roderick, the Head Master of the time, for a year's schooling, and lesser sums were paid to other Ushers. He boarded with Newborough, who charged £40. 17s. for three quarters' board for William and his man. He and other pupils were well dressed in the fashion of the time, and bills show heavy expenditure on clothes and shoes, and in Russell's case for a periwig and a cane. (He had two visits to a tooth-drawer, one for cleaning and filing his teeth, and one for extraction.) The books required throw some light on the curriculum; besides the Euripides that Barrett needed, there was Aesop's *Fables* for the younger boys, and Russell required Sir Walter Raleigh's *History*, Baker's chronicle and Cowley's poems, so that the curriculum cannot have been exclusively classical.[6] The bill of a boy called Patrick, dated 1688, mentions payments to the Writing Master of £1 for a half-year, but no payment to the Head Master or to Newborough, with whom he too was boarding. Presumably it was a bill for extras. It does include 9d. for a bat and Ram Club; the Ram Club would apparently annually hunt a ram and batter him to death at the time of the Election to King's and to Eton.[7] This unattractive custom no doubt reflected the more brutal attitude of the English towards animals in former days, but it was also perhaps seen as a safety valve for the boys' energies when games were limited and informal.* Cradock, in a letter of 1694, recalled that in Rosewell's time the Collegers would have wine bottles drawn up to their windows from what is now Weston's Yard, and that when Roderick was Head Master, the Collegers

---

* An account of a cricket match was published in a book of Latin verses, *Musicae Juveniles*, in 1706. The author, William Goldwin, was a Windsor boy who was a Colleger from 1695 to 1700. Cricket may have been played on College Field: the game described is similar to cricket in the mid-eighteenth century. It has also been claimed that in 1702, a third stump was added, as a result of an incident at Eton. The batsman had been required to ground his bat in a hole between the stumps before the fielder grounded the ball. After a serious collision, a crease to be crossed was introduced, along with the third stump where the hole had been.

forged a key in order to make midnight excursions, for which several were expelled.

There were evidently a fair number of difficult boys at Eton around this time. Sir William Culpepper was a baronet whose mother had remarried a sensible guardian, Captain Mason, RN. Mason wrote for advice to the maternal grandfather, who took an affectionate interest in the boy. Mother and son were inclined to take a private tutor at home, but the other two felt differently. Captain Mason wrote in 1683 to his father-in-law:

> You know that in this month he is fifteen years old; and the Culpeppers grow stubbornly ripe betimes. I am fearful by taking a tutor into the house that his mother's blind fondness will prejudice his learning. I doe fully agree with you that it is absolutely necessary that he should make himself master of the Latin tongue, for as 'tis the foundation of almost all our Christian languages, it is the key to unlock the cabinets in which are contayned the quintessence of all human learning.

The boy went to Eton but was soon in trouble. His grandfather wrote in vain: 'Submit yourself to the orders of your guardian, serve God with a perfect heart and keep orderly Company.' He left Eton having acquired extravagant habits which later obliged him to sell his family home.[8] Lord Hastings was another aristocrat who did not survive at Eton, disliking the life so much that he badgered his father to remove him – though unfortunately we do not know why. Letters about his sullen moods from Newborough indicate that he may simply have had an excess ration of teenage introspection.[9] After mentioning some failures, it is reassuring to read a commendation of Eton from Sir John Temple in 1695, which in particular implies that a reputation for severity should not deter prospective parents: his son Jack was seven years at Eton and never whipped – but perhaps a proud son kept any bad news from his father.[10]

Cradock died in 1695, a year after the completion of Upper School, to be succeeded by Henry Godolphin, the Vice-Provost, who had himself been an Oppidan at Eton, and who was also a priest and Doctor of Divinity, and thus fully qualified. He was a wealthy man and brother of the Lord Treasurer, Sidney Godolphin, which no doubt helped him to secure the royal mandate to be Provost. His long reign, until 1733, was distinguished by much new building, beginning with the restoration of College Chapel, towards which the Provost himself contributed £1,000. A new roof was built, the walls were panelled up to the windows, a new organ loft was placed across the building by the second windows from the west end (incidentally damaging the concealed wall-paintings at that point), and the pulpit was placed roughly opposite the north door; there was a great classical altar piece. The quality of the woodwork was high, and the Chapel was handsome in the style of that period.

It was Mr Gladstone's view that Eton was at its best in the seventeenth century, at any rate before the Glorious Revolution of 1688.[11] At that point he felt, not quite correctly, that Eton became too much the home of the aristocracy. At all levels, from Provost to boys, Eton under the Stuarts seems to have been open in recruitment. Indeed, the combination of Godolphin and Newborough, with Weston as Lower Master from 1693 to 1707 (a future Bishop, for whom Weston's Yard is named), was to take Eton far ahead of Winchester in popularity and esteem, though Westminster, then at the height of its fame, could still match Eton in numbers. Both Winchester and Westminster educated more Bishops than Eton, but under the long headmastership of the famous disciplinarian, Dr Busby, Westminster also became a nursery of politicians. Westminster had always emphasized Greek more than Eton, and under Busby Mathematics was taught; yet it was not the wider curriculum that drew parents: it was the character of Busby himself. Eton too had men of distinction in charge, and intellectual life was not as stultified as it later became, nor the academic curriculum so constrained. By the end of the century Fellows from King's were becoming more numerous, as Archbishop Laud's ruling that five should be Kingsmen was taken increasingly seriously. For the next 150 years the close relationship between Eton and King's was to have largely unfortunate consequences.

CHAPTER EIGHT

Eton under the Early Hanoverians

THE ACCESSION OF George I, together with Walpole's appointment as Prime Minister, inaugurated a period of 250 years in which the political influence of Old Etonians was, generally speaking, unmatched. Other schools, Westminster at first, and later Harrow, which was deliberately moulded to resemble Eton by a succession of Etonian headmasters between 1669 and 1785, were comparable at times, but overall Eton stood supreme. It is not always reasonable to claim that Eton was a good school during this period, and some critics would say that the pre-eminence of Eton was simply an illustration of the British class system. Yet not all the Etonian Prime Ministers were aristocrats. Eton did have some good qualities to secure the custom of parents, and to give its boys the confidence to achieve in politics, and in other fields.

Eton began the Hanoverian period in a position of strength, with the well-connected Godolphin as Provost. Newborough had just resigned the headmastership in 1713, to be succeeded by the High Church Tory, Dr Snape. In a bitter pamphlet war, he maintained the old orthodoxy against the latitudinarian views of the Bishop of Bangor; one Assistant Master, Thackeray, who shared the Bishop's opinions, had to resign but much later became an esteemed headmaster of Harrow. Snape did not compromise; his polemics were matched by his enemies, who attacked his origins – the Snapes had long been royal Serjeant-Farriers – and his pedantry: 'His every period, crabbed and severe, smells of the birch and terrifies the ear.' In 1719 he was rescued by being elected Provost of King's; the

Fellows of King's had established the right to choose their own Provost.

Snape's troubles were, however, the only cloud over a serene prospect. Godolphin, once more contributing much of the cost himself, was able to pave School Yard, which had previously been grass, and to dignify it with a statue of the Founder in Hanoverian Court dress, by Francis Bird (1719), which idealizes him beyond recognition.* The next year the College resolved to build a new library. After several schemes were abandoned, the present Library by Rowland was finished in 1729. The gallery on the south side of the Cloisters where the books were at that time kept was replaced with a building, correct on the outside and splendid within, capable of holding ten times the number of books then owned. This was an act of faith amply justified by many rich benefactions. Defoe in his *Tour through the Whole Island of Great Britain*, published in 1724, commented on the excellent state of repair of the College, and thought it the finest school for grammar in Britain, or perhaps in Europe.

The Hanoverian succession had followed closely on the Act of Union. There were already Scottish boys at Eton (the 1698 list shows a Mr Campbell, and the 1707 list a Lord Dalkeith), but now the numbers grew. Sir John Clerk, for example, an advocate of the Scottish Bar, a member of the Scottish Parliament, and a Commissioner treating for the Union, resolved to enter his son John, who survived the death in childbirth of his mother in 1701. In May 1715 young John was sent with a cousin, James Stewart, to Eton, 'which was under the direction of one Dr Snape, a very learned man'. Sir John was naturally enough uneasy, but felt that his son would gain if he understood the English language, besides having a fine opportunity of learning Greek and Latin. The boy was intended to stay two and a half years before returning to study Philosophy and Mathematics, followed by Law, and then to travel abroad. The father told the son not to start with French, nor to learn fencing until he had developed physically; to learn to dance, but to avoid swimming (it was the better swimmers who drowned, not those who could not swim at all), to shun wrestling; to be early to

---

* Horace Walpole dismissed the statue as 'a wretched performance indeed'. Oliver Van Oss more charitably thought it (for its absence of swagger) 'a very English work'.

bed, early to rise; to drink water and eat plain food; never to game, least of all for money; to be obedient to his Masters; to choose the best company, who would help him in his career; not to go to London; to buy books suitable for his current studies; to keep himself informed by reading news letters; to wear his clothes clean not fine; and to be circumspect about his pocket expenses.

The boy did indeed prove a paragon. His early expenses on books included dictionaries, Caesar's *Commentaries*, Aesop's *Fables*, and *Eton School Prayers* (only one shilling). The boy's maternal grandfather, the Duke of Queensberry, visited Eton in 1716: 'Nothing pleased me so much as to find at Eton so many fine young Scotch Gentlemen, among whom your son bears an admirable Character from everybody, both from being very far advanced in his studies and behaving himself every way as he ought.' By 1717 the boy's purchases of books had become more ambitious and more varied. And when the two and a half years were up, John stayed on at Eton. Early in 1719, Sir John wrote, 'I had an agreeable account of my son's great proficiency. Everybody spoke of him as the chief Scholar at Eton.' His paternal grandfather wanted young John home, and Sir John agreed: 'I knew there was this bad consequence from an English Education, that Scotsmen bred in that way would always have a stronger inclination for England than for their own country.' In October 1719 John left, with a cask of books in his luggage. What had occasioned the change of plan? No doubt the boy must have been successful and therefore happy, but it seems that his health was not good, and sadly he died in 1722.[1]

Under Snape the school numbers rose to 399 (he claimed there were 400). His farewell speech is said to have drawn tears from the boys. His successor, Henry Bland, was a Kingsman, but this time a Whig and of doubtful orthodoxy. Yet he too was a successful Head Master, and the numbers went up, only dipping when the South Sea Bubble broke (1721). Among Bland's pupils were William Pitt and his elder brother, Thomas. Their Tutor had to write a familiar-sounding letter to their father about Thomas: 'He has unhappily lost a great deal of time by his own negligence, but I think his natural abilities are so good that he may recover it at the University if he takes a good turn, which I imagine he will do upon his conversing more with men.' As for William, 'Your younger son has made a great progress since his coming hither, indeed I never was concerned with a young gentleman of so good abilities, and at the same time of so good a disposition, and there is no question to be made but he will answer all your hopes'.[2] There were in fact a number of very distinguished boys at Eton at the time, founders of political dynasties, rather than aristocrats by inheritance.* Yet others excelled in different fields: Frederick Cornwallis ended as an amiable but dim Archbishop of Canterbury. Thomas Arne was a distinguished composer, most famously of *Rule, Britannia*; he is said to have tormented neighbouring boys with his flute.† Ralph Thicknesse was a violinist who became an Assistant Master, and had the misfortune to drop dead playing a concerto of his own composition at Bath. There is, however, no evidence of systematic encouragement of music at Eton. Henry Fielding, the novelist, felt that he owed his style to the study of Classics at Eton. 'To thee [i.e. learning], at thy birchen altar, with true spartan devotion, I have sacrificed my blood.'[3] He is one of three boys in this period known to have run away, and presumably he was flogged on his return. Doubtless he began to acquire his expert knowledge of low life at Eton.

Dr Bland's successful tenure as Head Master ended when in 1728 he was appointed Dean of Durham, thanks to the influence of Sir Robert Walpole. His successor was his son-in-law, William George, a good enough scholar, but one who lacked skill in management. Within a year he had indeed provoked a rebellion, about which there is unfortunately little recorded. He seems to have been inconsistent, veering between weakness and undue severity. Nevertheless, Classics continued to be well taught.

The Provost and Fellows, however, rather than Dr George, must be blamed for what appears to have been the end of an independent choir at this time. After the Restoration, the Clerks continued singing at Windsor, and this became their main job; the boys became almost a junior choir awaiting promotion to St George's. Choral matins was abandoned by 1701, though the organ books of the time show that a range of anthems were performed at evensong. Increasingly men were appointed to both choirs at once, with a joint Master of Choristers from 1733.[4]

In George's early years, Eton could still seem an idyll to some of its students. Round about 1730, the first great sentimental

---

* Pitt did not send Pitt the Younger to Eton. He regarded Eton as really only suitable for the rougher boy.

† Arne wrote perhaps the earliest setting of *God Save the King*, used frequently at School Concerts nowadays.

friendships developed of which we have good records. These were known collectively as the Quadruple Alliance, between Horace Walpole, Thomas Gray, Thomas Ashton and Richard West. Gray was an only son in an unhappy family with a violent scrivener father in the City; he would be assessed by modern social workers as having boarding need, and luckily he had two uncles who were Assistants at Eton. Walpole was the youngest son of the Prime Minister, but also from an unhappy home. Ashton was a schoolmaster's son; West was less grand than Walpole, but of higher class than the other two. Their friendships were not exclusive, and were open to other contemporaries. They do not seem to have been based on any particular common interest, but all were bookish boys, who shared the growing amount of leisure that Eton permitted.

West was perhaps the most attractive of the four, but unfortunately consumptive. At Oxford he wrote a nostalgic poem:

> Lost and wrapt in thought profound
> Absent I tread Etonian ground;
> Then starting from the clear mistake
> As disenchanted, wake . . .
> Oh! how I long again with those
> Whom first my boyish heart had chose,
> Together through the friendly shade
> To stray, as once I stray'd.

Gray, who was somewhat deficient in passion, nevertheless wrote a sonnet when West died, and began his celebrated 'Elegy Written in a Country Churchyard'. Earlier he had written mostly in Latin, an expertise that he would have begun to acquire at Eton. Later, he wrote an 'Ode on a Distant Prospect of Eton College'. Its first sunny verses seek to capture the joys of an Etonian youth: the surroundings, cricket, rowing, even earnest bookwork for those with that bent, or 'the fearful joy' of breaking bounds. Then black misfortune is to break. 'Alas! regardless of their doom the little victims play'; 'Thought would destroy their paradise. No more; – where ignorance is bliss, 'Tis folly to be wise.'* Sadly, it was indeed the case that for both Gray and the more lively and exotic Horace Walpole,

---

* Gray's poems are presented to Etonians when they leave. Other poets are perhaps better qualified, but he remains Eton's laureate.

their schooldays were to be the happiest of their lives. Some contemporaries thought them effeminate; and it is the fashion of modern scholarship to argue that the friendships must have been homo-erotic, but that reflects current obsession rather than past reality. The friendship of Gray and Walpole, clouded though it was by a four-year quarrel (begun when they were on the Grand Tour together) which may have been caused by a betrayal of confidence from the much less amiable Ashton, was essentially born of a common experience: the discovery at Eton of affection that had been denied at home. Walpole appears to have had a physical relationship with a younger Etonian, the Earl of Lincoln, but only after both boys had left Eton. Lincoln had been a handsome and very spirited lad, often in fights and often punished, seemingly to his mother's delight: 'I was not displeased to hear of your exploits, tho' I'm afraid your poor B—— suffered for it.'[5]

There is also the first recording of a continuing problem at schools: in October 1736, Francis Cust reports to his older brother the appearance of a paedophile who tried to pick up boys in the playing fields. When this became known, 'almost all the School' went to the Christopher Inn where he was staying, and would have ducked him in Barnes Pool, had not Dr Sumner, the Lower Master, and his wife come by; he sent the boys into School, and dispatched the man under two constables to the Justices at Iver, where he was released with a severe reprimand for his folly.[6] The attitude of the boys is refreshingly normal, and similar to that of boys in the 1960s and 1970s, when Eton was troubled by a more persistent offender.

Under Dr George (1728–43) the numbers in the School fell. In 1731 a 14-year-old boy from Antigua, Edward Cochran, was stabbed to death by a boy called Dalton. His tombstone records an accidental stab with a penknife, but the Chapel Register states that he was murdered. One year later, a newspaper reported that Dalton was still deeply depressed 'and desirous of Death to make an Atonement for his Crime'. Subsequently he was found guilty of manslaughter. Even at an age when death was more commonplace, this unfortunate event cannot have helped Eton's reputation.

The more general fall in numbers would have affected Dr George's own pocket, since at this time he was apparently paid annually £62 as the Master, together with food and lodgings worth £30, and rent from boys who lodged with him worth £8; but he also received a 1 guinea entrance fee from all boys, and often a gratuity of 4 guineas from boys in the Upper School – though it appears that about one third of the older boys did not pay. While the Head Master's income fluctuated with the success of the School, the incomes of Assistants and still more of Dames must have varied more. It will be noticed that the income of the Head Master, despite his having to make payments to his Assistants, had grown far beyond the original provision of the Statutes. This was obviously inevitable, in view of sixteenth-century inflation – and desirable, if the best men were to be attracted to the job. From the seventeenth century prices changed little, and Eton boys' bills were remarkably constant. The Lower Master at this time received about £30 p.a. as basic income, augmented by the same sort of fees and gratuities from lower boys. He too paid his Assistants. Francis Goode, who was the Lower Master from 1717, and was liked by the boys, resigned in 1734, apparently out of distaste for Dr George's regime.

There was some royal patronage, but George I never visited Eton and George II came only in 1747; Eton had to be content with the Duke of Cumberland, who in 1730 had the doubtful honour of delivering the first blow with a ram-club. (The ram hunt was abolished in 1747; after one ram was chased into Windsor, causing the boys exertion thought to be a danger to their health, rams were hamstrung and simply beaten to death.) In 1735, the Duke also attended Speeches at Electiontide in Election Hall, following a very lavish breakfast with Sir Robert Walpole and many grandees. In 1733, Godolphin had died after a 38-year tenure as Provost.* Walpole secured the return of Dr Bland as Provost, and this occasion was Dr Bland's thank-you. One of the Fellows (it would seem) wrote an acid account, having been given no part in the occasion; he records that Speeches contained verses on the King and Queen, and on the Duke, but mostly on Sir Robert. The boys performed well and were rewarded with 140 guineas, the College with £100.

In 1742 Dr Snape died at King's; Dr George was narrowly victorious in the contest to be chosen as Provost of King's. The new Head Master was William Cooke, promoted from Assistant. After three brutal years, his health broke down, but he was consoled with a Fellowship of Eton within two years. Later he moved on to be Provost of King's, causing the uncharitable diarist William Cole to

---

* It should be recorded that Eton town is now a good place to grow old, partly because Provost Godolphin renewed the almshouses.

remark that it was not the first time a man's unsocial and bad disposition has been the occasion of his advancement. 'Cooke will be a schoolmaster in whatever station of life his fortune may advance him to.'[7]

Cooke was followed by Dr Sumner in 1745, and a year later Bland was succeeded by Dr Sleech. Both were Eton and King's men by birth as well as by education. Sleech was the son of an Eton Fellow, Newborough became his stepfather, Weston his brother-in-law; Sleech married a Fellow's daughter; one of Sleech's daughters married Cooke, her elder sister married a Hawtrey (which was to be another great Eton family) and a third married another Fellow.* In due course Sleech's son became Lower Master. All of this was a consequence of the Eton Fellows' being allowed to marry, and of the almost automatic progression from College at Eton to King's, back to Eton as a Master, and promotion to a Fellowship. The progress was attractive, the time as Colleger at Eton being the hard apprenticeship which secured the easy and idle future. In the eighteenth century it was quite general for what would now be regarded as positions of trusteeship to be treated almost as property rights, with the perks less to be questioned than the duties.

In 1731, Septimius Plumptre, the son of an MP and already an Oppidan, secured a promise from Provost Godolphin to allow his election to College. Soon Septi was asking his father for an allowance to supplement his food, for the provisions in College Hall seem to have become more meagre over the years. Next year Mr Plumptre sent gifts back for Septi to distribute, and the boy reported that Dr George had accepted the money, whereas Mr Goode had refused. Later still, in January 1734, Septi was writing to ask for twenty shillings a year to get to study by a fire; in the Long Chamber he needed to wear his wig to stand the cold. At the same time, young Plumptre was learning French from a Monsieur Julien, an extra for which his father paid. When he reached the Sixth Form, father Plumptre began to calculate the prospects of getting his son to King's; there would

---

* In 1734, Hawtrey was *not* chosen as a Fellow, since Harris and Sleech did not think that three brothers-in-law should be Fellows. Instead they chose John Reynolds, uncle of Sir Joshua and author of a geography book, who was a schoolmaster at Exeter. He did not have a coat of arms; in a window of College Chapel he is represented by a rebus – a fox – on the grounds of his benefactions to College Library, and his gift of a scholarship for Etonians at University.

need to be six vacancies at King's, such as might be caused by marriage, death or resignation, before he would be able to secure a place. This occasioned much correspondence to prevail upon the Kingsmen to move. Eventually in 1737 Septi was 'sewed up and unsewed' – a description of the symbolic tearing of a Colleger's gown as he left Eton; he had apparently earned much credit, and was the richer by £10 that the Duke of Cumberland presented, via Sir Robert Walpole. On to 1741, and Septimius writes to his father about the possibility of returning to Eton as a Master. It will be hard work, but as he priggishly remarks, 'Labour never was any scarecrow to me when either my own, or my friends' interest was in question.' A word or two from Sir Robert Walpole to the Provost might help. He felt himself best qualified for teaching Classics. His friends had warned him that Dr George's temper would suggest a roundabout and diplomatic approach. It was successful, and he became an Assistant Master; but he never achieved the Fellowship – not until the next century was there a Plumptre Fellow. Whether he would have become a Master in a more open competition is impossible to know.[8]

There was amazingly little to admire in the life of the Fellows. Holding church livings elsewhere, they grew rich; and by 1758 they were in a position to expand their residences by adding another floor to the north and east of the Cloisters. Ashton, the schoolfriend of Gray and Horace Walpole, behaved even worse. He had already, in 1753, displayed some of the acrimony of an under-employed man in a small community, in a rancorous quarrel with Provost Sleech. Now, in 1760, he proceeded to dispossess a Conduct of his room at the foot of his own apartments. The Conduct found that workmen had nailed up his door and plastered it over, and taken down a wall of his bedroom to enable Dr Ashton to have a pompous staircase to his grand rooms above. The locked door and the grand staircase remain to this day as evidence against Ashton, but the staircase leads only to the offices of the Bursary.[9]

There is one matter to the credit of the mid-eighteenth-century Fellows, however. They did allow visitors to College Library, unlike their nineteenth-century successors. A silly, illiterate servant, Taffy Woodward, was entrusted with looking after visitors until the Librarian could be found. When he did not know what any curiosity was, he had a catchphrase: 'Neither I, nor the Fellows, nor Provost can tell.' For example: 'This is Kikero, the poet, this is

Novid, the Orator; but who *this* is, neither I, nor the Fellows, nor Provost can tell.' When Taffy died, and his coffin was lying for public view, an Oppidan called Smith (son of a grocer and tea-merchant, who was later to create the part of Charles Surface in *The School for Scandal*) wrote on the coffin-lid:

> Here lie the remains of Taffy Woodward!
> But whether his soul's in heaven or hell,
> Neither I, nor the Fellows, nor Provost can tell.

For this impertinence the young actor was soundly flogged.[10] The boys also had the advantage of a bookshop in Eton:

> Jos Pote of Eton, a man of great renown,
> Buys a book for sixpence and sells it for a crown.

The family were to run the shop for some 150 years, and Etonians had an extra opportunity to develop literary tastes. The Pote boys usually spent a time as Collegers in order to get to King's.

The *Eton College Register* records sixty-eight boys with fathers in trade during the period 1698–1752, most of them Collegers. A fair proportion of them lived locally, and may have begun as day boys. The three bakers' sons, however, were from Nottingham, Southwark and Cirencester, but had been able to find someone to promote their cause for election to College. These humbler boys usually progressed up the social scale as adults, for example in the Church. Etonians not only came from a wide social range but from some distant parts. There were boys from America, Ireland and the Grisons in Switzerland. Politically, notwithstanding Walpole, there was a suspicion that excessively Tory leanings lingered at Eton, and this made Westminster more the establishment school of the time. In 1745, one Scottish Etonian, the 16-year-old John Murray, learnt that his father had taken up arms for the Pretender. He held the King's Commission in a newly raised Scottish regiment, and was keen to fight against his father if necessary, but the need did not arise. On the other hand, there is in the Churchyard at Upton, on the edge of Slough, a tombstone for Dame Bramston, which records that she dared to be honest in the reign of George II – presumably she was a Jacobite.

The reputation of the School was still low, but there was

apparently during this period a development of lasting significance: Masters began to act as Tutors to boys. Some rich boys arrived with their own private tutors, but now Masters prepared to fill this role more cheaply for the generality. It was an acknowledgement of the impossibility of learning easily in crowded schoolrooms, and it accompanied the decline in school hours. Boys prepared work under a Tutor in his house to be tested orally in school. For the Masters there was an important new source of income;* for the boys there might be a Master who would be not just a pedagogue but a counsellor and friend. William Pitt, as mentioned earlier, had a Tutor who wrote the type of letter to his parents that was later to become general practice. Quite how far Tutors had become universal by 1750 is uncertain.

After 1745 the numbers in the School strengthened slightly, standing at over 300 by the end of 1753, the reflection partly of a more assured political situation, and partly of improved roads. The Colnbrook Turnpike Trust had been set up in 1727 to cover the Bath Road as far as Maidenhead, but it did not take over the spur into Eton until 1766.[11] It needed, however, the promotion of Edward Barnard to Head Master in 1754 to create a new period of vigorous growth at the School.

* In 1766, John Hawtrey, a Master, wrote to his brother Edward, who was about to join him: 'Your Chambers consist of 2 rooms without any furniture. The furniture of your Pupil Room may be brought here – any Rubbish will serve.'

CHAPTER NINE

Dr Barnard

EDWARD BARNARD WAS one of those Collegers who did not secure a place at King's; he went instead to St John's College, Cambridge. Consequently he could not become an Assistant Master, but he was employed by the Townshend family as a private tutor at Eton, and he acquired other pupils, connections of the Townshends. When in December 1753 Dr Sumner announced his intention to leave the following Whitsuntide, the obvious successor was Mr Dampier, the Lower Master, a cultivated man who acquired the great architectural books of his time (now in College Library); but there is some doubt whether he was forceful enough to be Head. Mr Barnard persuaded the Duke of Newcastle, Mr Townshend and others to lobby the Fellows on his behalf. Dampier applied to the Earl of Guilford, whose son, Lord North, the future Prime Minister, had been his pupil, to rally others to his support. On 1 February Barnard wrote a letter to two Fellows promising not to apply for the headmastership, providing they would help procure him the post of Lower Master. Presumably his prospects must have improved, and the letter been cancelled, for Barnard did indeed win the contest: his patrons were the more influential, and just possibly the Provost and Fellows may have thought him the stronger candidate.

Certainly he had considerable assurance, though he was not as scholarly as other Head Masters of the century. He was a good mimic who, in one pupil's view, might have rivalled Garrick, had he been less ugly. He had a fine voice and wit, and he taught the Greek plays that appealed to his theatrical taste most effectively to the

1. Henry VI – a 16th-century portrait

2. William Waynflete

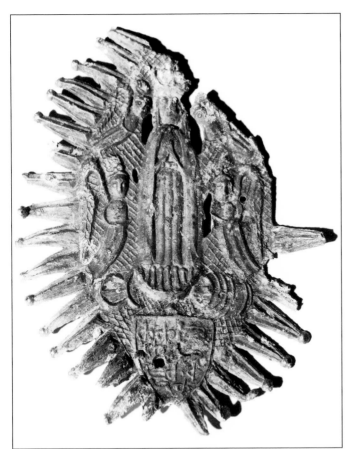

3. Pilgrim badge recovered from the Thames. The badge, which is of pewter, shows the Virgin of the Assumption

4. The Eton coat of arms, granted on 1 January 1449, but in use earlier, has three lilies, the flowers of the Virgin, on a black shield; the upper part has a golden lion on a red background and a golden fleur de lys on a blue ground, reflecting Henry's position as King of France as well as of England

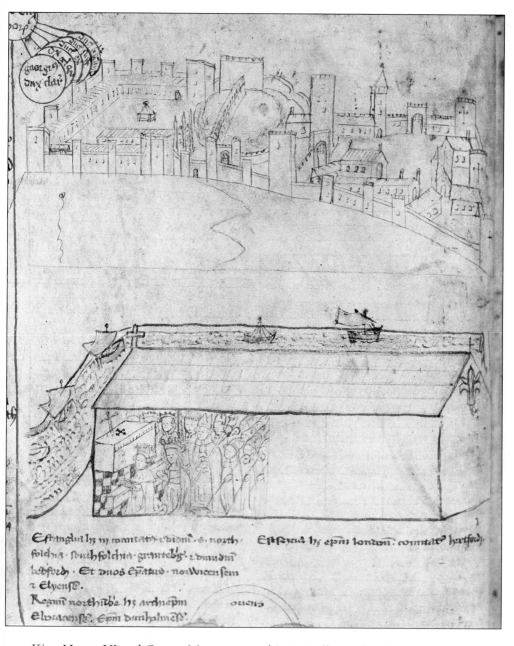

5. King Henry VI and Queen Margaret worship in College Chapel on the occasion of the consecration of William Waynflete as Bishop of Winchester, 30 July 1447. The representation of Windsor Castle, as well as of Eton, is the earliest known. For Sir Robert Birley it was 'perhaps the nearest thing to a snapshot which has survived from the middle ages'. Probably drawn by John Blakman who owned the manuscript

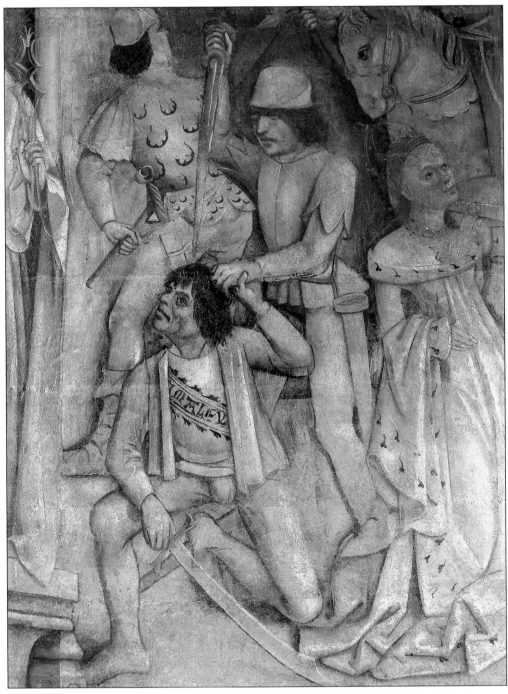

6. Wall-painting from the south side of College Chapel. The Empress is rescued by a knight, and one of her captors is about to meet his deserts

7. Wall-painting from the north side of College Chapel. A lady, unable to attend mass on Purification Day, has a vision in which she sees mass celebrated before the Virgin: here she is seen receiving a candle for her to keep

8. Sir Henry Savile,
by Gheerhaerts II, 1621

9. Sir Henry Wotton,
by an unknown artist

10. Sir Francis Rous, possibly by
Edward Bower

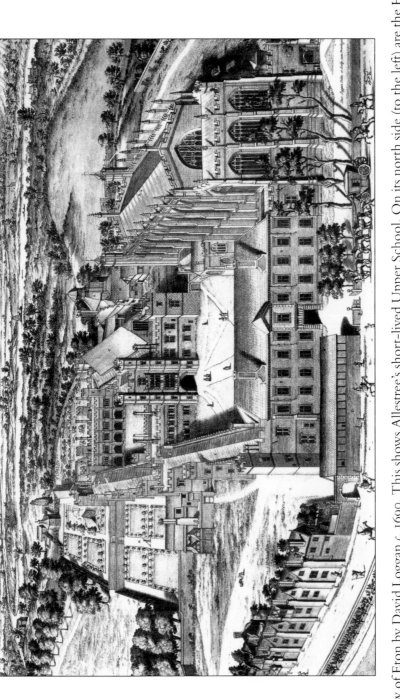

11. View of Eton by David Loggan c. 1690. This shows Allestree's short-lived Upper School. On its north side (to the left) are the Head Master's chambers; then the Long Chamber above Lower School, the original schoolroom; then the Lower Master's chambers. Across the east side of School Yard, with Lupton's Tower in the centre, is the Provosts' Lodge. Beyond that the Fellows' houses around the Cloisters. On the southern flank of the Cloisters was the gallery, which can just be glimpsed, and which was pulled down to allow the building of College Library, and behind it College Hall and the College kitchen. The north entrance to the Chapel in School Yard had only recently been added. Savile House can be seen lower left alongside the Slough road, and the old wharf where goods and materials for the College were landed is by the building on the Thames, far top left. Many of the structures that have now vanished were stables

Ode, on a Prospect of Windsor & the adjacent Country. in 1743.

Ye distant Spires, ye antique Towers,
That crown the watry Glade,
Where grateful Science still adores
Her Henry's holy Shade;
And ye, that from the stately Brow
Of Windsor's Heights th' Expanse below
Of Grove, of Lawn, of Mead survey,
Whose Turf, whose Shade, whose Flowers among
Wanders the hoary Thames along
His silver-winding Way.

Ah happy Hills, ah pleasing Shade,
Ah Fields beloved in vain,
Where once my careless Childhood stray'd
A Stranger yet to Pain!
I feel the Gales, that from ye blow,
A momentary Bliss bestow,
As waveing fresh their gladsome Wing
My weary Soul they seem to soothe,
And redolent of Joy & Youth
To breath a second Spring.

Say, Father Thames, (for thou hast seen
Full many a smileing Race
Disporting on thy Margent green
The Paths of Pleasure trace)
Who foremost now delight to cleave
With pliant Arm thy glassy Wave?
The captive Linnet which enthrall?
What idle Progeny succeed
To chase the rolling Circle's Speed,
Or urge the flying Ball?

While some on earnest Business bent
Their murm'ring Labours ply
'Gainst graver Hours, that bring Constraint
To sweeten Liberty.
Some bold Adventurers disdain
The Limits of their little Reign,
And unknown Regions dare descry;
Still as they run, they look behind,
They hear a Voice in every Wind,
And snatch a fearful Joy.

12. The manuscript of Gray's 'Ode on a Prospect of Windsor and the Adjacent Country', 1743, now known as 'Ode on a Distant Prospect of Eton College'

13. Dr Barnard

14. Charles James Fox by
Sir Joshua Reynolds. A
leaving portrait given to
Dr Barnard

15. A flogging in Lower School. Collegers were pressed into service as holders-down

16. Dr Keate, a pencil cartoon by Harvey KS inside his copy of Horace, 1828

17. Montem in 1820, by C. Turner. The procession is assembling in Weston's Yard. George IV can be discerned in the background with Goodall and Keate. It is melancholy to reflect on the fate of the three handsome heroes in the foreground: Lord Ingestre, a serjeant (on the left), was drowned with his horse in a marsh, when riding on the Prater in Vienna, 1826; Maturin KS, the Mareschal (in the centre), died in Corfu about 1830; and John Wilder, the Captain of Montem (on the right), became Vice-Provost in his eighties

18. Theatricals in Long Chamber, by Samuel Evans

19. Cricket on College Field by William Evans (mid-1830s)

20. The Fourth of June by William Evans (mid-1830s)

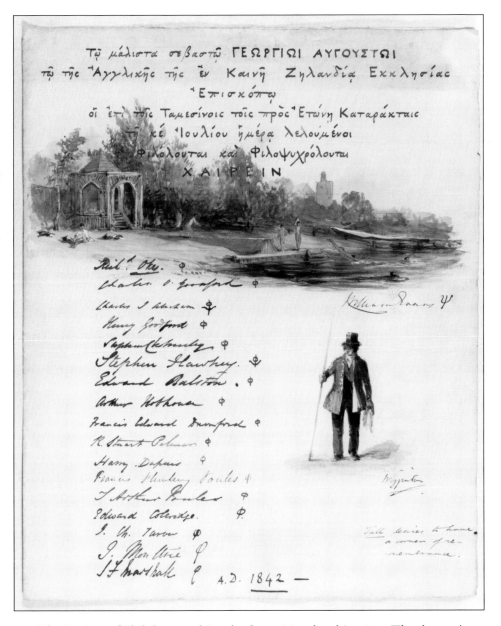

Τῷ μάλιστα σεβαστῷ ΓΕΩΡΓΙΩΙ ΑΥΓΟΥΣΤΩΙ
τῷ τῆς Ἀγγλικῆς τῆς ἐν Καινῇ Ζηλανδίᾳ Εκκλησίας
Ἐπισκόπῳ
οἱ ἐπὶ τοῖς Ταμεσίνοις τοῖς πρὸς Ἐτωνῇ Καταράκταις
τῇ κέ Ἰουλίου ἡμέρᾳ λελουμένοι
Φιλόλουται καὶ Φιλοψυχρόλουται
ΧΑΙΡΕΙΝ

[signatures]

A.D. 1842 —

21. The Society of Philolutes and Psychrolutes, Membership 1842. The decoration, by William Evans, shows the bathing place above Windsor and a waterman

22. M' Tutor's Sweepstakes by G.R. Winter (*c.* 1850). Sweepstakes would be arranged with some handicapping – pairing the young and the old for instance. Winter was in the Eton VIII in 1844 and 1845, became a clergyman and ended as Canon Winter

23. Messing by G.R. Winter (1850s). No shortage of fags

24. Speeches by G.R. Winter. Dr Hawtrey is seated in the centre of the front row. At this stage Upper School was being decorated with busts of eminent Etonians, the first of them being of Lord Wellesley and the Duke of Wellington, given by themselves

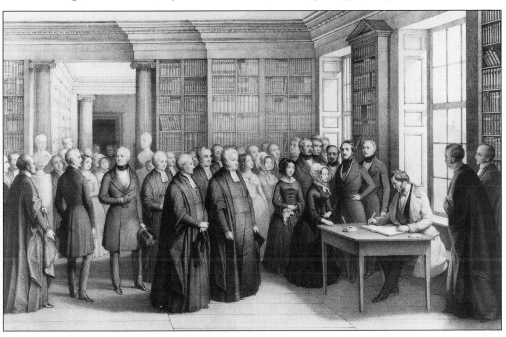

25. King Louis-Philippe in College Library with Queen Victoria and the Prince Consort in 1844. The Duke of Wellington on this occasion was lost in the crowd, but was rescued by Etonians headed by J.C. Patteson, the later Bishop and martyr. Dr Hodgson was host to the royal party

26. The Rotunda, built by Stephen Hawtrey at his own expense as mathematical schools. It was also used for lectures and theatricals. It was pulled down to make way for Queen's Schools

27. Boys outside the entrance to School Yard in what is known as the Long Walk, *c.* 1860. The one vendor shown was privileged; all others were driven out of the Long Walk by Dr Keate

Sixth Form. He could spot boys with unusual character, and the large number of distinguished pupils who presented portraits of themselves to him testify to his power of arousing affection and respect. Horace Walpole, in a letter of 1762, wrote that Dr Barnard was 'the Pitt of masters, and has raised the school to the most flourishing state it ever knew'. By 1765, at the end of his time as Head Master, there were indeed 552 boys, including a high proportion of aristocrats. One suspects that he showed rather more deference to them, and their parents, than was necessary, even in that class-conscious age.* Certainly the number of Collegers fell below the statutory seventy, a reflection of the discomfort of their lives; presumably this capable and vigorous Master could have done something to relieve the problem, had he been so minded. He is said with some reason to have reduced the amount of flogging, because he could speak to boys with great effect, yet he does not seem always to have been fair. Henry de Salis, one of the boys from the Grisons, left Eton feeling that he had been 'subject to the discretionary power of a partial pedant'. An 18-year-old in the Sixth Form with a good record, he was accused with others of breaking some windows; the evidence did not convict him, and he denied the charge, but Barnard flogged him for neglect of his business (Barnard's phrase apparently), although the boy had always been studious. There is some suspicion that de Salis's treatment was not the only miscarriage of justice.[1]

A consequence of the success of Dr Barnard in attracting Oppidans was that boarding accommodation was short. Boys of the same family had frequently to share. The grandees were very conscious of their social position, but they did not allow their boys to expect too much comfort. Lady Caroline Fox, soon to be Lady Holland, and her sister, Lady Kildare, had altogether four young boys at Eton in 1758 (accompanied by two servants): Stephen and Charles James Fox, Lord Offaly and William Fitzgerald. The boys boarded with Mrs Milward, who was trying to improve her accommodation and move into the College area from down the High Street. Lady Caroline Fox dictated the arrangements to her sister: 'Ste. and

* In one bizarre episode Dr Barnard flogged Viscount Hinchingbrooke for getting a Windsor girl with child – an inappropriate punishment, one might say. But hardly had Barnard started, when he stopped: 'Psha! what signifies him for being like his father? What's bred in the bone will never get out of the flesh.'

William are to lie together. Ophaly a bed to himself in the same room, and Charles in a little one by them; for neither Ophaly or Charles like to have bedfellows; besides they kick off the clothes so that the other boys don't like to lie with them, and I'm told Ste. and Fitz agree mighty well.'[2] (Parents might expect to pay an extra £2. 10s. on a basic £12. 10s. for a half year to secure a single bed for a son.)

Charles James Fox was perhaps the most characteristic Etonian of his time. By the time he was 14½ he was writing sophisticated letters home, showing an interest in the political scene as much as in school affairs. He did not find Eton at all agreeable, but felt that it was useful to him. His parents had been rash enough to take him to France, which cannot have made it easy for him to settle back. (Like some later Eton fathers, Lord Holland thought that Ste. and Charles wore their hair too long.) Stephen was a happy Etonian, but left early because of bad health; Charles had his way and left when he was 15½, at which age his portrait was painted by Reynolds and given to Dr Barnard. The boy looks old beyond his years, and already a rake. He was extravagant, but later, when he became bankrupt, his Etonian contemporaries helped to pay off his debts – an example of the usefulness of old schoolfriends. In a newspaper called *The World* one of Fox's contemporaries recalled his Eton career:

> Charles Fox left early as too witty to live there – and a little too wicked. As a scholar, he was not of the first rate – but better than his brother, who was asleep there. His companions were the same as they are now, Lord Carlisle, Stavordale and the etcaetera of Dame Milward's, who had them flogged constantly, for playing at chuck for guineas.

Gambling was a constant problem, and the best tennis player, Hulse, was reported in 1767 to have a match arranged with some gentleman for 20 guineas.*

Some boys put their leisure to better use. Joseph Banks, who had been briefly at Harrow, did become interested in Botany at Eton.

---

* This would probably have been played not in Eton but in Windsor; there is no clear record of a court still at Eton. In fact the gentleman was awed by Hulse's reputation and withdrew from the match.

His Tutor, Edward Young, reported that he could translate Latin into English readily enough, but that he was very deficient at turning English to Latin. Not only was the Harrow education to blame: the boy was inattentive and fond of play. But later in the year, Young reported that he had begun to read. Then after bathing in the river, Banks stopped in a flowery lane, and was captivated. Remarkably, three other Etonians of the time, Phipps, Woodward and Frankland,[3] were also sufficiently distinguished as botanists to have species named after them; Frankland made cowslip wine, but was also out badger-baiting at night. Banks boarded with Frances Yonge, who built up her house to forty boys, including other future Fellows of the Royal Society.

In 1761, when the school numbers topped 500 for the first time, there were 286 in the Upper School of whom fifty-nine were Collegers, with nine Oppidans delaying their entry to College because of the living conditions; of the Collegers, roughly half went on to King's. The Upper School included twenty-three sons of peers, three baronets and seven future baronets. (Perhaps the most surprising baronet was Sir Sampson Gideon, who was elevated while still a boy; he was the son of a Portuguese Jew brought up as a Christian, and promoted on his father's merits.) Ten boys came from the West Indies, sent over with the sugar, and two from America (from the richer Southern States).* There were also a number of local boys who boarded at home, or went into College young, thereby getting to King's by seniority, ahead of cleverer late entrants. Such boys were not charged an entry fee by Dr Barnard, but he would charge up to 10 guineas for sons of wealthy parents (and keep the takings for himself): 2 guineas was normal.

These same boys have been assiduously tracked down by R.A. Austen-Leigh; even his pertinacity, however, failed to elicit the subsequent careers of many (and some, of course, died young). Nearly half the Collegers, and about one fifth in all, took orders, some as academics or schoolmasters. (Of these two became Bishops.) Almost another fifth, mostly Oppidans, read for Law, but not all would have practised. Twenty-five became MPs and a further three were members of the Irish Parliament. Fifteen were soldiers and one, the Colleger son of the novelist Henry Fielding, a sailor who

---

* Thomas Lynch, who entered Eton in June 1764, was the most notable American Etonian: he signed the Declaration of Independence.

later turned to Law. Three practised medicine. Five were civil servants or diplomats. Industry and finance were unpopular; on the other hand a few tried literary careers. Large numbers would have returned to family estates and occupied themselves with county business. In judging these statistics it should be borne in mind that the School was larger than it had been, and, in proportion to the national population, larger under Barnard than it has ever been since.

In 1755 Barnard changed the summer holidays from Whitsuntide to the month of August, after the Election to King's. In 1759, the date of the Montem procession was moved from January to the Tuesday of Whitsun week, but it was no longer held every year. This was to increase the popularity of the ceremony with adults, and to enable more money to be raised for the Captain of Montem. For by now the purpose of the celebration was to make money, rather like a modern university rag day.

There is fortunately a long, if rather tedious, account of the curriculum written by a boy, almost certainly a Colleger, in 1766, the year after Barnard had given up the headmastership. Thomas James, later to be a distinguished Headmaster of Rugby,[4] gives a day-by-day account of the business in the different forms, which varied from week to week with the incidence of Saints' Days and other holidays. Certain generalizations remain. The number of lessons in an average week had fallen, and more work was done out of the schoolroom than had been the case 200 years previously. Boys could now be expected to have more books, which they would bring into school, where they sat on benches. This did not make for easy writing; so that most of the school business constituted the construing of texts prepared in advance, and the declamation of saying lessons learnt by heart. The writing of exercises and composition of verses, and the preparation of their schoolwork, at least for the younger boys, took place under tutorial supervision. Under Barnard the number of Assistants rose to ten, and every boy apparently had a Tutor.

The office of a praepostor, on the other hand, had diminished in significance, though the Sixth Form had some prefectorial powers to punish boys who broke bounds, drank and swore. There were still praepostors for every form, who were really administrative assistants for the Master, taking in exercises, marking out absentees and checking with the Dames to learn whether the boys were 'staying out' – if so, a Dame would write a note: 'James a cold, Mary Naylor'.* Two rather special praepostors from the Sixth Form attended on the Head Master and the Lower Master, being present at the execution when the boys were to be punished, but also calling over boys' names at Absences, and presiding at certain schooltimes, at which they were expected to ensure quiet. All praepostors served for one week at a time, and could themselves expect to suffer if they covered up for a culprit.

School hours were variable from day to day. It was characteristic of Eton that 6 o'clock lesson was retained for the younger boys, but ran from just before 7 until 7.30 a.m. All boys were in school from 8.00 to 9.00, from 11.00 to 12.00, from 3.00 to 4.00 and from 4.00 to 5.00 on whole school days. There might be half-holidays or 'play at four'. On Saturdays Chapel was from 2.00 to 3.00. On Sundays there was a service at 10 a.m. (Oppidans were expected to stay in their houses until then); at 2.00 the whole School gathered in Upper School, to be marked in by a praepostor, and the boys listened to a reading of the *Whole Duty of Man*; then there was Chapel again at 3.00. At other times on a Sunday, boys were expected to keep to their houses, which must have led to a quantity of disciplinary problems. Saints' Days caused a total rearrangement of the week, and the boys went to Chapel on the Saint's Eve and twice on the actual day; Absences ensured that the boys were in Eton, but they had more freedom than on a Sunday, particularly in summer. Oddly enough whole holidays and half-holidays were the times for lessons in classical Geography, Arithmetic, Algebra and Euclid (Geometry).

The youngest boys concentrated on Latin grammar with a little construing; they were also trained in writing. The Third Form was subdivided into Upper and Lower Greek, Sense and Nonsense. In the latter two sets they were introduced to verse composition; in Nonsense the target was to learn to scan and fit words to the metres, in Sense they began to think about translating words which could then become Latin verse. Similarly Upper and Lower Greek took the first steps in Greek, while continuing with Latin, construing and parsing, as well as translating from English to Latin in exercises. At this point they moved from the Lower School into the Upper School.

---

* The sample staying-out slip is evidence that James was indeed the author. He appears to have been writing his account perhaps for a Preparatory School.

The lessons became a little more sophisticated. Boys began to read Caesar and Ovid, and in Greek Aesop's *Fables*, as well as working at Farnaby, an anthology of suitable pieces. Gradually they extended their reading of classical authors, and their own compositions became more ambitious. Over Christmas, for example, they might have to write some eighty lines of Latin verse on a biblical theme as a holiday task. By the time they were in the Sixth Form, they were widely read in the Classics and would be able to quote extensively, a skill that would be useful to them in political life. They could also theoretically produce verses or epigrams on any subject set to them.

This almost exclusively classical syllabus was based on the belief, acquired during the Renaissance, that the classical authors offered the best models for style and content. Some Masters might have come to feel that there were English authors of equal merit, yet the Classics had the great advantage of being more demanding. In mastering grammar, boys were assumed to learn the habit of logical thought, as they had been in the fifteenth century. This was the theory, but many boys would not have reached the top of the School or had the advantages of wider reading of the best classical authors. Also, it is clear that the idle would often rely on cleverer contemporaries (or on bright younger boys) to help with the exercises done out of school.*

It is worth noting that there were rewards as well as punishments. A boy who wrote a distinguished exercise would 'Go up for Play' or be 'Sent up for Play'; the hero would be given a free school period to write his verses on gilded paper, and he would then take them to the Head Master and beg for a half-holiday for all.† This was popular with the Masters, too, in weeks which were otherwise short

---

* Only a few years later (1769) Dr Johnson exposed a complete ignoramus from Eton, Ralph Plumbe, son of a Lord Mayor of London. He failed many questions: 'Who then was the great Carthaginian General?' – 'Pigmalion, I think', says he – 'or Agamemnon, I forget which.' He died of consumption, aged 21, never apparently knowing which was of greater value, two shillings and sixpence or half-a-crown. It is important to remember that there was no formal entrance examination, though boys were tested on arrival.

† The reward, 'Sending up for Play', was supplemented by 'Sending up for Good', when extra half-holidays were not needed. 'Sending up for Good' continues at Eton, an example of the remarkable durability of the technical terms of the eighteenth century. Unacceptable exercises were 'torn over', then as now.

of holidays. Boys could also expect a financial reward if they did well in the Trials which preceded promotion from one form to the next. A shilling or half-a-crown was the reward, but it was recouped from the parents' bills. A boy with bad marks in the Trials would be kept back. Financial rewards were also occasionally given to younger boys for writing a good exercise, and Masters would sometimes give a book to a boy, to encourage excellence.

We learn of a rather different side of Eton from four curious manuscripts (slightly differing) dated 1766, known as 'Nugae Etonenses'.[5] Masters are listed, together with their nicknames, starting with Perny-Pojax Dampier, and including other instructors for writing and French. Alexander Cozens, father of the even better water-colourist J.R. Cozens, is mentioned as Drawing Master; Dancing, Fencing and Boxing were taught, the last by a formidable figure, William Stevens, The Nailor. There is a list of some sixteen private tutors. We learn of more sinister figures, such as the Poursuivant of Runaways with his assistants, and the Rod-maker, who was also the Clock-winder. Three Domines, of whom two were also Writing Masters, ran Oppidan houses, and ten Dames are listed. There are lists of tradesmen (and the favourite foods some of them supplied), the men who worked at the Christopher Inn and their dogs, watermen, billiard table keepers and medical men. There is a curious list of blackguards and of five young ladies who were the toasts of the School. Boys' nicknames, often crudely physical, are also noted.

At this time, the boys enjoyed many generally known children's games, such as hopscotch, marbles and tops, but also cricket, Fives (which was played around School Yard, and not just between the one set of buttresses that eventually became the standard form for Eton Fives courts), and football. Popular rides and places of resort include the Ascot Races, and Bachelors Acre and Bedford's Yard in Windsor for bull-baiting and cockfighting. There are lists of bathing places; the Thames had become a little cleaner, and it seemed that Eton now employed watermen to help make bathing safe rather than to assist boating – encouraged perhaps by Dr Barnard's experiences as a boy, when he was saved from drowning by another Etonian. Rowing as a sport was in its infancy, to judge from the scant references to it.

Some of the sights of Eton, and what were judged to be remarkable occurrences, reveal the heartlessness of many boys, and have to be set against more attractive characteristics such as interest in wild life, or regret for the fine elms lost in a gale.* Boys would go to see a criminal hanging in chains. They relished Dr Ashton's having a fit in Church, with the service accordingly cut short. There was little regret for Kent, a boy who died of scarlet fever, by virtue of which all got a week's holiday. In 1765 turrets were built on Lupton's Tower; one of the bells to be installed there fell, narrowly missing old Burton, the Vice-Provost. (This was when the clock was moved from a building near the north-east corner of the Chapel, where boys had been able to tamper with its time-keeping.) The following year, there was a major battle between Etonians and the butchers of Windsor; Henry Angelo, later the Fencing Master, says in his reminiscences that boys trapped in Windsor escaped only by dressing as women. More schoolboy fun: Hickford shut in his own dancing school; Brudenell swarming up a pillar in Lower School and defying the Lower Master until the praepostors and birch-desk keeper pulled him down; Dr Barnard cutting off Hare's pigtail in Hall with a greasy knife. This is not what schoolmasters should do, but it proves Barnard's standing that he accomplished this without causing much protest, though Hare was a bright spark and an exceptionally popular boy.† (Hare made his own protest by refusing to write his Latin Bacchus verses before Lent, writing an English poem instead; when forced to write in Latin, he dashed off 150 lines better than any other entry, and still had time to get to a Shrove Tuesday dance in Windsor.) The habit of pelting boys as they went into Upper School for the first time was already established, and was to prove a troublesome custom. There was something of the world of early schoolboy comics coexisting with the political sophistication of the older boys from the great Whig houses.

Among other occurrences mentioned is the visit in 1762 of King George III and Queen Charlotte. It did not start promisingly, for Their Majesties drove by the College, unaware that the whole School had turned out to greet them. The King was upset; a proper full royal visit was swiftly arranged, the King asked for holidays for the boys, and presented the College with two handsome silver cups, which hold a generous five pints each. This was the beginning of a

* Another natural wonder was the eclipse of the sun on 1 April 1764; a boy skipped Chapel, and claimed darkness as his excuse.

† Hare, a Colleger, was a friend of C.J. Fox. He became an MP and diplomat (Minister in Warsaw).

long friendship which brought pleasure to the troubled King and useful patronage to Eton.

In 1765, Dr Sleech died and Dr Barnard succeeded him as Provost. He addressed the boys for the last time as their Head Master, ending: 'Stet Fortuna Domus and God bless you all!' The boys were much moved. His reign had been a happy period for Eton, but his time as Provost was to be much less successful, beginning with the unwise selection as Head Master of the scholarly Dr Foster.

CHAPTER TEN

A Dark Time, but with Gleams of Light

FOSTER WAS THE son of a Windsor tradesman, and may have been unpopular partly because of this, but he was probably rather more handicapped by his small stature and poor eyesight. He is said once to have mistaken a black pig for a Colleger. He lacked any sense of how to manage boys, and could not see when their grievances were genuine.

Thus towards the end of 1768 occurred the worst act of rebellion in Eton's history. Accounts of it exist, one deriving from the Head Master, one from a rebel, Milles major, and there are a few contemporary letters by Pierce Taylor, a participant.[1] The trouble began when boys in the Sixth Form, who had duties as praepostors to ensure that boys were not in Windsor misbehaving, fell foul of Norbury, an Assistant. By this time a ridiculous custom had developed that boys who were out of bounds were expected to 'shirk' Masters; a Master would overlook the breach of bounds, which was not normally regarded as heinous, providing the boys made a gesture of respect by retreating out of sight, for example into a shop. Norbury complained of a boy in the Sixth Form who had failed to shirk him; the boy claimed it was an accident, and that he was legitimately present. Another two complaints from Masters of other praepostors followed, whereupon the conflict between the Sixth Form and Masters spread to Chapel. A Master complained that a praepostor, who was – perhaps noisily – quelling the young there, was guilty of indecency during the service, and of offensive behaviour to the Master afterwards. It seems this was the very boy who had clashed with Norbury in Windsor. Dr Foster flogged the boy, to the very open satisfaction of Norbury. The other praepostors all protested and resigned their office. Two days later they refused to take part in Speeches. They tried to negotiate new rights, accepting that they deserved to be punished if they were discovered in a tavern or at a billiard table or the like, but otherwise reaffirming their privileges. Dr Foster refused to treat, particularly disliking the combination of boys in defiance.

The Sixth Form duly marched off, and most of the Upper boys, perhaps 170, followed. Some Masters' windows were broken, and one or two Masters were actually manhandled.* Then the boys went on to the inn at Maidenhead Bridge, where their behaviour was quite decorous, and they even remembered to tip the servants. One Master, Roberts, rode out to try diplomacy. He did not succeed, since Foster had offered no concession. The next morning, after one more attempt at defiance, the rebellion began to fall apart. Some of the leaders made their peace 'to their eternal infamy'; others, perhaps more honourable, were sacked. Of those who did return, many left shortly afterwards. Milles, admittedly justifying himself after being expelled, remarked that 'the secession was conducted by a calm and deliberate reflection; not by youthful impetuosity and levity. The [Head] Master behaved with the warmth of youth: the boys with the prudence of a more advanced age. The boys desired either to be convinced, or to convince the Master by reason; the Master refused both.' Reading all accounts, the historian tends to sympathize with the boys, who appeared generally more reasonable and – in the case of Milles and Pierce Taylor – undeniably more eloquent than their opponents.

Dr Foster never recovered from this disaster. A year later Pierce Taylor, after admitting that he had been deservedly whipped for going on a shooting party, reported that fresh riots caused Dr Foster more trouble: a boy, Lord Petersham, hissed and Foster lost his temper; several boys were faulted in translating Homer, and 'I will not say he whipped them, but he butchered them'. Pierce Taylor's Tutor, Heath, sought to advise him to moderation, but he replied with admirable sense that he had to care what Dr Foster did, because

---

* The boys are reported to have thrown their schoolbooks in the river, though Thomas Grenville would not part with his Homer; he was later First Lord of the Admiralty and a famous bibliophile, and a brass commemorates him in Chapel.

some boys had been punished without reason. By 1773, the numbers in the School were less than half the strength Foster had inherited. He resigned, his health collapsed and he was soon dead.

There are many anecdotes connected to the rebellion, which came to be remembered with some hilarity: quite a number of them involved some episode of flogging. Now it all seems alien and reprehensible, but that was not so then. There were other punishments available, for instance writing lines, but flogging was accepted and expected. The degradation was then seen as part of the punishment. There was also something about it akin to the ancient Romans forcing their captives under the yoke. Accepting flogging was a gesture of submission on the part of the boy, and if he would not submit, then it was time to leave. Dr Foster flogged Burke, a popular Irish boy, thought to have lampooned him in the press; when he then also expelled Burke, this was seen as ungentlemanly behaviour, and noted as yet another fault. It would also seem, from Taylor's letter, that Foster showed sadistic tendencies of which other Head Masters were free.

His successor was Dr Jonathan Davies, who, like Foster, was of humble origins. His father had been a barber, and Davies himself was nicknamed 'Barber'. He survived as Head Master for eighteen years, but was not particularly successful. He did restore prizes for Holiday Task and for Declamation, which had recently lapsed, and founded two scholarships for departing Collegers. He was renowned for his stentorian voice and for his fondness for good living. Although the numbers in the School crept up, he too had to face a rebellion, but he handled it more successfully than Foster had done.

Probably it suited Dr Barnard as Provost not to have a Head Master of any great distinction. He presided with a rather bullying manner over the College, and did not, for some reason, send his own son to the School. (He was somewhat embarrassed when the boy, who was being tutored privately at home, welcomed in Etonians to give a theatrical performance in the Provost's Lodge in his father's absence; theatricals were popular with Etonians at this time.) Dr Barnard was able to attract a particularly notable royal visit in 1778, though on the day he was laid up with gout. Speeches were performed in Upper School, and Lord Wellesley, who had migrated to Eton after being sacked from Harrow, made a great impression with Strafford's final speech at his impeachment, which drew tears from the audience. This was an early instance of a Speech given in English rather than in Latin or Greek, and Queen Charlotte, who let it be known that she was happier with English, helped to encourage a greater frequency of English Speeches.*

Dr Barnard died at the end of 1781, leaving a large fortune. While Dr Davies might have expected to succeed him, Thomas Dampier, son of Barnard's Lower Master, had the support of Lord North. As his father had found before him, this was not enough. The King was determined to appoint William Roberts, a Fellow and the former Assistant Master who had tried to mediate in the 1768 rebellion; the King had become friendly with Roberts. Roberts soon found himself again required to attempt conciliation, for in 1783 the Masters rebelled against Dr Davies, offering their resignations. As Provost, Roberts had no authority in this sphere, but he was prepared to act as a go-between. In fact, many of the Oppidans took advantage of the absence of any control from the Masters to disobey the rules they did not fancy. The Masters were shocked into returning to their posts, and order was restored. Davies prudently closed the School early for the Christmas holidays, but Eton's reputation was further damaged.†

Roberts was not yet 50 when he became Provost. He could claim to be a poet with several volumes to his credit; a poetical essay on 'The Existence, the Attributes, and the Providence of God' suggests that he took his poetry seriously, but he wrote no more poetry after becoming Provost. His account book survives to show that he and the Fellows were rich men.[2] His stipend was only £279, fixed in the

---

* A letter stating her case, was written by Lord North, the Old Etonian Prime Minister. Wellesley loved Eton so much that he arranged to be buried there where boys would daily walk over his grave. The Latin verses he composed for the tablet were translated by another Old Etonian Prime Minister, Lord Derby:

> Long lost on Fortune's waves, I come to rest,
> Eton, once more on thy maternal breast.
> On loftiest deeds to fix the aspiring gaze,
> To seek the purer light of ancient days,
> To love the simple paths of manly truth,
> These were thy lessons to my opening youth.

† In 1789, Stephen Hawtrey was doubtful whether he could entrust a son to Eton or King's: 'The total neglect of discipline at each of these places is shocking.'

seventeenth century and worth less in real terms than the £75 laid
down in the Statutes. He received £300 p.a. from the College living
of Farnham Royal, situated conveniently close to Eton. As Provost
he also had a double share of the 'fines', the premiums extracted
when leases on College properties were renewed. (The practice of
sharing these among Fellows dated back to Sir Henry Savile's time,
and furnished growing rewards as, thanks to rising prices and
increased prosperity, tenants were prepared to pay more.) The sums
were variable, but in 1784 Provost Roberts received an income of
£1,800, as well as housing and other benefits – nearly £100,000 in
today's money. He was also able to ensure that his sons returned as
Masters. Furthermore, the elder was promoted Fellow aged only 24,
and the younger would doubtless soon have followed had not Dr
Roberts himself died in 1791.*

This time Davies was not disappointed. He became Provost and
Dr George Heath, known to the boys as 'Ascot' Heath, was chosen
as Head Master.† He did not make any great impression. The best-
known anecdote suggests that he was a coarse man: a boy was to be
flogged for playing cards – 'You shuffle and I cut', he said. Indeed,
he was an excessive flogger who yet failed to ensure good discipline.
On the other hand, he did attempt to appoint a Master who had been
an Oppidan and then at Oxford, but the Provost and Fellows
insisted on maintaining the old Colleger/Kingsman closed shop.
During Heath's time the numbers in the School rose to 499 but then
fell to 357. The Lower Master who was already in office, William
Langford, cannot have been a very effective help, since he was not
only a Canon of Windsor, but Chaplain to the King, which gave him
an excuse to be at Court, even in London, or in Weymouth, where
the King went for the sea bathing. He often chose to reside in the
Cloisters at Windsor, and lower boys had to go there to be flogged.
In 1801 and 1802 vacancies arose which enabled both Heath and
Langford‡ to be appointed Fellows with the consequence that
Joseph Goodall became Head Master. He was the first Master who

---

* The Roberts sons were known to the boys as 'Hog' Roberts and 'Peelipo'
because of their conflicting views about the treatment of potatoes in College
Hall. Should they be served in their jackets, fit for hogs, or peeled?
† Heath's brother had been Headmaster of Harrow from 1771 to 1785,
when he returned to Eton as a Fellow.
‡ Langford subsequently fell into debt and had to take refuge at Holyrood
House. His daughter became one of the best Dames.

can certainly be said to have been a Housemaster, with boys boarding. John Keate became the Lower Master, and both appointments took effect in 1802.

During the second half of the eighteenth century, several questionable characteristics of Eton life are documented, which one suspects have existed at most schools and at most times: bullying, fighting and fagging. Two arrangements at Eton may have added to the danger of bullying. Boys were grouped for work according to ability rather than age, and small clever boys might find themselves with stupid older louts; in such a case they might find the best solution to their problems would be to help the older boys with their out-of-school work. Secondly, the houses were uncontrolled except by their Dames; boy prefects with responsibility do not seem to have existed in the way that they had done in the sixteenth century. A Dame could appeal for help from a Master, and senior boys might exercise a benign influence, but bullying, which may occur even under a vigilant regime, must have been more than usually prevalent. Houses varied substantially, and yet there was a strong feeling within the School that College was worse than elsewhere. H.J.C. Blake, who came as an 8-year-old Oppidan in Langford's time as Lower Master before moving to College at 13, reckoned that College was rougher, but he also felt it was livelier.* College did entrust the Sixth Form with some responsibility, but it was not taken seriously. The boys were not supervised by the Head Master, under whose direct authority they came; they were simply locked up at night and left to their own devices.

Fighting was frequent, and became the normal way in which disputes between boys were settled. It should be remembered that prize-fighting was very popular, and that the fighters were given some of the adulation that the young now direct at professional footballers. (And were they always less admirable role models?) The best fighters among the boys were well known. The Duke of Wellington, who arrived at Eton under the original family name of Wesley as a 12-year-old in 1781, is best remembered as an Etonian for his defeat of an older boy, Bobus Smith, elder brother to Sydney Smith, the cleric and wit, who was educated at Winchester. Wesley

---

* Reportedly the stupidest boy in the School, Blake nevertheless rose automatically to the Sixth Form. He became a clergyman, and in old age wrote *Recollections of an Etonian*.

had thrown stones at Smith while the boy was swimming. Another famous fight arose between two boys who boarded at Goodall's: John Musters did not like T.A. Smith growling at him; they fought for one and half hours, but were happy to have tea together afterwards, as defenders of fighting expected.[3] There were also more general mêlées between Collegers and Oppidans, and between the boys and townspeople of Windsor. Although football was played, it was, according to Blake, extremely violent.

Blake had a fight on his first full day at Eton, and he was also recruited at once as a fag. Henry Angelo speaks of fagging in Dr Foster's time. Morley Saunders, an Irish boy in Third Form, wrote home in 1767:

> Dear Papa Eton is a very bad place and I should be glad to leave it. Besides I lead a very unhappy life for I am force to wait upon the Big Boys while they are at supper and to goe down for every thing they want and If I do not do it directly they beate me very much and I dare not tell. I and two other boys wait upon them as a Servant.[4]

Saunders's letter ended pathetically: 'I assure you Papa I will not keep company with bad Boys but indeed their is very few good ones in this Place.' (Nevertheless he remained at the School until 1771.) It is hard to believe that small boys were not performing jobs for big boys from much earlier. When the system was humanely operated, it worked well – as a type of feudal exchange of services with the fagmaster acting as protector. Again fagging seems to have been more onerous in College. James Gifford in 1783 reckoned his fagmaster kind, but his pride was sadly affronted by having to fetch water in the morning and food in the evening. Then he had to watch out for the Head Master, and might return to Long Chamber to find his bedclothes gone.[5]

Another complaint that weighed particularly on the Collegers was the poor quality of their accommodation and food. In 1785 Lord Godolphin left £4,000 to improve the diet of the boys. Pudding was provided on Sundays and slightly more mutton, but that did not account for all the interest. It is a slight surprise that the Fellows did not spend it on themselves, but of course their diet was already ample: Godolphin's legacy was allowed to accumulate. The fundamental weakness of eighteenth-century Eton lay in the low quality of so many of the Fellows and Masters, and this in turn was attributable to the stranglehold of King's, which only recruited from uncompetitive Eton Collegers, and had no graduation examination requirement.

Yet there were developments to praise. Fagging grew alongside the amiable habit of boys sharing meals with their friends. 'Messing together' for breakfast and tea may have been going on for some time, but in the 1790s we learn from two boys in Goodall's house, Michael Hicks Beach and Charles Metcalfe, that their Tutor was reluctantly manoeuvred into permitting tea in boys' rooms. Collegers might have rooms in Dames' houses where they too could mess together; but tea may have been expensive for them.

The social life of the boys extended to theatricals; they also had fairly easy access to drink and could look forward to meals out. In the School year of 1786–7 there occurred the first example of boy journalism. Collections of Latin verse, *Musae Etonenses*, had been published officially; but now four boys masquerading under the name Gregory Griffin produced forty numbers of about 10 pages each, entitled *Microcosm*. It was intended for a wider public, not just for boys, and was similar in style to the *Spectator*. The four boys, George Canning, John Smith, Bobus Smith and John Hookham Frere, sold the copyright for 50 guineas, and the *Microcosm* was reprinted several times, even as late as 1825.* In February 1827, 'Gregory Griffin' wrote angrily to refute the criticism that the authors' literary work had been looked over by Ushers. 'Slaves cannot live in England; Ireland enjoys an immunity from toads; in a similar degree is the climate and constitution of Eton utterly unadapted to the existence of Ushers.' Indeed, the good things at Eton came about largely through the unaided initiative of boys.

Still, boys could be well trained as Classics. The famous scholar Richard Porson came to College from Norfolk aged 14, encouraged by his local clergyman. (Most Collegers were from the home counties in those days.) He displayed his astonishing facility and memory, but he had entered too late to gain a place at King's; at Trinity College, Cambridge, he soon acquired as great a reputation

---

* At the time of the last reprint, the authors were all distinguished men and MPs, and Canning was Foreign Secretary before briefly serving as Prime Minister in 1827. John Smith, known as Easly Smith from the way he pronounced the word 'aisle', was not related to Bobus; both were Collegers.

for drunkenness and eccentricity as for scholarship. While at Eton he did write a drama, *Out of the Frying-pan into the Fire*, satirizing some of his more obnoxious contemporaries, but he claimed only really to have enjoyed rat-hunting in the Long Chamber. Curiously Goodall, his contemporary, considered Lord Wellesley, the Duke's brother, to be the better scholar at Eton.

In 1800, Charles Metcalfe began a diary just after his fifteenth birthday. He must have been a boy of some character as well as ability, for he had ridden through Eton on a camel. His diary tells not only of his conflicts with Goodall over tea, but the extent of his reading – for example, Rousseau in French. In one long entry he compares Eton, a Public School in the sense that it drew boys from all over the country, with the private schools, which provided local education:

Wednesday 19th (March). Whole school-day. Read Homer. Virgil. Read a dissertation on Rowley's *Poems*, tending to prove from the language that they were not written in the 15th century, but by Chatterton. Gave Neville, Hervey, and Shaw tea. Wrote a letter. Entered into a train of thoughts on public schools in general, and Eton in particular. I conceive the advantages of a public school to be so great, that I shall here take an opportunity of enumerating them. Many have objected to a public education, with the idea that it gives an inclination to extravagance, dissipation, and vice, which would never be acquired in private schools. I will not pretend absolutely to deny it; but still, how much more dangerous is it to rush from the close constraint of a private education to the unbounded liberty of the world . . . Secondly, at a public school every vice and every virtue which we meet with in the world is practised, although in miniature, every deception is triflingly displayed which one would be open to in life; we learn to abhor vice, consequently shun it; we learn to admire virtue, consequently imitate it; we learn to beware of deception, consequently to avoid it; in short, a public school is but a humble imitation of the theatre of the world; it is what one conceives of a drama acted by boys, where the actors are small . . . Thirdly, where is that emulation at a private which is the great actor [? factor] in a public school? The praise of others naturally excites us to wish for the same ourselves, and to obtain it we must deserve it; if a friend or a rival be superior to us in some respects, we naturally wish to render him inferior; if inferior we naturally wish to maintain our superiority; this is the great stimulus to industry, and, consequently virtue; this is the stimulus which acts as well in youth as manhood; it guides us through life to glorious and virtuous deeds . . . Fourthly, the very freedom, the very pleasures of a public school, which have been so constantly objected to it, are additional arguments to my assertion. From study to relaxation, from relaxation to study, is delightful transition; in the other way of education one trudges on in the usual method of teasing application and when study no longer becomes a merit it loses *all* its pleasures; if study arises from free will, it is always brisk, happy, and successful; if from force, it is dull, tedious, and seldom I may say never, retains what it is meant to acquire . . . From the above, I would infer that public education is a much better mode than private, and that the very freedom of the former is a great cause of its superiority.

That this freedom may be carried too far, is an undoubted fact; I have witnessed it at Eton, and, from the little I have seen of Westminster, I will venture to affirm that it is still more dissipated than Eton; but nevertheless, take all the advantages and disadvantages, the former will preponderate in every public school; for, exclusive of the others which I above have mentioned, the advantage of making acquaintance who will be of service through life is no contemptible one; every one remembers with retrospective joy the years passed at Eton, and a friendship there formed and established will be maintained throughout life.[6]

A few days later, Metcalfe left Eton for service in India where he joined the school in Calcutta set up by Wellesley, who had become Governor-General, to instruct the East India Company's servants in oriental languages. It is hard to think that many 15-year-olds today could achieve such maturity. For those able to use the opportunity for self-education, there were great rewards.* Charles Metcalfe

---

* Metcalfe is widely recognized as the greatest administrator of British India. By the age of 27 he was the Resident at Delhi, administering an area roughly equal in size to the north of England. He stopped the slave trade and the burning of widows, and abolished capital punishment; he lightened the tax burden and prosperity increased remarkably. He himself gave credit to his Eton education, where he had developed his independence of thought and action. Happily, he became friends with Goodall, and they were regular correspondents.

retained happy memories of Eton, and was always grateful. The same could be said of Lord Wellesley and of many others.

One last example of gratitude: in 1799 Eton was to receive a most remarkable benefaction: Anthony Storer, who had been a boy in Barnard's time, bequeathed his books and prints to Eton. The 2,800 books almost filled the remaining space in College Library, and include many of its greatest glories. Such a collection is a responsibility, and a drain on the College's funds rather than a source of wealth. But by caring for it Eton enriches scholarship and the national heritage.*

---

* Storer was the son of a wealthy merchant from Jamaica. He was a good scholar at Eton, whose verses were circulated among less good scholars for years after he left. At Cambridge he was the best gymnast, dancer and skater. He had a brief political career, but then his health suffered and he became an antiquary. Eton was fortunate to receive his books, for he would have left them to Downing College, Cambridge, had its foundation Charter been granted before he died.

CHAPTER ELEVEN

Dr Goodall and Dr Keate

JOSEPH GOODALL WAS Head Master for only eight years, from 1802 to 1809, but continued as Provost from 1810 to his death in 1840. His influence on the history of Eton was therefore extended, but, it must be confessed, largely negative. His character was formed at an early age, and did not change. He was a good scholar, and thus competent to teach the Sixth Form, where indeed he was said by the later Head Master and Provost, Hawtrey, to have a gift for bringing out the best in boys of potential; he was also said to encourage boys to read widely. He was, however, lazy and conservative; he would only change his stance if to do so were less trouble than preserving it. He had good manners and geniality, towards boys as well as adults – particularly if they were well connected.

Two Masters did not regard Goodall as a worthy Head Master and resigned; one of them, Peter Hinde (or Hind), returned to his Fellowship at King's, and was so permanently offended by an apparent slight from Goodall that he pursued a vendetta which was to cause Goodall much trouble. One boy equally distressed Goodall, but this was to prove to his advantage: the boy had written 'No Goodall' in Upper School, along with other more gross and slanderous remarks; he had also as a prank put in some explosive candles, for it was afternoon school. Eventually new candles disclosed and drew attention to the inscription, and, after a long pause, Goodall said: 'I thought I had to deal with gentlemen. Is this proper treatment for your Head Master?' Most boys disclaimed the remarks. Goodall said that, had the opinion been general, he would have resigned; 'If the individual who has done this will come and apologise to me after school, I will freely forgive him.' When the boy did so, it transpired he was a favourite of Goodall, which was a particular grief, but the boys appreciated Goodall's generosity.[1]

There was, however, a hint of weakness in his dealings with the boys, and this emerged in another episode, when one Ponsonby was sentenced to be expelled. Hal Pearce, a natural son of Charles James Fox, rose to accompany Ponsonby, and many others followed. Goodall, alarmed, did a deal with the senior boys, agreeing that the sentence should be reversed provided one in ten of them should submit to a flogging; this decimation was very mildly carried out. Indeed, Goodall was a mild man. In 1806 the Sixth Form sided with one of their members in trouble; Bransby Purnell wrote to his father that it 'ended as it generally does with his crying and yielding to the boys' – not what a Remove boy should be writing about his Head Master.[2]

In 1803, Goodall did take an initiative to raise volunteers among the boys to meet the threat from Napoleon. Eventually 190 were enlisted, with the numbers in the School again rising towards 500. Keate, and possibly other Masters, took lessons from a drill sergeant. Many boys left to fight,* and some actually had commissions while still at Eton – this was particularly likely if they had been royal pages. Goodall noted that he had the honour one morning of flogging a Major in His Majesty's service. That is a reflection on the arrangements for the army, rather than Eton.

In 1809 one of the recurrent great floods inundated Eton, and swept away the Fifteen Arch Bridge on the Slough Road. (This was subsequently rebuilt with only three arches, but it retains its old name.) The boys were left by Goodall to their own devices in their houses, and teaching ceased; this inactivity was felt to be symptomatic of his idleness. For five days the boys lay in bed, played cards, and experimented with fire balloons.

George III's relations with Eton, always warm, became even closer at this period. His health had recovered, and he was greeted so enthusiastically by the boys when he came to Eton in 1804 that he declared, 'I was ever an Etonian, even from my cradle, but

---

* Goldwin Smith saw a letter from a 14-year old Bathurst, who went straight from Eton to Waterloo: 'Dear Mamma, Cousin Tom and I are all right. I never saw anything like it in my life.'

henceforth I shall be so from the gratitude I owe you for the reception you gave me yesterday, which I never shall forget.' The boys enjoyed being treated almost as comrades. One hurrying back for absence ran full tilt into the King, and was delayed by the need to apologize; the King therefore wrote a note asking that the boy might be excused. Another, caught by a keeper coursing a hare in Windsor Park, was locked up for the night; Goodall enjoyed speculating with the boys whether the miscreant would be tried for treason; but in fact the boy escaped all punishment, as the King and the Head Master left action to each other.

Goodall profited himself from these happy relations. His letters to his brother[3] reveal that he had almost an obsession with promotions and payments. He was delighted when in 1808 he became a Canon of Windsor. Then when Provost Jonathan Davies died in December 1809 and Spencer Perceval, the Prime Minister, nominated Benjamin Heath, who had been Headmaster of Harrow, the King insisted: 'No, he will never do, for he ran away from Eton.' Instead the King consulted Goodall's old friend, the Marquess Wellesley; thereupon Goodall received a letter: 'You are Provost'. By Christmas, Mr Keate (as he then was) had been elected Head Master.

Keate and Goodall were good friends, and Keate had indeed met his wife, Fanny Brown, when she and her sister Margaretta were staying with the Goodalls in 1802.* Fanny was a strikingly beautiful woman, and Keate was pleased and amused when one of the best cricketers in the school called his bat Mrs Keate:

> Without a flaw, without a speck,
> Smooth as fair Hebe's ivory neck,
> It was withal so light, so neat,
> That Harding called it – *Mrs Keate*.[4]

Keate was also every whit as good a scholar as Goodall, and had won most of the awards available to Kingsmen at Cambridge. Physically and temperamentally, however, the two men were very different.

---

* Dr Brown, later Sir Charles, who was probably born in 1746, was thought to be a natural son of Bonnie Prince Charlie. He had become Court physician to the King of Prussia. This, rather than Fanny Brown's undoubted charms, may explain why she was embraced by Blucher when he was at Windsor after the Battle of Waterloo.

Goodall was ample and genial, but by nature supine. Keate, known to the boys as the Baffin because of the noise he made coughing, was small and, in public at least, bad-tempered; more than one record refers to days when he was 'savage'. In private he emerges as kindly from the diaries that were kept by Margaretta Brown, and boys who were invited to his table experienced his better nature, while others found an unexpected sympathy. He was also far from supine; his moral and physical courage were considerable, and if something seemed to him wrong, it was to be fought. Goodall was the last Head Master to wear the conventional wig, Keate the last to wear a cocked hat. The most famous description of Keate is by Kinglake:

> Anybody without the least notion of drawing could still draw a speaking, nay scolding, likeness of Keate. If you had no pencil, you could draw him well enough with poker, or the leg of chair, or the smoke of a candle. He was little more (if more at all) than five feet in height, and was not very great in girth, but in this space was concentrated the pluck of ten battalions. He had a really noble voice, and this he could modulate with great skill; but he also always adopted this mode of communication in order to inspire respect . . . His red, shaggy eyebrows were so prominent that he habitually used them as arms and hands, for the purpose of pointing out any object towards which he wished to direct attention, the rest of his features were equally striking in their way, and were all and all his own.*

It is tempting to think that Keate knew many of the faults of Eton in his time, and would have put them right but for the negative influence of Provost Goodall. There is perhaps some truth in this, but really the men were not so very different in their policy: Keate was a little more progressive than Goodall, but almost anyone must have been. Keate accepted the constitution of Eton as it was at the end of the eighteenth century, and he was determined to make it work.

Keate had a predictably difficult first year in office. Indeed there is some evidence that a campaign of rebellion was planned even

---

* In Cairo Kinglake had met a lad who claimed to be able to call up the image of any person Kinglake chose to name. Kinglake nominated Keate and the lad replied: 'I see a fair girl with golden hair, blue eyes, pallid face, rosy lips.' Kinglake offered the readers of *Eothen* his own description. Keate was in fact about 5ft 4ins tall.

before he took up his appointment. In March 1810, Richard Gosling wrote home to his mother that 'hissings from the boys were the constant companions of our wise and *lofty* Head Master. He is generally disliked as Goodall was esteemed.'[5] Boys are conservative creatures – particularly when the old ways are easy. Then in May worse troubles developed. A jeweller called Levi, or possibly one of his employees, stole five links from a boy's watch chain. A group of boys were proposing to duck him in Barnes Pool, but he escaped to Slough; and so the boys broke his windows. According to Gosling, 'Keate sent for the constables who drove the boys from the house, and Keate tucking up his gown ran after them. The next day he imposed a new absence on about 120 boys in our part of the school [Gosling was in the middle ranks of the Fifth Form] instead of the higher ones who were most culpable, but of these he undoubtedly was afraid.' The result was booing and another new Absence for the Gosling group; Gosling himself was out with his parents at the time of the booing. Eighty-seven boys refused to answer this later Absence,

> unwilling to put up with such injustice. About 20 boys answered and were accordingly despised. I am sure you will not be angry to know that I was in the 87, for if I had not, I should have been totally neglected, and perpetually bullied . . . Then followed another thing which surprised everybody: the same evening, Keate flogged *the whole 87* hard amidst the loudest hissings, and several *eggs* which were thrown at, and hit him, by boys in the fourth form. 40 rods were used on the occasion, and not withstanding the rigour of the flogging not a face, or tear was to be seen. Everything is pretty quiet now and though the flogging effected no good, yet quiet speeches from the assistants have produced tranquillity.[6]

'Mr Keate's conduct in this affair seems to be highly approved by everyone, he has certainly shown great firmness and judgement,' commented Miss Brown, whose 'everyone' evidently did not include all the boys. As with most collective punishments there was certainly some unfairness. The 'boo' had become a favourite Etonian misdemeanour because it was almost impossible to pin down to the actual guilty parties. The cowardice of the crime may mitigate the injustice of authority.

At the end of June a boy called Harris was in trouble for driving a tandem, the fastest and most strictly forbidden vehicle, through Eton. Harris declared he would leave, but Keate said that he must hear from the mother first. The boy was then so insolent that Keate did indeed expel him, whereupon his uncle arrived to ask for the expulsion to be revoked. The uncle set himself up with his nephew at the Christopher Inn, and proceeded to behave as badly as the boy. Only on 7 July did Harris and his uncle depart. The previous day, Margaretta Brown had been cheered by the King's speaking most approvingly to Keate for his firmness: he knew all about the Harris affair. (Sadly, it was one of the King's last rational moments.)

In the autumn there was more trouble, caused by older boys loitering at Chapel, but it would seem that Keate had established an uneasy equilibrium, which nevertheless fell far short of good order. Keate's desk in Upper School was nailed up, but picking up his gown, he vaulted over it – a considerable feat which earned applause. On another occasion the door by which Keate normally entered was locked and he had to come in by the boys' door and pass through the boys, who set up a boo. Keate again resorted to collective punishment, which induced the perpetrators of the original crime to own up; they were not among those set an extra exercise, which certainly embarrassed Keate enough to remit the next week's exercise for those who had wrongly been punished.

Keate was not vindictive over acts against himself. He did, however, almost automatically flog boys who were complained of by any of his Assistants. It was particularly unfortunate that some of these were of such poor mettle. 'Botch' Bethell was an ignorant man who could not be trusted to correct boys' work properly, and Keate had in effect to introduce a system whereby work was corrected not just by the Tutor but the Division Master also. Bethell and others could not command the boys' respect, and Keate felt that he needed to back up his Assistants in that one way. The actual floggings were not normally severe, and were not feared by most boys. Keate should have realized that Eton needed more, and better, Masters. If he could not be rid of the weaker ones, he could have improved the average standard by adding good new men, while smaller classes would have made control easier for all.* Some of his

---

* Some of the worst, including Bethell, were promoted to Fellow, where the damage they did was limited to their lamentable preaching.

appointments were successful – notably of his eldest daughter's fiancé, Edward Coleridge, who was an Oxford man; in an act of justifiable nepotism, Keate nevertheless persuaded the Provost and Fellows to accept him. Coleridge was to replace William 'Slinker' Heath, third son of 'Ascot' Heath who was obliged to resign. Only three boys boarded with him, which Keate had earlier thought inexplicable; but Miss Brown, who sometimes enjoyed the indiscretions of boys, knew better. The failure to increase the staff was really caused by economic considerations: more Masters meant fewer tutorial pupils for each, and therefore less income. The Head Master also had to pay his Assistants a small stipend out of his own income, and Keate, for family reasons, was not as rich as his predecessors. In 1820 Keate did subdivide the Upper Division of the Fifth Form, appointing an extra Master; he himself had been teaching nearly 200 boys, and this reduced the number to roughly 120. There were eight Assistants to the Head Master and Lower Master, together responsible for some 600 boys, but there were perhaps twice as many private tutors, who were certainly some help.

One Master was both popular with the boys and gifted. However, Ben Drury, son of a headmaster of Harrow, unfortunately had serious problems of personal behaviour. He and Knapp, who was another ineffective schoolmaster, liked to slip up to London for the theatre, leaving on Saturday afternoon and returning for Monday early school, sometimes the worse for wear. Drury liked the excitement of fighting, and once reportedly appeared very damaged at the Head Master's Chambers, alleging that it was a result of a cricket ball hitting him in the right eye; Knapp mischievously remarked that the ball must have cannoned, for there was also a dreadful bruise under his left ear.[7] Drury and Knapp also claimed to be ill when in fact they were simply taking time off. By 1820, Drury's exotic life-style was affecting his finances, and in the summer holidays of 1823 he took himself off to the Continent.* Miss Brown reported his departure with relief: 'What a happiness that such a disgrace to the School should *at last* be obliged to quit it – but how I wish he had gone some years ago, or could have been sent away.'

---

* He did repay a substantial sum that Keate had lent him, but left many unsatisfied creditors. He took his wife and children with him, and he was apparently shamed by the ruin he had caused them. Oddly, his uncle and cousin, Harrow masters, had to escape to the Continent in 1825.

Keate, who referred to him as '*il gran peccatore*', said that he would have dismissed Drury, but for his innocent wife and children; that is an honourable sentiment, but Keate's primary responsibility was to the boys to whom Drury, for all his gifts, had not set a proper example.

There were further difficulties with staff before the end of 1823. Successful Masters, who received £110 p.a. for a boarder (£200 for two brothers), wanted to take up to forty boys. Keate, however, with the support of Goodall, wished to limit the number of boys in Masters' houses. Keate thought that twenty-four was as many as one man could manage, but he was prepared to allow the Lower Master twenty-eight. Keate had his way, but this was to be a recurrent problem. One of the Masters most opposed was Yonge, yet Keate was generous enough to make Yonge Lower Master on merit in 1829. Unfortunately Yonge died in 1830. A fine memorial by William Pitte in the north porch of Chapel was erected by his sorrowing pupils to show how fond they were of him in life, and how much they missed his strength of mind, softened by unrivalled charm, and his fine scholarship, enlivened by a wit entirely his own. Their words (in Latin) suggest that there could already be the bond between Tutor and pupils on which Eton was later to pride itself.

Before then, Keate had faced another rebellion. The year 1818 was notable for rebellions; all but one Public School suffered. At Eton in October behaviour was generally bad. There was an epidemic of hunting, shooting and tandem-driving; Keate himself rode out in an unsuccessful attempt to catch some villains. He decided to bring forward the hour of lock-up from 6 to 5 p.m. This created further commotion, and Miss Brown was frightened in the street by the loud and riotous behaviour; a window in the house of Green, another moderate Master, was smashed by stones, to the accompaniment of violent shouting. A popular young boy who was involved with tandem-driving was then sacked: 'He was in Drury's house – the worst place he could be.' On Sunday afternoon, 1 November, when Keate assembled the boys as usual for what he called 'Prayers', which the boys knew as 'Prose', they threw eggs and were again rowdy. Rowdiness was often worse on Sundays because Keate did not flog on that day. On the Tuesday, Keate's desk was found smashed to pieces. A young Colleger had been spotted nearby, and was questioned for an hour before he broke down and revealed the names of the culprits, four Oppidans and two Collegers, all of whom were then expelled. Another malcontent, Palk, in the Sixth Form, said 'Never', when Keate said that he hoped the expulsions would be a lesson to the boys to behave better. Overheard by Drury, he too was sacked.[8]*

On Tuesday, 3 November Edward Stanley wrote to his sister:

I have indeed been very lazy of late, but we had such disturbances, and so much to do, that I have not really been able to find time. Keate has thought fit to put a new absence at 5 o'clock, which naturally made a good deal of row, and was not particularly admired. A boy named Marriott was sent away for not going home when one of the Masters told him. The boy being very much liked, the next day when all the boys were assembled, one of them in a loud voice called out – 'Where's Marriott', followed by a volley of hisses and shouts; this drove the Doctor from his Elevation, but he was not allowed to descend in quiet, for, before he reached the Door about 4 or 5 eggs were thrown at him, tho' I believe very little touched him.

After he had gone out and left us in the School, the work of demolition began; the forms, which are nailed to the floor, were broken up by a sledge hammer, and the pieces thrown about. Presently, after the Doctor returned, accompanied with all his satellites, viz., six of the Masters of the Upper School, with their assistance he was enabled to proceed for that time without further molestation. He threatened to expel publicly the first boy who after this should do anything which could possibly be laid hold of by the Masters to send him away. However, at five the next day all not choosing to retire quietly to their habitations, assembled near the road, they pulled down part of the wall, and broke a good many of the School windows; one of the Master's looking thro' the blinds of his house to mark who he should see throw a stone. One of the company, observing his situation, threw a stone at the window, and hit the very pane of glass he was looking out of, broke the blind and very near hit him on the head.

Things, however, were patched up in a way till this night, when the Doctor said he would expel a boy who he knew to have been

---

* 'Palk's rebellion' became the familiar name for the whole affair. Some historians take his side and regard him as unjustly punished. He was soon commissioned in the army.

in the crowd, though he had not been seen throwing; and likewise several others. This was considered as a breach of a kind of Agreement which had been made by the boys being quiet, and Keate saying that he hoped there would be no more disturbance, and that all was over; however, having threatened to expel this boy, this morning they went into the School, and with a crow and large hammer knocked down the Doctor's Throne. The unfortunate man when he arrived was extremely astonished at the disappearance of his accustomed seat, and ran about like one of the guinea pigs at the Poultry Yard. – A poor wretched little Colleger was caught coming out of School about the time this was done, he, being carried away triumphantly, was bullied, badgered and baited by all 10 Masters till they got a kind of confession of who was concerned in pulling about the Doctor's Desk down about his ears.

After church to-day we all assembled in the School, and six boys were expelled publicly for being concerned in it. After they had marched, Keate was prosing, and said he hoped it would make the remainder more quiet, to which one of the Sixth Form said 'never' to himself, and was immediately likewise publicly expelled. The Doctor threatens to send away a good many more who were in the Assembly, tho' they did not throw stones or destroy anything else. I have only just time to write this before the post.[9]

Unrest continued until the end of the year. One placard which was displayed and left in people's houses read: 'Floret Etona. Down with Keate! Floreat Seditio Maryott Palk Jackson Pitt Elton Elton May White. *These* names will be soundly revenged by all Etonians. Down with the Tyrant! No five o'clock absence! No disrespect of the 6th Form. To Arms – Revenge!'[10] In December, Keate sent round a letter to parents justifying the Absence. Lady Stanley reported that her twin sons seem 'to have enjoyed the fun amazingly', as she also clearly had. 'I admire Dr Keate's firmness extremely, tho' I might perhaps have thought him rather too severe if I had had a son expelled.'

There was another, lesser rebellion in June 1832, when a popular boy called Munro refused to write a punishment, but went instead to watch a boat race. Keate was then going to flog him, but Munro refused to submit and was therefore expelled. When the boys knew at the next Absence that his name had vanished from the roll, they set up a boo and calls for Munro. Keate responded by ordering extra

Absences. Some 150 boys resolved neither to attend nor to be flogged. At night, however, small groups of boys were taken from their beds, and all were flogged, except for two who submitted the next day; twenty-one who claimed that they did not know about the Absence were excused. Keate had successfully divided the young opposition and enforced his rule. One boy, having submitted, felt cheerful enough afterwards to share supper with a friend at a neighbouring Dame's. The next day the boys cheered Keate in recognition of the fact that they had been fairly defeated.[11]

In 1829 there was a much happier occurrence. The Duke of Newcastle founded a scholarship for the ablest boys at the top of the School, with papers in Divinity as well as Classics. Religious education had been very limited, but here was a real incentive to self-education. A new seriousness was coming into public life, and Eton was going to be affected by it. The Duke wrote to Keate in 1828 about his plans:

> My whole and only object is national ability and if by this means young men who have been educated at Eton shall take with them a first knowledge of and affection for a Religion which shall regulate their future conduct, the scholarships will not have been established in vain and I perhaps may live to know and perceive the great benefits which may result from the influence on Society of a large body of Etonians who in addition to their classical attainments, will be otherwise qualified to uphold the Religion which now too many but nominally possess.[12]

The scholarships were initially worth £50 a year for three years, a very generous sum. Previously the only religious teaching had been via the very indifferent sermons and Keate's one hour 'Prose' each Sunday. Now Tutors would help boys to acquire some background knowledge of Divinity, particularly Coleridge, whose pupils were more successful than those of other Tutors. Coleridge thus brought much jealousy on himself, particularly when he brought back the first winner to help coach his pupils. At first Oppidans were more successful than Collegers, a reflection on the low state of College in those days. The second year a sweepstake was got up, and Miss Brown was pleased to draw two runners; but neither won. In the third year Creasy, a King's Scholar, was the first Colleger to win; Miss Brown reports that he almost killed himself with work.

Meanwhile Goodall had also had his problems. Hinde in 1813 led an appeal from King's to the Visitor, against Eton College. Fellows of King's were less well off and would willingly have moved to Eton. They were therefore opposed to the reduction in the number of Fellows from the original ten to seven. The particular issue, however, was that the Fellows of Eton held benefices as well as their Fellowships, which aroused envy among the Fellows of King's. In 1815 the Visitor confirmed Queen Elizabeth's dispensation which permitted the Fellows to hold a living, though he did (justifiably, we would say) decree that they must not hold more than one. The brevity of the Visitor's judgement contrasted with the vast expense incurred by the Colleges (who were joined by the *Amicabilis Concordia*). One of the Eton counsel argued that the Fellows needed to be rich if the boys were to have a proper esteem for the Church of England.

Hinde then encouraged the politician Henry Brougham to investigate Winchester and Eton as part of the work of his 1818 Select Committee on the Education of the Lower Orders. Neither College was doing much for popular education, but it could be argued (probably erroneously) that by their Statutes they should be. Unquestionably those who were Collegers were not being adequately provided for. Whereas the Fellows were receiving 110 times what the Founder provided for them, the Scholars were costing the College only twelve times what the Founder had stipulated. The gains from ownership of land had accrued to the Fellows, not to the boys. The main reason for this was that the College had not increased its rents (which paid the annual maintenance of the College, including the upkeep of the boys), but had taken large sums in premiums, which the Fellows had then shared among themselves. Really the only defence that could be offered, but which Goodall did not deploy well, was that it was clearly impossible to run a school on the basis of salaries and allowances laid down in the fifteenth century. Goodall relied instead on casuistry: the Head Master could not *demand* payment, but he could *receive* it, for example. As for the sharing of the fines (premiums), the Fellows would make up a deficit on the annual income and expenditure account; but that only acknowledged they had taken too much out over the years, instead of allowing the wealth of the College to accumulate. All that could be said for the Fellows was that other corporate bodies acted in the same way. The Select

Committee felt their enquiry 'unquestionably shows, that considerable unauthorised deviations have been made, in both Eton and Winchester, from the original plans of the founders; that those deviations have been dictated more by a regard to the interests of the Fellows than of the Scholars'. In 1819, a pamphlet analysing Provost Goodall's evidence was published anonymously, but presumably written by Hinde. Luckily for Goodall, however, only some humiliation was suffered: no reforms were enforced.

Goodall lived on amiably enough, taking some interest in the collection of shells that he built up. In 1832 William IV, who was almost as fond of Eton as his father, told Keate in Goodall's hearing: 'When he goes, I'll make you him.' Goodall, bowing gracefully, responded, 'Sir, I would never think of *going* before your Majesty.' Nor did he.

By 1834, Keate was exhausted by his stewardship, and determined to resign. His departure may have been encouraged by a fall in numbers from over 600 to about 450 at the end of his reign. This may have been occasioned by cholera scares in Windsor, or by the decline of the Lower School to just eighteen boys under the ineffectual Knapp. Keate was now 61 and he represented the old order. Dr Arnold had been Headmaster of Rugby since 1827, and was by now becoming widely known; he reflected the new aspirations of the educated classes. From 1830 criticism of Public Schools in general, and Eton in particular, had begun to grow. The curriculum was criticized as too narrow; bad behaviour in Chapel led one critic to argue that attendance should be voluntary; conditions in College were found wanting, and the subversion of funds by the Fellows was again attacked. In *Eton Abuses Considered*,[13] Keate himself was faulted for his cavalier manner towards the older boys, treating them as though they were liars rather than to be trusted. Flogging boys older than 13 was condemned. The leaving money given by boys to Keate on their departure was also criticized. Nevertheless, Keate's own departure occasioned a great display of affection. Generous presents came from many quarters,* and he was greeted

* Twenty-eight portraits of Keate's favourite pupils are gathered in Election Chamber at Eton, together with a later portrait of Mr Gladstone, who did not much like Keate. The silver that he was given on retirement was, years later, purchased by the College and is back at Eton. The value of the leaving presents must have amounted to nearly £100,000 in modern terms. Later attempts to raise a memorial to him in Chapel were unsuccessful, but Chapel was the Provost's concern, and Keate was not seen to advantage in there, where he is commemorated only by a modest brass.

warmly at any Etonian gathering. When Goodall died in 1840, Keate refused the offered provostship, since he felt he could not afford it. He lived on at Hartley Wespall in Hampshire as Rector, occasionally going to Windsor for residence as a Canon. He died at his rectory in 1852.

Keate had somehow managed to be an effective teacher of boys who had the aptitude to learn, and this was a very substantial part of his daily routine work. Etonians did go on to achieve considerable academic success at University; nevertheless it is for the control of the School that he is assessed. For many people he was the typical flogging schoolmaster:

> In general, from almost every point of view, it must be admitted that the nineteenth-century Busby was a failure. He did keep better order than most of his contemporaries. Occasionally he educated a few boys – or, to be more precise, got credit from aged alumni for educating them. On the whole, he educated neither morally nor intellectually; indeed the harm he did by lending his prestige to the conception of the cruel, suspicious master was of incalculable harm to future Public School education. If he kept order it was at the price of rebellion, fear and hate.

So wrote Edward C Mack in the 1930s; but he does excuse something to the villain: 'Allowing for Keate's personal deficiencies, which were many, we must still impute his failures to the deficient methods of discipline, instruction and moral training that he inherited.'[14]

This is a very different picture from 'the dear doctor' or 'the good doctor' to be discovered in Miss Brown's diary; nor does it really match the man encountered in boys' letters home and diaries (for we should not trust reminiscences too far.) Most boys recognized in Keate someone whom they could fight, but who was essentially their flesh and their spirit. In a famous judgement, Sir Francis Doyle, who went to Eton in 1823 and left at Christmas 1827, compared Keate with Dr Arnold:

> There was one qualification for a head-master which Keate possessed but Arnold did not – I mean the knowledge of God Almighty's intention that there should exist for a certain time, between childhood and manhood, the natural production known

as a boy. Now though Keate was not good at manufacturing youthful infallibilities of the normal Arnoldian type, he was perfectly aware that boys existed, and that they always must be boys, not manikins, like the little Master Laocoons. He was rough with them I admit, but neither unkind nor unjust beneath that roughness. He had no favourites, and flogged the son of a duke and the son of a grocer with perfect impartiality. He was also thoroughly manly and right-hearted in the depths of his nature.[15]

CHAPTER TWELVE

Life at Eton in the Age of Keate

THE BACKGROUND OF Etonians at the beginning of the nineteenth century was not so different from 1761, and more uniform than that of Etonians today: most were from the landed gentry. It is not easy to track down the sons of squires in the school lists; but in 1826, a year chosen at random and quite typical, there were eleven peers, eight baronets and forty sons of peers in a total of 562 boys. Clergy, army officers and a few professional men were among the parents, but these would mostly be younger sons of the gentry. Some successful entrepreneurs of the Industrial Evolution aspired to give their sons a similar background. Local tradesmen might send their sons, sometimes as day boys, usually as Collegers, though there was limited financial advantage to the Colleger. Geographically most Collegers came from the Home Counties, but Oppidans from all over the United Kingdom.

The boys arrived at more varying ages than would today be the case: 10 or 11 would be perfectly normal, though many started at 13 as now.* Preparatory Schools existed, to some extent catering for children locally and to some extent preparing boys for particular schools. Other boys had been taught at home with private tutors,

---

* The record for young entry is usually attributed to Repkombe (or sometimes Reebkomp), a natural son of the Earl of Pembroke, who arrived at Eton in 1767 before he was even 5. The poor little bastard did not stay long enough to escape from the Lower School, but joined the navy and became a Captain. His illegitimacy would not have occasioned much problem as there were enough other Etonians similarly placed.

who might accompany them as tutor at Eton; this was an expensive option, since a room would have to be hired for the tutor as well as for the boy in a Dame's house. More usually boys boarded with a Master, who would act as Tutor, or with a Dame or Domine (a male Dame), in which case the boy would also need a Master as Tutor. For example, Henry Everard arrived in 1831 at Hexter's: Hexter, known as 'Hag sty', taught writing, Arithmetic and Mathematics, the last to a very low level, and he did not rate as a Master; Everard accordingly had Chapman, a good man, as Tutor, to whom he was a private pupil: that is, he had Private Business, distinct from ordinary school business, in Chapman's house in a more informal atmosphere (though Private Business on Sunday was at 7 a.m.). Everard's parents were dead, and his elder brother Sam acted as guardian; his letters to Sam have a frankness and immediacy that few boys achieved in writing to their parents.[1]

Everard had a room to himself, about 15 feet by 9. The furniture comprised a bureau,* a bed which folded up in daytime, a wash stand, a deal table and two chairs; this is not so different from the standard of today. Some boys, particularly brothers, might share. Collegers, on the other hand, started in a dormitory, the original Long Chamber little changed from the time of the foundation.

A boy was excused fagging for his first fortnight, but then the fag-master became an important figure in his life. For Everard he was 'my Master' with a capital M; his requirements were slight and handled by several fags. He actually played his proper part by ensuring that his fags were not bullied by 'the Cock of my Dame's', whose strength enabled him to give smaller boys a good licking or to fag them illicitly. Yet bullying and fagging could be much more of a problem – they were, for example, to Milnes Gaskell, who arrived at Eton in May 1824, aged 13, a keen scholar from one of the better-known Eton Preparatory Schools.[2] He boarded for his first half with a Mrs Atkins, and his Tutor, who had no room for him at first, was Okes. Within a week he found himself bullied. His deter-mination not to swear, his piety and his zeal even to exceed the set work, did not help him. Mrs Gaskell must have dreaded the almost daily arrival of letters from her Milzy, describing his suffering from

* A very beautiful late eighteenth-century bureau, which served two gen-erations of Malmesburys, was given to Eton by the late Lord Malmesbury. Its condition suggests that Eton life may have sometimes been less rough than is generally assumed. A bureau came to be known at Eton as a burry.

both blows and taunts. Just occasionally there is reference to a kind friend, and more frequently he speaks of the commendations of his good work regularly made by Mr Okes. In July he moved to board with Okes, where the fagging was less troublesome, and bullying – though bad – less persistent. In general Tutors were thought to have more controlled houses than Dames. Even so, Milnes missed the Michaelmas Half, perhaps from sickness, for he was not strong and his doctor, Sir John Chapman, was frequently called for. Bullying still troubled him the next year, as did his health, and his parents removed him to stay at Brighton. He returned in the summer of 1826, and life was easier. He had, for instance, a garden down the Eton Wick Road to which he could retreat. Better still, he discovered a group of intellectual friends, and by 1827 the early misery was so far behind him that on leaving (not yet aged 17) he could speak of the happiness and enjoyment at Eton that he had found at least with them: he had grown up.

Another boy famously bullied was the poet Shelley. He arrived at Hexter's late in the Summer Half of 1804, aged 11, and was placed in an advanced division for his age. He thus was not expected to fag for long, but refused at first even to do what was required of him. Certainly his contemporary, the future Head Master Hawtrey, speaks of Shelley's having been conspicuously bullied. Yet after one year Shelley seems to have had a successful fight with Lyne, the son of a tailor in the Strand, and this established him.* The idea that his whole career was a misery, and that he was a rebel all his time, would seem to be an invention: it was felt that romantic poets should be unhappy at school. By the end he was himself a fagmaster, a kindly one; but he was certainly acting illegally when he harnessed some lower boys to bring down a brass cannon he had bought at auction in Windsor.[3]

The life of young Collegers was undoubtedly tougher. The Long Chamber was a rat-infested home to fifty-two boys. Their beds were made up of boards; desks were provided but not chairs. The windows were high up and often draughty from broken panes, though there were two great fires. The boys almost inevitably needed a room at a Dame's house, for which they would pay. Some

---

* Gronow, an unreliable witness, describes another inglorious fight in 1809 against Sir Thomas Style, which ended with Shelley running away. It seems, however, that Style had left Eton by 1809.

would even rent a room in the town, to get some peace. Similarly, though they were fed free in College Hall with mutton, bread and weak beer, this needed supplementing by personal food – some of which would be bought of an evening from a tradesman hawking his food and porter at a grated window. The Oppidans, by contrast, at least received a more varied dinner at the end of the morning and would be served more food at it if they so required – indeed, they would occasionally 'brosier' their Dame: that is, try to eat her cupboard bare. Fagging in College was more arduous, extending over the entire waking day, and could include making a bed, fetching water, cutting wood, serving food, keeping watch against the arrival of Keate (who would occasionally let it be known that he was not coming round to spare this task). Because the ratio of fagmasters to fags was so much higher than for Oppidans, the young Colleger was more put upon: any failure might mean a slapped face. Bullying was also worse. Boys were tossed in blankets, but some did not mind; indeed, some Oppidans would come along for the thrill. It could, however, be dangerous, and one boy coming down on the end of his bed was scalped; luckily the skin was reattached and the victim lived. A few years later Fortescue Wells could report without comment in letters home, 'I saw the stars last night', and for most the experience was just something taken for granted. All Collegers were identified by the letters KS, King's Scholar, in George III's reign, possibly as a complement to the King.[4]

Where a boy started in the School was determined by the Head Master, who examined new entrants personally. Lower boys would be placed in the First, Second or Third Forms; the Third Form was divided into Upper Greek and Lower Greek, according to ability in that language, and to Sense and Nonsense, which took their names from whether the Latin verses written were required to make sense or merely to scan. These divisions were all quite small and were taught in Lower School, but not each with a separate Master. Progress from them could be rapid, for example if an intelligent boy had been misplaced because he had been to an indifferent preparatory school. The Fourth Form was where most boys started, and it had three removes, subdivisions through which boys advanced during the course of a year. Similarly, Remove was divided in two parts, and progress was made after Trials at the end of December or in June. Gaskell started in Remove, Everard in Fourth Form. Boys in Remove were taught in particularly crowded circumstances beneath Upper School, sitting on benches in tiers, which doubtless made the kicking of luckless boys all the easier. Escape from Remove meant progress to Upper School and the end of fagging. Normally a year would be spent in the Lower Division of Fifth Form, and a year (post 1820) in the Middle Division, depending again on Trials for promotion. Those who stayed then moved into the Upper Division for a period determined by whether there were any vacancies in the Sixth Form, which might comprise about twelve Collegers and twelve Oppidans, though numbers were not fixed as they were to be later. Shelley, for example, spent some time in the Upper Division of Fifth Form before admission to the Sixth Form. Oppidans would leave, probably at 17 or earlier, but Collegers would have to wait longer if they wished to progress to King's. In 1826, for example, there were twenty-seven in Sixth Form, the senior twelve being Collegers, with three other Collegers among the Oppidans. There were eighty-nine boys in the Upper Division of the Fifth Form and eighty-eight in the Middle Division. Boys in the Middle Division could start to use fags. There were 121 boys in the Lower Division of Fifth Form, 114 boys in the Remove, and seventy-four in Fourth Form. The rather unbalanced distribution of boys throughout the School, was influenced by their leaving earlier than they now would. In some cases they were expelled for bad behaviour or lack of academic progress; but often they were withdrawn by parents, possibly because they were unhappy: quite a number did not stay three years. A surprising number died, more than one boy a year on average.

All the Upper School were taught in Upper School, and Keate himself taught over a hundred boys depending on numbers in Sixth Form and the Upper Division of the Fifth Form. Boys sat on benches rather than at desks, and could not therefore write work. Junior boys did the written work, mainly composition of Latin verses, in Pupil Room in Masters' houses, where they also prepared to construe, and wrote out 'derivations' (parsing the words and attempting to comprehend the grammar). Naturally, few boys could be 'called up' (tested in school); it was a sufficiently rare event for William Gladstone to record each instance in his diary. (Before 1820, and the formation of the Middle Division of Fifth Form, the situation was worse. Edward Coleridge was one of 198 boys taught by Keate, and was only called up to construe twice in the half.) Equally, learning Latin by heart, or 'saying lessons', which was also an important part of the curriculum, could not be universally tested. Lower boys had a more varied curriculum and went into school more. They and the Fourth Form had 7 o'clock school, which began somewhat later. Other boys began at 8.00, after which there was breakfast. Further schools on a whole school day were scheduled at 11.00, 3.00 and 5.00, interspersed with tutorial periods. The younger boys might have some twenty schools a week, but it is impossible to be precise because almost every week had a holiday. In the week of January 1827 in which Gladstone was confirmed, every day but Wednesday was a holiday, and this allowed him to complete reading Clarendon's *History of the Great Rebellion*.[5] The Fifth and Sixth Forms had fewer schools, divided between Latin and Greek, and worked more on their own. It was a very leisured life. To be fair, though, quite a number of boys took extra lessons, for which they paid extra. Most commonly they studied French, which was seen as useful. It was taught in the eighteenth century by Frenchmen, the best known being Porny (originally Pyron du Martre), who founded a free school for local children in Eton, and later by the Tarver family. The Evans father and son taught Drawing, but there was no proper provision for Music. There were voluntary Science lectures by a visiting speaker. For the Sixth Form there were lectures on Greek plays from Keate, which earned him his reputation as a good teacher. Also, those who paid extra for Private Business had more informal tuition in small groups with their Tutors. This helped create a closer relationship between boys and Tutors.

Chapel played a modest part in boys' lives. On Sunday at matins a Fellow would preach, probably inaudible to most; but Gladstone heard enough to record the sermons in his diary. Their standard was low. At evensong there would be a choir borrowed from Windsor. On half-holidays and holidays the Chapel services really served to ensure that the boys were in Eton, rather than for religious worship. On a holiday there would be services morning and afternoon, perhaps with Communion if the holiday was a Saint's Day – it normally was. On half-holidays the service was in the afternoon, before boys went to games. Behaviour was tolerable on a Sunday, but lamentable on weekdays. Stories abound of inattention and worse: for example, of rats and other animals released. It was the convention that Collegers newly in Sixth Form distributed 'church sock' – almonds, raisins and so on – to their fellows to consume during the service. Peers and sons of peers, who sat in stalls so far as their numbers allowed, also enjoyed church sock when a newcomer took his seat. (Peers did pay extra, and the separate, more comfortable seats were all that they received in recompense.) Additionally there was Sunday Prayers, 'Prose', with the Head Master; but that was more an assembly for announcements and the reading of an improving book than a religious occasion. Boys were confirmed with little preparation, the timing depending on the random arrival of the Visitor. The ceremony was usually unimpressive. With Confirmation often later than is now the case, and with the Church not enthusiastic about the Sacraments, Holy Communion played a small part in boys' lives.

The amount of leisure that boys enjoyed was indeed astonishing, and considerable freedom existed, which (unsurprisingly) was often abused. Absence in theory ensured boys' presence at various times, but it was possible to shirk and with luck escape detection. Games played a larger part than previously, but they were essentially voluntary activities. Cricket was mildly encouraged; Keate had enjoyed playing himself, and would sometimes hold Absence in the playing fields to facilitate the game.* Miss Brown's diary and Gaskell's letters report on it. Collegers played a particularly large part for two reasons: they had the use of College Field, and they stayed longer. The Captain of the Cricket XI was always a Colleger until 1837, and he organized Upper Club, for which the subscription was 5 shillings and sometimes more. Lower Club existed for younger Oppidans and Lower College for younger Collegers. An unpleasant aspect in early days was cricket fagging, a time-consuming chore, involving marking and returning balls from the boundary.

In 1805 there was played at Lord's the first cricket match against Harrow of which scores survive. It was more of a social occasion for the teams. Lord Byron played for Harrow, and had to record: 'We were most confoundedly beat.'[6]† There had in fact been one-sided school matches against Westminster between 1796 and 1801. More usually, visiting teams of adults would play the XI at Eton. Boys were spectators: 'I think an Eton boy would be almost criminal if he

---

* Keate scored 0 and 4, but took two wickets in the 1791 match against the Maidenhead Club, which Eton won by 4 wickets. This match was reported in the *Morning Chronicle*.

† College Library possesses a letter written by Byron in 1812 to an Eton boy: 'I never even in my boyish days disputed your [Etonian] superiority which I once experienced in a cricket match.' Mere flattery?

were not to attend to see their glory in beating other clubs,' wrote Bransby Purnell, showing that enthusiasm for school sporting heroes was already evident in 1807.[7] Parents might also applaud such athletic pursuits. Richard Gosling's father wrote to him: 'Your mother thinks cricket a very dangerous game, but it certainly is a fine manly amusement and I should be sorry if you did not like it, for in my opinion it strengthens a youth, conduces to his health and gives him courage to meet the difficulties of life.' By the end of Keate's time, regular matches with Winchester and Harrow at the beginning of the summer holidays had become established, in which Eton was slightly the more successful.

The river provided an alternative outlet for active boys in the summer. Swimming had always been popular and continued at a variety of bathing places. It would appear that the School did provide some guards and instruction, but nevertheless seven fatalities occurred in the first quarter of the century. One should remember that most boys would not have had the chance to learn to swim before they arrived at Eton. The most famous instructor was Shampo Carter, and watermen thereafter tended to be called Shampo by the boys as a sort of generic name.* Boys were not afraid to bathe even in cold weather, and the swimming season began at Easter. By 1828 a society had been formed, started by Old Etonians at Cambridge but including boys still at the School, called the Philolutic Society; it was possible to be a Philolute, a lover of bathing, or to go further and become a Psychrolute, a lover of cold water.

The occurrence of accidents may have been the reason why successive Head Masters opposed boating. It is also possible that boating, initially in the hands of working watermen, was not thought to be a suitable activity for gentlemen. Towards the end of the eighteenth century, however, boys began to take to the river of their own inclination, hiring boats from local owners. Boys were in theory out of bounds when they went boating, but if they observed the courtesy of shirking any Master whom they passed, there was in practice no opposition. In the 1790s, processions of boats began, after the fashion of a Venetian carnival, with flags

---

* Dr Warre, Head Master at the end of the nineteenth century, thought that the original Shampo was a Frenchman, Champeau, also known to the boys as 'slip-gibbet'; others say that the origin is in the word 'shampoo' which arrived from India in the nineteenth century.

flying; in 1793 six boats with splendid flags were pulled by boys in some semblance of fancy dress on 4 June, the King's birthday. In the course of time, that date and Election Saturday at the end of the Summer Half became the accepted occasions among the boys for processions, and naval dress was adopted, the coxes as officers, the oarsmen as seamen. The destination was a pub, the Surly Hall Inn, just above Boveney on the Windsor bank. (There was no lock or weir at Boveney until 1838.) Vast quantities of alcohol would be consumed, sometimes given by a member of the royal family who would take a seat to be rowed up. Amazingly, nobody died on these occasions.

Some other rowing took place. In 1798, for example, boys deliberately missed Absence to row to Maidenhead; Dr Heath, who had tried to dissuade them, flogged them all soundly (as indeed they doubtless expected) on their return. Racing developed more slowly, using boats of various sizes, and not especially slim; 6-oared boats were as common as 8-oared at first, and the 10-oared boat which led the processions, and acquired the name 'The Monarch', was the most prestigious. (The royal barges also had ten oars.) Up to 1828, the long boats were often stroked by a professional waterman. In those days racing was more of a physical combat, with no holds barred, and opponents could be forced into the bank or legitimately rammed. The races might be the outcome of a challenge, perhaps for money, or a race in skiffs would be a sweepstake.

In 1829 and 1830 a complete record of the School's rowing was kept, in *Greek*, by T.K. Selwyn: the three volumes which survive were translated by Dr Warre in 1903 and, with his notes, run to 350 pages![8]* The problems confronting a Captain of Boats were clearly considerable; for instance, the *Hibernia*, captained by Waterford (an Irish peer), seceded because the members wished to be exclusively Irish. Keate was particularly keen to prevent rowing before Easter, as the weather was dire and the river dangerous. He spoke to the Captain, who, with his Second Captain, did manage to stop all but Waterford and his friends; but boating soon restarted, to Keate's fury, provoking a rage so great, even by his standards, that it occasioned a practical joke against him: the boys hired seven cads (in those days the name given to workmen with boats) to row masked,

---

* Thomas Kynaston Selwyn was the younger brother of George Augustus Selwyn, of whom more in Chapter 13; he won the Newcastle Scholarship in 1830, but sadly died a scholar of Trinity College at Cambridge in 1834.

and thus successfully duped Keate and other Masters, who were then booed by a whole crowd of laughing boys. In the Summer Half of 1829, one can also read of two duck-and-green pea nights, convivial occasions which became a tradition. At the end of the half, Eton raced Westminster – 'for 100 sovereigns a side', according to a contemporary paper, but that may well be untrue. Keate apparently did not know of the race until Edward Coleridge's St Bernard was brought to Absence wearing the light blue rosette the boys had worn; when this was explained, 'he smiled, and, as usual, said – "Foolish boys"'. In 1830, the season was more trouble-free, and there was a full programme of racing, by now mostly in eights or smaller boats, often with betting on the side.

Henry Everard much enjoyed his boating, though he did not learn to swim until his second year. He had his adventures. For instance, after a splashing combat, he arrived late for Absence with a boating jacket on; quickly he borrowed another boy's coat – 'I was much afraid [Keate] would swish me then if he had he would have found me with a check shirt on, that would not do at all. Fortune favoured me, and I got off with writing out the Psalms [presumably those set for that day] and bringing them to him at five o'clock.' In October 1832,

> I got a *Black Eye* . . . from an impudent snob throwing a stone at me whilst sculling. I an my companion immediately got on shore, and gave chase to this impudent clod, at length we caught him, my Billy Rufus (passion) being on tip-toes, I pegged right and left into this Gemmen's face, I make little doubt, both his eyes were every bit as bad as mine.[9]

Boating was the cause of much trouble with the local community, but fighting was not restricted to the river.

Rowing was an expensive hobby, and Collegers played little part in it. Indeed, many boys may have shirked all summer exercise, for the number that could play cricket was limited by the shortage of playing fields to fewer than 100; some oarsmen also played cricket, or a variety of it, known as 'aquatics'.

Football was not so well organized, but the Wall Game was codified at about this time, and the annual matches between Collegers and Oppidans date from this period. Quite when the game began is uncertain, but it was probably in the mid-eighteenth century. It is said to have been a more lively game in those days than it has since become, despite being confined to an area between the wall (which was built in 1717) and a furrow only about six yards away. The Field Game was developing in the fields west of Eton, but the games were apparently informal and are not described; Bransby Purnell says that he played football most days in the autumns of 1806 and 1807.* Keate acted to preserve the common land for this use by boys. Hockey was more regarded, and in 1832 it was said to depend for its existence on being played at Eton and the RMC Sandhurst which, with its better-drained soil, was the more suitable place for the game. Fives was played only between the buttresses of College Chapel, which inevitably limited the growth of the game, though lower boys would play in the corners of School Yard. Additionally, boys certainly walked, ran, and jumped in the countryside

Many, of course, found what Gray had called a 'fearful joy' in poaching and other illegal activities. Henry Everard was still a new boy, when Sir John Anstruther, a 13-year-old, was shot dead while taking turns with a hired gun. Everard was impressed by what Keate said on the occasion. Fighting with the townsmen was, of course, a major excitement, and was most common at the time of the Windsor Fair: 'the time for larks, cracker flying, china stalls overturning, Keate flogging, Masters jawing and billing'. After that came Guy Fawkes Day, but the School authorities were fairly successful in suppressing its celebration after 1804, when Lord Cranborne killed Grieve minor, a son of the Tsar of Russia's doctor: a practical joke miscarried and fireworks exploded in Grieve's pocket inflicting horrible injuries. It was an act of folly rather than malice, and no prosecution followed.

Boys' fights continued, most famously the battle between Charles Wood and Anthony Ashley at the end of February 1825.[10] This began when Ashley trod on Wood's heel as they pressed to get into

---

* Purnell was grandson of an iron founder, but he quickly proved a typical Etonian of his time. In Michaelmas 1807 he was in trouble for staying out, pretending to be ill, and visiting a billiards salon in Datchet; he was flogged (which he accepted) and moved down six places in the School order (which he did not). Later, he was caught out shooting, early in the morning. His father was summoned; he promised to reform and 'sap up for Trials'. His Tutor, Drury, however, thought (wrongly, it would seem) that he did not want to stay and therefore lacked self-discipline. (Who was Drury to find that fault?) Purnell was removed to a small private school, but was sacked from there too. Happily, he ended as a respectable JP.

Upper School for Prose on a Sunday. Wood hit Ashley, who hit back, and they agreed to fight the next day. Ashley's two older brothers, and Taunton, a close friend who acted as his second, supported him. Before the fight, the eldest Ashley gave Taunton sixpence to buy brandy, which he did, obtaining a small phial of brandy and a lemon. Leith acted as second to Wood, who was a 14-year-old in the same part of the School as Ashley, but a bigger boy, and the best part of a year older. The fight lasted over 40 rounds, for about 2½ hours. In the last stages both combatants were so exhausted that they could hardly exchange blows, merely pushing against each other, and the end came when Ashley fell face down, Wood on top of him. Ashley was carried off back to Knapp's, his Tutor's. Later, the brothers and two friends were playing at cards, when they suddenly realized that Anthony had ceased breathing. He could not be revived. Wood, who had also fought bravely, was in little better state, but survived. Wood and Leith were brought to trial, Wood apparently still showing bruises a fortnight after the fight, but no evidence was offered against them. As it happened, the fathers, Colonel Wood, an MP, and the Earl of Shaftesbury, were political foes, which may have accounted for the protracted nature of the fight. Shaftesbury was praised for not pursuing the matter, but his other sons could not be free of blame. Rumour had it that much brandy had been consumed – this was not the case, according to Taunton, who should have known. Certainly the eldest son should have stopped the fight. Keate made exactly this point in speaking to the boys, with an effect that impressed them all: 'It is not that I object to fighting in itself; on the contrary I like to see a boy who received a blow return it at once. But that you, the heads of the School, should allow a contest to go on for two hours and a half has shocked and grieved me.' He went on to speak with genuine eloquence of his sympathy for the bereaved parents. One and all trooped out of Upper School, says Doyle, with a thorough belief and confidence in Keate.[11]

Enough, at least for the moment, of what has given Eton a bad name. Boys could, and did, use their time to advantage. Acting, for example, was popular. It was a regular entertainment in Long Chamber, but groups of Oppidans and Collegers together would hire a room suitable for acting. In 1817 one group took a warehouse in Datchet Lane. They certainly committed themselves to their plays as wholeheartedly as their successors today.

Shakespeare they felt to be above them, but tragedies were put on, as well as comedies, and Sheridan was perhaps the favourite dramatist. With their minds trained by saying lessons, the word-perfect learning of parts was no trouble. Finally, when audiences were attracted from outside the School, and a band and choristers from St George's were hired to provide music, the theatrical enterprise was stopped; Goodall, rather than Keate, is usually blamed; but one suspects that Keate must have concurred. Drama did not die, but it did not again reach the levels of the first decade of Keate's rule.[12]

Another initiative that did have Keate's blessing was the founding in 1811 of the Eton Society by Charles Fox Townshend.* This attracted a group of serious-minded boys, who educated themselves. It was a little more than a debating society (and there seem to have been other debating societies at the time and earlier);[13] the members met for breakfast once a week in rooms, at first in Mrs Hatton's sock shop – 'popina' in Latin, equivalent perhaps to lollypop shop in English. The club, initially known as the Literati, soon became known instead as Pop, under which name it has survived with some ups and downs and transformations of character, to this day. The debates, profoundly serious, were historical or literary; Keate did not permit discussion of religion or of matters of the last fifty years, but issues from the past could still divide boys on present political lines. The minutes survive, and speeches, other than a few that were made extempore, could be very long. One looks in vain for awareness of contemporary social issues, but members were universally patriotic and lovers of liberty. The Roman Republic was admired above the Empire.

William Gladstone was a member from the autumn of 1825 until he left in December 1827. He wrote then: 'It has been our good fortune to behold the golden days of this Society.' He spoke often and at length, usually (but not always) on the Tory side. He had a passion for fining any member responsible for a minor breach of the rules; even his great friend Hallam, the subject of Tennyson's *In Memoriam*, had to submit, although he was the President of the day (the office rotated).[14] Some philistines mocked, but to boys like Milnes Gaskell the Society brought profound happiness. Indeed, he

---

* Townshend died aged 22 at Cambridge of consumption, when he was already parliamentary candidate for the University.

it was who stimulated political interest in others. The fact that Collegers could join with Oppidans was in itself an advantage.*

A few years earlier Winthrop Mackworth Praed had been a member. He was grateful for the reading that preparation for debates had encouraged him to undertake. On 1 February 1821 he wrote to his sister of his plan to establish a subscription library, primarily for the use of Pop, but eventually for the top hundred boys in the School. This institution lasted and was the foundation on which the present School Library developed for the use of the boys. Harrow and Charterhouse, at least, were ahead of Eton and gave Praed his idea.[15] George IV, who was not fond of Eton, presented the Delphin edition of the Classics; boys were more grateful for the holiday that celebrated this event.

In 1804–5 a group of boys led by Stratford Canning, cousin of George Canning, attempted to repeat the success of the *Microcosm* with *The Miniature*. It ran to thirty-four numbers and was republished as a volume dedicated to Dr Goodall, but was not financially successful; the editors were rescued by a bookseller, John Murray, who bought up the unsold stock.† The next major periodical was the *Etonian*, which coexisted in 1820 with another publication called *The Salt-bearer*. It was the inspiration of W.M. Praed, who wrote prose and verse with astonishing facility; when he went to Cambridge, and the *Etonian* ceased, his reputation was higher than any other Etonian since George Canning.‡ In 1827 Gladstone and his circle produced the *Eton Miscellany*, which was of a lower

---

* In old age Gladstone revisited the Pop Room with the President of the time. 'Do you have any athletes in Pop now?', he asked. 'We used to have a few, to show we were not down on athletics, if they were not too dull.' By then Pop, however, contained few who were not athletes.

† This generous act brought Murray useful contacts and led to the starting of the *Quarterly Review*, and the success of his publishing firm.

‡ Praed's letters reveal him as a happy Etonian almost throughout his time. His blackest moment occurred in 1814 when, as a 12-year-old, he was forcibly stripped and made to bathe, though he was terrified of the water. He enjoyed chess, he wrote verses successfully in Latin or English, and his academic progress was so rapid that he apparently became a fagmaster at the age of 14. After Trinity College, Cambridge, he returned to Eton as a private tutor in September 1815, for 15 months of enjoyable existence. Later he became an MP. His nostalgic poem 'School and Schoolfellows' ends with the words: 'That I could be a boy again – a happy boy – at Drury's'; but he had in fact boarded with Miss Langford, and his Tutor was Plumptre: Drury was more convenient for scansion and rhyme.

quality, and in 1832 and 1833 there were further magazines, less literary but more informative about life at Eton.

Boys also wrote individual works, often poetry. In Goodall's last year as Head Master, Charles Sumner, an 18-year-old Colleger, later Bishop of Winchester, published a novel, *The White Nun*. He was surpassed by Shelley, who published *Zastrozzi*, a gothic horror novel, before his 18th birthday. In the time after he had ceased to be bullied, he had pursued an individual career. Botch Bethell had become his Tutor, but he had found much more instruction independently from a Dr Lind in Windsor, who taught him Chemistry and charmed him with unorthodox views on life. Still, though explosions were a particular interest to Shelley (as to other contemporaries), he played no part in the insurrections of Dr Keate's first year. Instead, as a respectable Sixth Form boy, he departed with a successful Speech from Cicero's denunciation of Catiline, and a leaving dinner for his friends on which he spent the £40 he had earned from *Zastrozzi*.

The Procession of Boats on Election Saturday made that the greatest day of the year. The Oppidans below Sixth Form knew that they were going on holiday, but the Collegers had to wait until after the Elections to King's on the Monday, and the selection of new Collegers. On that day Speeches were given, the intellectual climax of the year. Of course, going to and from Eton must often have been a major experience in itself with prolonged, uncomfortable boat and carriage trips. Just occasionally, boys with their friends might hire a boat to take them to London – a day's journey, but with luck a rather special day.

The Fourth of June was growing in significance by the end of George III's life, though he was no longer able to come to Eton, and his past benevolence was what endeared him. After his death the birthday celebrations, coming at a convenient moment in the calendar, were continued. That Eton still wears mourning for George III is certainly a myth (even more demonstrably than that other unlikely story, that Wellington said the Battle of Waterloo was won on the playing fields of Eton). The boys put on mourning at his death, as they did after deaths in their own families, but, mourning over, they reverted to their more colourful dress; they put on mourning again for George IV, who was little loved.

Every third summer there occurred an even grander celebration, with no real excuse but tradition behind it, Montem. Boys assembled in picturesque fancy dress which had some military connection.

(Gladstone in 1826 showed his sympathy for the Greeks, by appearing in something like the dress of the evzones.) They then, as ever, paraded to Salt Hill in Slough, raising money for the Captain of Montem to spend at Cambridge – except for what he had laid out on organizing and entertaining his troops lavishly. Parents who lived near enough attended, and doubtless gave most, but up to £50,000 in modern terms was raised, and sometimes, one suspects, from those less well off than the beneficiary. After Montem, boys could wear their red coats for the rest of the half. On top of these regular great days, there were visits from royalty which would often occasion requests for holidays. By the end of Keate's time, William IV was proving as generous as his father had been. Foreign celebrities would also come to Eton and ingratiate themselves by similar requests.

With so very many holidays occurring, Sending up for Play became less common, but Sending up for Good remained a notable honour for boys. A selected exercise was read to the other boys, and £1 was given to the scholar. Three Sent up exercises secured a book prize, as they still do. Boys were also rewarded for promotion in Trials with cash prizes; but these seem to have been indirectly funded by the parents, whereas the book prizes would have been paid for by the Head Master.

The standard penalty for inadequate work was to write out the construe which had not been adequately learnt. But a boy might find himself in the Head Master's Bill, and therefore liable to be flogged. A new boy could plead to be excused for a first offence, sometimes more than once; but flogging was a standard punishment for bad work, just as it was for bad behaviour. It should, however, be remembered that boys did survive Eton without being flogged, and that Masters were not allowed to use corporal punishment. At Harrow, in contrast, housemasters would beat boys, and (from about 1800) monitors would cane them; caning was unknown at Eton, except possibly in College. Even the jolly Henry Everard does not report being flogged, though he would surely have told his brother if he had been. Milnes Gaskell more than once wrote to his mother that no merit would save him, and yet he does not seem to have been flogged either. Gladstone in old age told A.C. Benson that he had been flogged but once, when he was praepostor for his division and deliberately failed to mark out three boys who were absent, and who had persuaded him to cover for them. Yet in 1823, when Gladstone was still a young boy, W. Farr, a friend of Gladstone's, recorded in his diary 'Gladstone flogged for leaving out the voices' – presumably his derivation of words (parsing) was at fault.[16] On the other hand, many boys were flogged frequently, and sometimes more than once in a day. (One such boy was Charles Keate, the Doctor's nephew.) This suggests that they did not much mind, and that the punishment was ineffectual. The first time might be frightening, but thereafter the alarm and shame felt would fall. Some psychiatrists would argue that certain boys became habituated to flogging, and that they developed an addiction to flagellation. This behaviour pattern was known at the time, but was not a matter of such fascination as it would be today.*

The discipline maintained by the Head Master with his Assistants was not really supplemented by any effective discipline among the boys. Sixth Form had vestigial duties, and in College they would occasionally punish misdemeanours by setting epigrams. Curiously, and ludicrously, Sixth Form could expect the same courtesy as Masters: that they should be shirked by boys out of bounds – they could, indeed, give a younger boy his 'liberties', or the freedom *not* to shirk. There was no routine of corporal or other punishment among Oppidans, but in practice big boys might thump smaller ones. Some boys undoubtedly exercised influence, and not just by size; these might include Captains of their houses, or such heroes as the elected Captain of Boats. The absence of a prefectorial system differentiated Eton from other great schools at the time. Despite the system of fagging, Etonians saw themselves much more as living in a republic than an oligarchy, and thought themselves lucky, for example compared with Harrovians. It was the extraordinary freedom amounting in the worst cases to licence, that was the distinctive characteristic of Eton.

The better-off among them undoubtedly maintained a high standard of living. Drink was readily available, and there were a number of shops providing food. Thomas de Quincey, son of a Manchester draper, was urged to become an Etonian by George III (no less) when he was staying with an Etonian friend Lord Westport and walking at Frogmore; but de Quincey thought its moral tone poor

---

* Certainly the birch had an unhealthy grip on the mind of some Old Etonians. It was, however, perhaps just a jape when Lord Waterford in 1838 returned to Eton with some friends and stole the block on which, after his many adventures, he had often knelt. It was carried away to Ireland. Lord Melbourne is reputed to have been too fond of the birch.

and went instead to Manchester Grammar School. Early in 1803, however, he had run away to London and thought to get a loan from his old friend at Eton. After a night sleeping rough on the road from Slough to Eton, he found no Westport but another 17-year-old Etonian, Lord Desart, whom he had met before. A magnificent breakfast was provided for him, which his unaccustomed stomach could not accept. He asked for some wine instead, which was also brought. Some advice and help was given. De Quincey seems typical of some teenagers 200 years on; Desart, on the other hand, is eighteenth-century in his generosity and urbanity – and yet also modern, in that the attitude to his age-group overcame any class barrier.[17] Within the School there was a brotherhood of Etonians, which enabled the poorer boys to live alongside the rich without too much discontent. Another magnificent breakfast figures in Disraeli's novel *Coningsby*. Disraeli took trouble to learn about life at Eton, and did not think it out of place to have his hero and friends debating the Reform Bill over a roast goose.[18] There is something piquant about contemplating 16-year old Etonians debating great issues like middle-aged London club members, and yet perhaps kneeling later in the day on the flogging block.

Sexual peccadilloes figure less than in later periods. Two old Collegers, Tucker and Wilkinson, later clergymen, speak of dreadful indecency in Long Chamber, but they may have meant little more than that conversation was very smutty. Edward Coleridge recalled: 'Evil songs were sung, and there were many things done, which one cannot but remember with horror and regret. And yet there was a kind of safety in the indecent publicity of our lives.'[19] In 1826, Miss Brown records trouble at Dupuis's: 'something *very unpleasant*'. One boy, Mr Devereux, was in Sixth Form (there were two Devereux brothers, and which one is unclear, but 'he was always a bad boy, I know'); the other, Lord Lindsay, was in the middle of the School.[20] There is one other hint of something similar in her diary; it all amounts to very little. Most boys were more concerned with the girls they met in the shops or saw around Windsor, but boys developed physically a little later and left the School earlier than is now the case.* Gladstone in old age recalled that Milnes

---

* Shelley was said by Gronow to have remembered the excellent brown bread and butter at Spiers's, a well known sock shop opposite the entrance to Weston's Yard, but also to have thought the beautiful Martha 'the Hebe of Spiers's', and the loveliest girl he ever saw.

Gaskell and Hallam, with whom Gladstone messed, though they were in different houses, were both enamoured of the same girl. Gaskell, ever timid, abandoned her to the dazzling Hallam rather than risk losing Hallam's friendship.[21] The word 'enamoured' describes a relationship which would certainly not have been physical; and it was characteristic that the school friend mattered more than the girlfriend. To sum up, in the unsurprising absence of evidence, one can tentatively conclude that sex caused fewer problems than to the young of today.

When the moment to leave came for those who had stayed to the end, there was a ritual of gifts and farewells. Best friends, or 'cons', would expect to be given a book.* The Tutor and Head Master, like the domestic servants curiously, would receive money. There was a ritual, indeed, of taking leave, a ceremonial signing off. Right to the end a boy knew he was subject to school discipline: In 1823 Hawtrey complained of three boys in his house because they were out on their last night; Keate flogged them and then took leave; Miss Brown (and probably therefore Keate) felt sorry.

The background of the boys' life was a very pleasant adult society, reminiscent of Jane Austen's novels. There were cricket matches between the private tutors and the boys; there were elegant parties, perhaps with a little music, and dances, though Keate did not approve of dancing during term-time. Romances often ripened, contributing to the inbred quality of Eton. For the private tutors with a little more leisure, but less consequent income, than the Masters, it was an enchanting world. The best-known of them, Henry Wagner, was employed by the Duke of Wellington, a supportive father. His charges were generally satisfactory, but the younger did once lie to Wagner, bringing down a formidable rebuke on the boy. Wagner was able to marry, and after he saw the boys to Oxford he became, by the Duke's influence, Vicar of Brighton, having enjoyed a happy, not too taxing, prelude to his working life.[22]

It would be wrong to assume that the constructive behaviour of the best boys was anything like universal, and for a salutary reminder of this, we need only look at the career of a boy called Tom Hoseason.[23] Miss Brown's father, Sir Charles, had taken a stake in

---

* Shelley gave two brothers Smith (later bankers) fine volumes possibly abstracted from his father's library. One is the Baskerville edition of Gray's poems.

some marshland south of Kings Lynn. (The drainage project failed, and was the prime cause of Dr Keate's having to support his sister-in-law as well as his immediate family.) The Hoseasons were neighbours; and Tom found his way into the hearts of both Fanny Keate and Miss Brown, who saw in him a resemblance to their own unsatisfactory brother, who had boarded with Goodall and died on military service in the West Indies. Tom arrived in January 1821, aged nearly 13, and boarded with Mrs Atkins, with Okes as Tutor; he was placed in Fourth Form. It was a melancholy half to arrive since no fewer than four boys died, two of sickness, one drowning when out in a skiff, and one burnt when his nightshirt caught fire.

Tom immediately caused problems. Miss Brown had agreed to keep an eye on his money, but he soon spent it. By March, he had used up his first fault, and was flogged soon after for not being able to say his piece of the Greek Testament. On 13 March he was involved in a fight, which left his hand still damaged on the 25th. It was quite a casual affair, which Tom made light of, but his eyes were closed up and he 'was so disfigured that I should not have known him had I met him'. His work was adequate, and he seems to have been helped by Keate himself. He continued to be welcome at the Keate table through his unsatisfactory career. In June, he was flogged twice on the same day: a lesson not done and noisy in Chapel. By July, he owed money at three sock shops, and was difficult with his Dame; Miss Brown lectured him, but with little lasting effect. In the next half, he was said to be better, but he was by no means perfect. The sock shops promised not to offer him tick, but money was still a problem.

In February 1822, when there was much trouble in Mrs Atkins's, Tom appears for once on the side of the angels. But shortly afterwards he stuck a pin into Trower, a friend of his, in Chapel; when Trower retaliated, Tom repeated the assault with a knife. He moved to board with Okes, but hopes that closer male control would help were disappointed. He was bad with the servants. Then in July, he apparently flung a stone at a 4-year-old, who needed to see a doctor – for whose services Tom offered to pay £1. Two days later, Miss Brown thought she detected Tom with an older boy going to a bathing tryst with two girls. Soon afterwards he was again spending too much on clothes. In November, Tom was lectured by Keate and barred from dinner for bullying a boy. (To be fair, it does not seem that this was his main line of wickedness.)

A year later, when Tom had reached the Fifth Form, he disclosed to Miss Brown that he had the use of a rope ladder for nocturnal escapades. (She did reveal where it was stowed.) Trouble continued through 1824. He was not playing football or hockey, being more attracted by riding at the barracks in Windsor, and by fencing; he decided he wanted to join the army, but that was not what his father wanted. About this time Mr Hoseason sent some pheasants for Mr Okes, but Tom failed to pass them on. Then he was up late in Drury Lane, and Miss Brown saw that he had taken to driving a tandem (the nineteenth-century equivalent of driving a sports car). His work still passed muster, but only because it was largely done for him. By now Milnes Gaskell was with Okes, and he may have been conscripted to help. Certainly Tom provided refuge for Gaskell from his bullies, and they played chess together.

In February 1825, a man masquerading as a soldier was haunting Eton, leading Tom and other boys astray with drink, and with playing billiards (which was thought very wrong, perhaps because of the gambling involved). During the half Tom spent £15 on tandem-driving, an extravagance that infuriated his father, who (perhaps foolishly) gave him no spending money. Dr Keate warned Tom that he might have to leave. On the Fourth of June, Tom became tipsy, and hit a man over the head: Miss Brown provided a sovereign for him to settle the matter. (He already owed £5 to three boys at this time.) He was promoted to the Upper Division of Fifth Form, though Milnes Gaskell reckoned he did no work.

Now Fanny Keate lost £5 and shortly after £4 was missing from Miss Brown's desk. The culprit was almost certainly Tom, who doubtless eased his conscience by saying to himself that he could make it good. In the Michaelmas Half of 1825, Miss Brown abruptly but temporarily gave up keeping her diary, and it is tempting to think that Tom's behaviour shocked her. Okes was certainly speaking to his house about the disappearance of money in September, and in November Tom was sacked. For some reason the Hoseasons felt that Okes had behaved badly; perhaps he had drawn Tom into a confession, supposedly in confidence, and then he had decided Tom must go. It is all a sorry tale. Chandos in *All Boys Together* reckons that Tom was a psychopath, but for Miss Brown, almost to the end, he was a dear, giddy boy. Given the ready resort to violence of the time, one does not necessarily have to count him psychopathic. He was a physically strong, morally weak boy who was led into extravagance which the liberty of Eton made so alluring to the hedonist. Two other boys were expelled during that half, one also for stealing and one for the more typical offence of being drunk and unruly in Chapel.*

It is supposed that schoolmasters often say that a boy will come to a bad end, and Tom did indeed do so. The British army was barred to him by his financial disgrace, but apparently he was commissioned in the Indian army. He remained in debt, even trying to borrow £100 from Dr Keate in 1841. In 1855, when he wrote affectingly to Miss Brown after a long silence shortly before her death, he was still destitute.

Hoseason's adult life, however, was not typical. Oddly enough, in view of the bad behaviour in Chapel and the low level of religious instruction provided, the commonest career for Etonians was to take orders in the Church of England. Of the boys at Eton in 1826, a number died young, including Hallam, the most admired by his contemporaries. Others disappeared from the records, sometimes overseas. Roughly one in five was ordained, of whom three became Bishops. Some would have combined the life of clergyman with that of schoolmaster or academic, others that of rector and squire. A few became active in the religious controversies of the day. Charles Simeon, the formidable evangelical, was a friend and contemporary of Dr Goodall; he claimed that he lived a profligate life at Eton, and that he would never send a son there. Edward Pusey, a leader of the Oxford Movement, left in 1817, having reached Sixth Form.

Forty-three Etonians of the 1826 year were for a time Members of Parliament, but other than Gladstone they made small impact; even the long-serving Milnes Gaskell only achieved minor office. Only one peer was active in government, though there were several Etonians who were prominent in the Empire. Fifteen could more or less be described as civil servants in this country, and about the same number went out to serve in India. About one in ten was commissioned in the army, but none of the 1826 boys achieved any prominence. Two joined the navy.

Nearly fifty became barristers, but only seven became solicitors; eight were bankers, while five were in medicine. Fifteen were academics, and others had an academic interlude – for example, as

---

* Trollope, in *Doctor Thorne*, was to create in Louis Scatcherd a wastrel as bad as Tom Hoseason, but at Eton a little later.

Fellows of All Souls. Only three became at all involved in forward-
ing the Industrial Revolution, one a coal magnate, one an iron
founder, one a manufacturer. This is a most serious deficiency.
(Possibly, though, some of those with careers unrecorded were
employed in industry, without achieving eminence; it is clergy and
barristers who are more easily tracked.) There are a number of odd
careers: auctioneer, stockbroker (unique in 1826, but not later), wine
merchant, merchant seaman, actor (Charles Kean), singer, officer in
the Austrian army, Portuguese diplomat (he was Portuguese), and
owner of a lunatic asylum.

Lastly, large numbers lived out life on their country estates, where
they were often involved in public service. Many were Justices of
the Peace and Deputy-Lieutenants; many served in their local yeo-
manry or militia. Thus the lives of the 1826 Etonians proved not
very unlike the lives of their parents. They felt the Etonian bond,
and many would turn out for the Eton Anniversary, an Old Etonian
dinner in London, held in May, which would attract two to three
hundred at this time.

Some historians say that only sentimentality accounts for the generally favourable attitudes with which Etonians later regarded their
schooling. Against this, there are examples like Shelley, who at the
time were probably reasonably happy, but felt later that they should
not have been. The more thoughtful of them were aware that Eton
had conspicuous faults. They knew that the vast majority were
indolent, and that the moral tone left much to be desired even before
Victorian values became fashionable, but they were not censorious.
They mostly approved of fagging, realizing that if they knew what
it was like to have to obey, they were better-placed to give orders.
They had cultivated friendships, not just in a narrow group of the
same age, as was to be the case in more regulated schools fifty years
on. Above all, they recognized that their parents had sent them away
to School to learn to stand on their own feet, and this they had done.

CHAPTER THIRTEEN

Dr Hawtrey

EDWARD CRAVEN HAWTREY, the senior Assistant Master, was chosen
to succeed Dr Keate. He was one of the best products of the long
association between Eton and King's; indeed, he was descended
from an Edward Hawtrey who was at both in the early seventeenth
century. That Edward's son was a Fellow of Eton from 1680 to
1715; the grandson had married Provost Sleech's sister; the great-
grandson, another Edward, became a Fellow in 1792. This man had
two sisters who were Dames, and he married the sister of Foster, the
Head Master. Their son, born in 1789, was E.C. Hawtrey, who
arrived as an Oppidan in 1799: his Tutor was 'Crumpet' Sumner,
later Archbishop of Canterbury. Because young Hawtrey came
from one of the inside families, he only moved to College when he
needed to qualify for King's, which he duly did in 1807. After a
short time tutoring he became a Master in 1814. He was not such
a good scholar as Keate, but he was widely read and an exceptional
linguist, familiar with French, German and Italian. His manner was
urbane, and his boarding house particularly popular with the aristocracy. He was something of a dandy, and used scent, but this could
not conceal that he was an ugly man, known to the boys as Plug.
F.C. Burnand described him thus:

> His face was of a somewhat monkeyish type, for his forehead
> receded sharply, and his upper jaw was heavy and protruding, his
> features being as hardly cut as those of the quaint little figures
> carved out of wood by a Swiss peasant. He used golden-rimmed

eyeglasses suspended round his neck by a broad black ribbon. He wore a frill which feathered out in front, suggesting the idea of his shirt having come home hot from the wash and boiled over. His collar and cuffs were of velvet. He invariably stood, and walked, leaning to one side, out of the perpendicular, as if he had been modelled on the plan of the Tower of Pisa.[1]

Fortunately Hawtrey saw the need to respond to the criticism of the School which had been voiced so loudly in the last few years. In August 1834 he wrote to Dr Butler, the famous Headmaster of Shrewsbury, for advice.[2] Butler represented the best of the old classical tradition, rather than the enthusiasm for radical change personified by Dr Arnold. How competitive were the internal examinations at Shrewsbury, and did they go all the way up the school (as Eton's did not)? Was Butler's Sixth Form chosen on merit or seniority? Were the lessons a set routine, or were authors chosen for extended reading by Dr Butler? More interesting than the questions was Hawtrey's admission that the Provost's attachment to the old course of things meant that any reform would be limited, and that the maximum benefit must consequently be extracted from the reform.

In September he wrote again, after receiving advice, to say that the Provost had agreed that the Head Master might divide Dr Keate's vast flock and himself teach the top thirty-two boys only. Exams the Provost opposed, since they would mean fewer lessons; but Hawtrey did institute a system of divisional reporting. Boys had a form of conduct card, a first step towards what became the fortnightly order cards familiar to generations of Etonians. Hawtrey would like to have revised the list of prescribed books read, but again the Provost was an obstacle. Dr Keate's advice was also sought on Hawtrey's scheme of improvement; he blessed it, and said that he himself would have liked some of the changes. But had he really fought for them?

Hawtrey remained in Savile House, where he had boarded boys, and the house from which Goodall and Keate had ruled reverted to a boys' house, known as Keate House. Savile House was to be the Head Masters' base for sixty years. Hawtrey moved his more select division into what is still the Head Master's Schoolroom, known in those days as the Library, though in fact it was not a library: its bookshelves were bare, but it did contain the birch cupboard and the block. Where previously a rather uncoordinated system of team-teaching had prevailed, boys were now clearly assigned to particular Masters in the various parts of the Fifth Form. The new division Masters were given separate rooms, and more freedom to pursue their own courses, while the Fourth Form was herded into Upper School. There were some losses in grammatical discipline, but boys benefited in other ways; Hawtrey was a great encourager of both boys and staff, which Keate never was. He was never allowed to appoint a non-Kingsman, though he tried twice with Goodall's successor, Hodgson, whereas Keate had smuggled two past the Provost.

Hawtrey needed to appoint a new Lower Master, since Knapp, like his old friend Drury, had had to depart hurriedly because of his debts. He chose the conservative Dupuis. Then in 1836 he appointed his cousin Stephen Hawtrey, who was not an Etonian, to teach Mathematics. (Since the man had been his second choice, the Head Master need not be criticized for nepotism.) Stephen Hawtrey was only allowed to teach the Head Master's division (if they so wanted), a concession that permitted the senior boys to prepare for Cambridge, where (outside King's) Mathematics was required.* In the rest of the School, Mathematics Extras (voluntary studies outside the normal school hours) were still the monopoly of the ignorant Hexter. When the compromise was seen not to be working, Hexter was induced to retire in 1839 with a pension of £200 p.a. This was paid by Stephen Hawtrey, who also built the Rotunda, which stood in what is now the quadrangle of Queen's Schools. From 1843 he began to pay and employ his own staff of Mathematics Masters, making a separate charge on boys' bills. In 1846 the Tomline Prize for Mathematics was founded, and in 1851 the subject entered the curriculum formally. At this point, Stephen Hawtrey was promoted to the same status as the Classical Masters, but *his* assistants were not allowed to wear academic dress, and could only complain of boys through Stephen Hawtrey; for this pettiness Provost Hodgson was responsible.

Goodall had died in 1840. He had always been regarded with affection, even if it was recognized that he was not helping Eton in reputation or in actuality. Even before Goodall's death Lord Melbourne, the Prime Minister, had suggested as Provost a former

---

* Quite a few Etonians became Wranglers at Cambridge in spite of having learned nothing at School; that would be less easy now.

Oppidan – who was not therefore qualified; he had then thought of Archdeacon Hodgson, who had been through Eton and King's, but was neither a Doctor nor Bachelor of Divinity; thus he was nearly but not quite qualified. The Fellows were keen to have a Tory, and approached Dr Keate on the day of Goodall's death. Keate was Canon in Residence in the Cloisters at Windsor, but would not be drawn. The Vice-Provost then sounded out Dr Lonsdale, one of only seven other fully qualified men, and received some encouragement. Meanwhile Melbourne had consulted Lord Wellesley, who had been responsible for Goodall's elevation – Keate was the man, but Keate refused again. Accordingly, on 6 April 1840 the Fellows received a letter stating that the Queen had nominated Hodgson; on 7 April the Fellows declared him ineligible and elected Lonsdale. By now, however, Lonsdale had had second thoughts: Hodgson was his friend, he did not want a quarrel between College and Government, he was happy at King's College, London – and the uncharitable said he wanted to be a Bishop (which he soon achieved). So he withdrew, and the Fellows were left without a candidate. Archdeacon Hodgson was admitted to the degree of BD at Cambridge by royal mandate, and he duly became Provost.

He had been an Assistant Master briefly in 1807, but at the time of his appointment he was Rector of Bakewell in Derbyshire. One claim to fame he possessed was that he had been a close friend of Byron, and he was indeed something of a poet and a literary figure himself. He had earlier hoped to be a Fellow of Eton, but had lacked sufficient influence. Now at 59 years old, he was to give up his clerical appointments and to turn enthusiastically to his new job. Fortunately he was, like the Head Master, a moderate reformer, but he felt particularly that he had a mission to do something for the Collegers – unlike most of the Fellows, who seemed to think that the hardships that they had survived had made them the men they were. At the end of the long journey south, as he came into sight of the College, he exclaimed: 'Please God, I will do something for those poor boys.'

Three sorts of improvements could be made: to the food, to the buildings, and to the provision of pastoral care. The first was simplest; twice a week, beef was served instead of mutton, and the supper meal, which became a little more than cold mutton, was moved from 6.00 p.m. to 8.00 p.m. – a more civilized time which has remained the hour for eating.

Rehousing the Collegers was more important, but required the raising of a large sum of money. The College could only provide £2,000 (say, £100,000 now), a meagre sum that in itself serves to condemn the management of the College. The Provost and Fellows and Head Master gave another £2,100. Within three years a further £14,000 was collected which enabled the New Buildings (as they are still known) to be begun. King's College gave £500. Among notable personal donors were Queen Victoria (£500) and Prince Albert (£100), Lord Melbourne, Dr Keate and Mr Gladstone. In 1844 Prince Albert laid the foundation stone, unfortunately while wearing a pair of lavender gloves which, to the boys' delight, were ruined.[3] By 1846, rooms were available for forty-nine Collegers, the intention being that twenty-one should remain in a large part of the Long Chamber as a dormitory. The New Buildings provided a higher standard of comfort but were less idiosyncratic than the typical Dame's house. There was heating and plumbing; there were sick rooms, and a tea-room; there was provision for a resident matron and staff. All of these facilities had been totally absent before.

Carter's Chambers, which had housed the Lower Master when he and the Head Master were required to live at either end of the Collegers' accommodation to provide supervision, had provided some supplementary room for the boys since early in the eighteenth century, though until Hawtrey's time they had had to pay a guinea a year rent to the Lower Master. (The Lower Chamber on the ground floor was important to the boys because it enabled provisions to be smuggled in after lock-up.) Now these rooms, together with the southern part of the old Long Chamber, were refurbished for a Master in College to sleep under the same roof as the Collegers. This was a salaried post, less rewarding than the holding of a boys' house (which drew fees from the parents). An effective Master, Charles Abraham, however, gave up his successful house to become Master in College, and by his influence established a more humane regime; he provided the level of pastoral care that the Oppidans in good houses enjoyed. The direction of the boys' work remained with their Tutors, just as it did for boys in Dames' houses, and the Tutor rather than Abraham (a future Bishop) prepared the boys for Confirmation.

In fact in 1841, there had only been two applicants for College – one of whom had to be baptized hurriedly in order to be properly qualified – and there were only thirty-seven Collegers altogether. Such was the reputation of Long Chamber. Once the reforms were public, numbers of applicants rose rapidly and it was possible to select by competitive examination; thereafter Collegers began to replace the Oppidans as the intellectual leaders of the School. Regrettably the price of this was that candidates for College had to be trained at expensive, and thus upper middle-class, Preparatory Schools. Reform thus excluded the poorer boys who had hitherto occasionally entered Eton.

Room was also found at the north end of the New Buildings for a library, which is where the remains of Dr Newborough's library, together with Praed's books, were moved. This School Library was further enhanced by gifts of books, including many from Hawtrey himself (he was a bibliophile), and in 1850 by stuffed birds given by Dr Thackeray, Provost of King's, which were to form the nucleus of the School's future Natural History Museum. A rather fine heraldic stained glass window was presented by the Head Master and Lower Master.*

In 1844 a sanatorium was also built, by the Head Master rather than the College. The cost was paid off by an annual charge of £1. 4s. on every Oppidan. At the same time, the College did provide new drainage to supplement the original great sewer, and this emptied into the Thames. Eton continued to be regarded as unhealthy, for example when compared with Harrow, but the number of deaths of boys declined. Scarlet fever was the principal killer.

In 1842 a very important exchange of property took place between the College and the Crown. The land bounded roughly by Barnes Pool, the Slough Road and the houses bordering the north side of Keate's Lane, known as Cock Close, which belonged to the Crown, was now exchanged for land on Primrose Hill in north London, which had belonged to the College. Curiously, the College had not owned the land on which the Oppidans lived, and it did not completely do so until after the Second World War. In the middle of Cock Close stood the Christopher Inn, which, with its courtyard, was in a sense the hub of Eton. As Brinsley Richards wrote:

* The window was recently rediscovered in an attic above the Natural History Museum. It must be hoped that an honourable position can be found for it.

To the Christopher came, many times a day, coaches and post-chaises from all points of the compass; on Fridays, which were market days in Eton, the farmers held their ordinary there; and squires, drovers, pedlars, recruiting sergeants, and occasional village wenches who came to be hired as servants, clustered under the porch . . . Add to this the noise made by criers of news – men with long red coats and post-horns – who, alighting from the coaches on days when there was any stirring intelligence from Town, would spread about, blowing fierce blasts and offering their special editions of the Times or Morning Chronicle, at a shilling apiece . . . But the Christopher was also much resorted to by boys of the School. Boys were always slinking into the inn for drink. If caught, they had been to see friends from London, or to enquire about parcels sent down by coach.[4]

The Oppidans indeed had a club at the inn which met in a cellar at half past two every day, for bread and cheese and ale, and where tradesmen's signs, carried off as sporting trophies, were kept until reclaimed by their owners.

Dr Hawtrey was anxious that the College should not renew the lease of the Christopher, and indeed, he thought it a good site for a parish church. The College, however, saw it as a source of income and refused at first. Later he tried again, after getting almost all the Masters on his side – though some asses felt that the existence of temptation within reach of the boys was morally bracing. This time Hawtrey won his point. Apparently nine-tenths of the landlord's income had come from Eton boys. The buildings were reassigned for Masters' accommodation and the Eton Society moved there. Subsequently boys were able to remove their drinking to more regulated premises, known as Tap, in the High Street.

At this very busy time the College also set in hand a restoration of the Chapel. By now the Oxford Movement was active and some High Churchmen were critical of the existing arrangements. The Provost was strongly Protestant, and so were most of the Eton community except Edward Coleridge. Thus consent was only given to changes in the structure, to bring the rather handsome seventeenth-century furnishing in line with the gothic taste. The reredos went first, and a new altar and altar rails were installed. Boxes provided for the servants of the College, segregated by sex, were swept away. The seats occupied by the nobility and the Sixth Form were removed from the walls to make way for oak stalls with canopies along each side; other walls were left bare.

It was in the course of this operation that the medieval wall-paintings were uncovered. The workmen were busily scraping away the top row when John Wilder, a Fellow, chancing to enter the Chapel, stopped them. (The services were being held in a temporary building opposite Barnes Pool, known as the Tabernacle.) The Provost, shocked by the superstitious subject matter, allowed the destruction to stop but only on the understanding that the paintings were to be covered by stalls. He would not even permit an arrangement suggested by the Prince Consort whereby they would have been covered by sliding panels, so that scholars could have seen them while the boys were shielded from their supposed dangers. All that was granted was that a careful record could be made by a draftsman – and indeed the paintings were not seen again until 1923, the time of Provost James.

Hodgson did allow the Ten Commandments and the Beatitudes to be painted on the bare wall at the east end. Stone flags replaced the black and white marble, and the medieval lectern was consigned to the Antechapel. The 1700 organ loft had crossed the aisle near its west end, incidentally damaging some of the wall paintings; this was replaced by a new organ suspended on the south side. Worst of all the changes was the introduction of stained glass windows. The great east window was commissioned from Willement, and the boys were induced to pay for this from their pocket money. It is hard to imagine a more odious levy, hated by all, but most of all by the senior boys who were charged with the task of collection. The window was dreadful. Other windows were given by Wilder, and were also bad. The only good window (which, by divine providence, alone survived Hitler's bombs), was one at the west end window given by Edward Coleridge. The glass in the Antechapel, which was from the start seen to be superior, was by a different artist, Hardman.

This is almost entirely a sorry story, and the sorriest part of it is that the services in the Chapel were left unreconstructed. The moving of the pulpit to its present position, with a sounding board over it, marginally improved audibility; but the services and the sermons remained at their existing low level.

Changes within the College were matched by an ultimately more significant change in the outside environment – the coming of the railways.[5] Even before Dr Keate retired, two schemes were floated for providing railways to Slough and Windsor. The scheme to Windsor, which was favoured by the Old Etonian MP for Windsor, Ramsbottom (who had had a son at Eton), soon came to nothing; but the Great Western Railway linking Bristol to London through Slough, with a branch line to Windsor, ultimately triumphed. The objections of the College were that it would be easier for boys to go up to London, that boys would be in danger from the trains owing to the natural foolhardiness of youth, and that there might be an increased danger of flooding. (At a meeting in Windsor, Keate added that he thought the passengers on the trains might be in danger from vandalism from boys; Ramsbottom poured scorn on all objections, observing that a railway would permit larger importations of birch should this prove necessary.) The College used the large number of Old Etonians in Parliament to press its case, and a letter exists, no doubt similar to many others written, from Keate to Gladstone, appealing to his loyalty. In 1834, the Great Western Committee felt obliged to drop its branch line to Windsor, but the next year secured permission for its main line, but only at the cost of some very irksome conditions: no new line to approach Eton without the specific permission of the Provost and Fellows; no station within 3 miles; a 4-mile-long fence, policed by company employees to prevent Etonians from coming on to the line, and maintained at the company's expense. The College had made itself ridiculous, but it had through its influence secured a temporary victory.*

In 1838, however, the Great Western thought of a scheme for enabling its passengers to embark or alight at Slough, then a small village within the parish of Upton cum Chalvey. Tickets were to be obtained at a pub, five minutes' walk from the stopping place. (A more adjacent inn was then found, whose landlord agreed to construct a veranda for travellers waiting for trains.) The College brought an action to prevent the company stopping its trains within 3 miles of Eton. When the Lord Chancellor considered the case at

---

* The evidence of Cookesley, an Assistant Master, to the House of Lords Committee contained the interesting observation that the railways represented a greater threat to Eton than to Winchester. 'The system at Winchester is one of great restraint and coercion compared with ours . . . The prosperity of Eton is mainly owing to the practice of giving the boys as much freedom as possible consistent with discipline, and in the event of a railway passing within a short distance of us we should be compelled to alter the system.'

the end of 1838, the College was able to produce evidence that the company had most of the identifiable features of a station, such as a board with letters SLOUGH and lamps. Nevertheless, the Lord Chancellor found for the railway, and advised the College to come to terms with it. They had weakened their own position by having to request that the GWR lay on special trains to take Etonians to Queen Victoria's coronation in June 1838, but they appealed against the Lord Chancellor's judgement. The appeal was dismissed with costs, ironically on the Fourth of June 1839.

The College now capitulated, and in February 1840 they permitted a proper station to be constructed at Slough. Naturally, it was much used by Eton, and at the end of that Summer Half the GWR arranged enough carriages to carry 600 boys. Relations were indeed more friendly until the GWR's plan of a branch line to Windsor west of the College was revived in 1845. By then the London and South Western Railway was planning to approach Windsor from Staines, always a preferred approach in the College's view. In 1848, a Commons Select Committee considered both applications, with formidable opposition to the GWR not only from the Provost and Fellows but from the Head Master and all his Assistants bar one (William Johnson). The line would inflict an irremediable injury, without any countervailing advantage whatsoever. The Committee, however, permitted both lines, and Bills were accordingly passed through Parliament, in the case of the GWR with many provisions to protect the privacy of Cuckoo Weir where the boys bathed (naked, of course, in those days), and to ensure that the boys could not easily get on to the track. The line was rapidly completed, at first on wooden trestles, which were replaced by brick arches between 1861 and 1863. In 1886 a requirement for special constables to patrol the line was dropped.* The outstanding consequence of the development of railways countrywide, and also the connection of Windsor to London, was the greater ease with which boys could attend Eton. Certainly Etonian parents had always been prepared to subject sons to difficult journeys to get them to School, and there was among the boys a certain prestige in having travelled from afar. Now it would be cheaper for the less wealthy to send their sons, and boys would not be so cut off from their homes. This helped to

---

* The principal hazard to the health of the boys proved to be the practice that developed of smokers retreating under the arches for their illicit activity.

stimulate the growth in numbers at the School from 444 to 777 in Hawtrey's time, which occasioned much new building of boarding accommodation.

Side-effects of the GWR were the rapid growth of the town of Slough, and the ease with which excursions could be made from London to attend the Etonian festival of Montem. In 1841 large crowds of sightseers came down by train, and this lent urgency to a debate which had been continuing for some time. It was fairly generally reckoned that there was a case for reforming some of the abuses of the festival: its extravagance, the over-indulgence of the boys who lunched all too well after the procession reached Salt Hill, and the wanton destruction which would follow lunch as boys attacked the gardens of the two neighbouring inns with their swords. (This was apparently a manifestation of dislike for an unpopular Captain of Montem, who had to pay for the damage, but it seems to have become almost traditional.) In 1841 the Captain was Edward Thring, later a famous reforming Headmaster of Uppingham. His 'salt', or collection, was £1,269, and expenses were £640 plus payments to some of the other boys. On this occasion the mindless destruction of a garden took place, even including the felling of an apple tree. Thring did not misuse his sudden access of wealth, but the 1844 Captain, Bernard Drake, a boy with glittering talents, 'played Ducks (and Drakes) with his money, went to the bad altogether, and died of debauchery'.[6]

By 1846 Hawtrey had been converted from one who had genuinely tried to limit excesses to an abolitionist. Okes, the Lower Master, and most of the Assistants agreed. The Provost had always wished to end the ceremony and three out of seven Fellows were with him. (Plumptre, the maddest of them, believed that the procession replaced pre-Reformation processions to a shrine of the Virgin; he therefore felt that Montem must be preserved as a protest against popery.) The Provost felt that this was close enough to a consensus to sound out the Queen's views. She had attended in 1841 and 1844 with Prince Albert. The royal couple were ready to accept some reform, but reluctant to see the ancient ceremony, which they must have enjoyed, abolished. Hodgson did not give in and tried again. Lord John Russell, the Prime Minister, told the Queen that most of the world sided with the Provost, and the Queen accordingly said that she would not oppose a decision of the College. Supporters of Montem held meetings, and rumours were rife of demonstrations by undergraduates and boys. Police were assembled on the evening before what would have been Montem, but outsiders were largely indifferent and Hawtrey handled the senior boys well. The newspapers, not for the last time, published accounts of events at Eton that had not actually occurred. Etonians behaved themselves with a Victorian sense of responsibility that their grandfathers might well not have matched. Hawtrey, with characteristic generosity, gave £200 to the boy who would have been the Captain of Montem; he also gave a dinner in Upper School to those who would probably have been his guests at Salt Hill.

Hawtrey's reign did see some increase in the opportunities for leisure within Eton. The most valuable reform was achieved by G.A. Selwyn, a private tutor, and William Evans, the Drawing Master. Both were philolutes and psychrolutes.* Selwyn was commissioned by Hawtrey to improve the arrangements for bathing, to promote the teaching of swimming, and to provide guards. In 1840, Charles Montagu was dragged into the river by a barge rope right by Windsor Bridge and drowned. While William Evans took a postchaise to London to break the news to the boy's parents, Selwyn drafted laws for 'Passing', which Hawtrey accepted immediately. Boys would in future only be allowed on to the river if they had passed a test: a header into the water, a longish swim breaststroke, a swim backstroke, and treading water (the last to enable a capsized boy to use his talents to clear any encumbrance). Since 1840 only two boys have drowned, in neither case because of an inability to swim. That same year boating became legal – not that it made a great difference. The technology of boats and racing continued to develop, and there were irregular races against Westminster, mostly at Putney, with mixed results. William IV watched Eton lose at Datchet in 1837; he was already ill and shortly thereafter died. (The King was certainly upset by the result, but there was a touch of arrogance in the boys' assumption that their defeat had caused the King's death.) Internal house races and small boat races became more regular occurrences.

At cricket Eton played Harrow each year, and tended to have the

---

* Selwyn was an early muscular Christian. There was one bush by the river bank over which he would dive, a feat which no friend would emulate despite his advice: 'You must fancy yourself a dart and you will do it with ease.' At St John's, Cambridge, he rowed in the first Boat Race, and walked to London nonstop in 13 hours.

better of the game. Harrow, however, was in a lean period in its fortunes (which no doubt contributed to the growth in Etonian numbers). Matches against Winchester also became annual events, and again Eton tended to win. Football on the fields west of Eton continued to grow; in Michaelmas 1842 Edward Melville Lawford[7] played football most days. Sometimes the games would be within his house, the sides not balanced in numbers, sometimes between houses or between scratch teams. What was played would be recognizably the Field Game that has survived to this day. Scores were by goals or by rouges; the defending captain would decide whether a rouge had been scored, or an offence committed, and would grant an appeal by the attackers accordingly. (It is not always clear even to an umpire whether a rouge should be given, for it depends upon contact either of ball or of attacker with a defender.) Fives, too progressed; in 1847 some courts, replicating the original space between the buttresses of College Chapel, were built along the Eton Wick Road on the initiative of two Masters. Hockey, on the other hand, expired. It was said that the game was considered dangerous by the authorities, but it can hardly have been more dangerous than football, where 'shinning', deliberately kicking an opponent's shins, was legitimate.

Lawford was an all-rounder, competent but unexcited by his work, yet able to enjoy music. He would note his appreciation of the occasional anthem in Chapel, or go up to Windsor to hear one at St George's. He found a violin teacher, in Windsor presumably, whom he liked. His brother is Lawford mi in his diary, but that did not betray lack of affection; surnames remained the convention. He was not particularly well behaved, and was always at odds with the housekeeper of his Tutor, Durnford. Lawford was required to write 50 lines each day for a week for telling the lady that 'she was like an ugly man in a picture'. Not very many years on, he would probably have been – deservedly – beaten by the Captain of the House. Her function was in essence that of the modern Dame, with some responsibility for the health of the boys as well as for catering and domestic staff management. The counterpart in a Dame's house might be a living-in, private tutor, but that was changing.

In 1839 William Evans,[8] who had been teaching Drawing in succession to his father since 1823, was persuaded by his friends George Selwyn and Edward Coleridge to take on a Dame's house of fourteen boys across Keate's Lane from his dwelling. He had in 1837 lost his wife in childbirth, and was so distressed that he was likely to leave Eton had not this new interest been created. The building was probably typical of most Dames' houses, with sanded floors and, dirty linen. The dinner meal was very moderate, and the boys expected to buy all but rolls and butter for their breakfast and tea. Evans determined to change everything: he borrowed to pay for improvements to the accommodation and served good meals in a proper dining room. The numbers wanting to board in his house rapidly rose to fifty, and he could thus pay off his debts without charging more than other Dames. One of them habitually called out of her window when she saw him, 'Oh, William Evans, William Evans, you are ruining us *all*!'. In practice, his example forced those who could improve their standards to do so; others were bought out by Assistant Masters, whose numbers began to rise with the growing size of the School.

Evans inherited a Captain of the House, Lord Lewisham, who had a private tutor. Evans, despite his friendship for Selwyn, thought that this detracted from his own position, and fortunately Lewisham soon decided that his new Dame had made the tutor superfluous. During the 1840s, private tutors disappeared from Eton. The Duke of Athole, who as Mr Murray had had a private tutor in Keate's time, told Evans (his friend as well as his boy's Dame) that whereas the cost of Eton with private tutor was £1,000 p.a., the son's expenses were only £170. No regulation directly forbade the private tutor, but it was decreed that all should have a Tutor from among the Masters; few boys wanted to work for two tutors, and few parents wanted to pay for two.

Lewisham was neither a big nor a strong boy, and a larger lower boy knocked him down when sent on an errand. Evans told Lewisham to box his ears, which would have been a normal act at that time; but the lower boy knocked Lewisham down again. Evans, who was a very large man, might well have dealt with the lower boy, but in fact he had primed his eldest son, a Colleger and also very strong, to frog-march the delinquent to College, where he was given what was called a College hiding. There was no further disciplinary problem. After this episode, William Evans continued to trust his senior boys with a responsibility that was not otherwise prevalent in the School, but which was to become general. Thus in pastoral as well as material care, higher standards were set.

In general, life at Eton seems to have become less harsh. Violence

and fighting became less common, and bullying was generally reckoned to have been much reduced. Cricket fagging was dying out.
For Oswald Smith, the main duty was attending his fagmaster's
breakfast – and tiresomely, he messed on the opposite side of the
School. Later, when Smith was Captain of his house, he had thirteen
fags; half served him at breakfast, the other half at tea. On his arrival
in the School he had been deeply shocked by the gross immorality
of one boy, 'backward in lessons but not in vice'. As usual it is not
quite clear what the boy said or did, beyond that he was obviously
trying to show off to younger boys in the only way of which he felt
himself capable. Thereafter, there is no more mention of immorality, and Oswald Smith had an excellent academic career, being
placed as a 17-year-old in the Select for the Newcastle Scholarship,
after which he left (never having been flogged). By then he knew
more than his Tutor, Eliot.[9]

Eliot was amiable enough, but evidently would not have been a
Master had he not come from King's. In 1845 Hawtrey made a more
interesting appointment from King's, William Johnson,* who had
been Cookesley's pupil before winning the Newcastle Scholarship as a Colleger in 1841, when Gladstone was examiner with
his brother-in-law, Lord Lyttelton. At Cambridge he became the
Craven Scholar. He was contemplating the Bar as a profession,
thinking London might prove a healthy change equally 'from
Cambridge sloth as Eton excitement'.[10] On receiving Hawtrey's
invitation to return to Eton, he was uncertain: 'There are heavy
temptations for an Eton Master towards love of money, gormandis-
ing, jealousy, intrigue and imposture,' he wrote.[11] Yet he decided to
face the temptations. His famous lines, *Heraclitus*, were thrown off
for boys doing the Greek construe book during his first half. All was
not easy, however; 'The noise of 200 boys and 4 masters in the
Upper School is so great that . . . the instruction can be but fragmen-
tary, and the great bulk of the division is learning nothing.'[12] By the
summer of 1846 he wrote gloomily to his mother about the need
for his own schoolroom, and spoke of the general wish among his
colleagues for more Masters, and the hopelessness of persuading
Hawtrey to increase the staff adequately.[13] With his weak voice and
poor eyesight he was not a natural schoolmaster, but the interest of
what he told his divisions, and the wisdom of his thinking about

* Some 25 years later, after leaving Eton, he changed his name to Cory.

education, were to have considerable influence. He did not persevere with boarding boys, but he had many pupils and became a remarkable Tutor. He was also exceptional in Victorian Eton because he did not take orders.

It is fair to say, however, that Hawtrey himself made the greatest general impression on boys. His Sixth Form did, admittedly, tease him, but in genial fashion. His addresses to the boys might sometimes be mocked, but they had humour and could be more effective than Keate's railing. When he did flog boys – and that certainly remained a standard punishment – he did so with a curious underarm stroke, and the flogging was 'tighter' than Keate's normal retribution.[14]* When boys came to leave he was courtesy itself. He would give a leaving book, and the Oppidans would respond with a cheque. Hawtrey would affect to be blind to these donations: 'It's rather warm. I think I'll open the window,' he would observe, and as he did so the boy deposited the envelope with its cheque. For the next boy Hawtrey would say, 'Don't you think it's rather cold? I think I'd better shut the window.' He would also ask for leaving portraits, often by George Richmond, but these were regrettably returned to the families after Hawtrey died.

Hawtrey deserves more than anecdotes. He founded an English essay prize. With his linguistic abilities he had a wide circle of distinguished friends from all over Europe, and was delighted when Prince Albert in 1841 founded prizes in French, German and Italian, to encourage the voluntary study of these languages. The French and German prizes continue as Her Majesty The Queen's Prizes, and they have certainly had an admirable effect over the years.

Provost Hodgson died in December 1852, and Hawtrey was nominated to succeed. Crown and Fellows were at one this time. William Johnson was later to assess Hawtrey as Head Master in a famous passage:

> Such was the man; not an accurate scholar, though versed in many tongues; not thoroughly well informed, though he had spent

---

* An impudent young lordling who knew he was to be flogged is widely reported to have put on a show for his friends. At Hawtrey's first stroke, he executed a kind of leap he had practised accompanied by a yelp. Hawtrey begged the boy's pardon – 'touched some nerve no doubt – go home and be quiet – better send for Mr Ellison, my Lord ' (Hawtrey was a snob). The boy departed triumphant.

thirty thousand pounds on books; not able to estimate correctly the intellectual development of younger men, though he corresponded with the leaders of England and France; not qualified to train school-boys in competition with a Vaughan or a Kennedy possessing the advanced knowledge of a later generation, for he had never been a University man, only a Kingsman; not one that could be said to organise well, for from first to last he dealt in make-shift and patch-work; yet, for all that, a hero among school-masters, for he was beyond his fellows candid, fearless, and bountiful; passionate in his indignation against cruelty, ardent in admiring all virtue and all show of genius; so forgiving, that for fifty years he seized every chance of doing kindness to a man who had tormented him at school; and so ingenuous, that when he had misunderstood a boy's character and then found himself wrong, he suddenly grasped his hand, and owned his error magnanimously. Many men have laughed at his rhetoric, and made themselves a reputation for wit by telling stories of his behaviour. Such men have probably never read the second part of *Don Quixote*. The knight was, after all, a true gentleman of fine mind, and his death was pathetic. Our Head Master was worthy of a high-souled poetical nation in its best age; and old men who had been his compeers in society wept at his funeral with younger men who had been only his humble yoke-fellows.[15]

CHAPTER FOURTEEN

The Establishment School

THE NATURAL SUCCESSOR to Hawtrey was Keate's son-in-law, Edward Coleridge. He was a distinguished schoolmaster, and a particularly successful Tutor. He was later to say:

> There must be a constant conviction that there is hope for any boy whatever he may say, whatever he may do and whatever he may think. That conviction of hopefulness breeds a necessary sympathy between the teacher and the taught; that sympathy once inspired begets influence, and influence good. You thus possess a power of drawing out whatever elements there may be in the boy's nature, and not only by bringing them out by your own exertion, but of putting into him as it were a power of teaching himself, which I consider to be one great end, if not the great end of public instruction, namely to make the boys teach themselves.[1]

A complete list of his pupils survives, and many achieved distinction both academically and in public life. Coleridge must have kept up with most of them, for he was aware that a large number predeceased him. Though he was not a great scholar himself, he undoubtedly had the ability to excite scholarship in others.

He had been in Sixth Form with Edward Pusey, and he was powerfully influenced by the Oxford Movement. His religion meant more to him than to the generality of his clerical colleagues. In his house he introduced 'family prayers' in the evening, a practice which was eventually copied even by lay Housemasters. He also began Sunday Private Business on Sunday mornings, in his case the reading of the Greek Testament. This became universal in the 1850s, though it was left to the Tutors to decide their own subject matter. Sunday Private was to be an important feature of Eton life for over a century, though it ceased to be essentially religious. Coleridge was as much a friend of G.A. Selwyn as William Evans was, and he shared with Evans the desire to provide an agreeable environment for his boys. His wife looked after all the domestic arrangements: 'No such vermin as a Matron or Housekeeper was ever known to crawl about my House.'[2]

In 1850, he had become Lower Master despite the opposition of some of the Fellows. One, Dupuis, advertised in the papers for a Lower Master. There was no doubting the hostility that Coleridge's Puseyite views aroused among the extremely Protestant majority; some of his less successful colleagues also remained jealous of the academic triumphs of his pupils. In fact the Lower School had shrunk to fifteen boys, but it was to revive remarkably as a preparation for life in the Fourth Form; one of Coleridge's Assistants, John Hawtrey, devoted his house to lower boys, in effect running a Preparatory School, but there also remained boys of 10 or 11 among the other houses. By 1859 there were 115 boys in the Lower School, though these would not now be regarded as old enough for Public School – a fact that should be remembered when considering the remarkable growth in numbers at Eton in the mid-nineteenth century. When Hodgson died in December 1852, damaging rumours immediately circulated that Coleridge was about to become a Roman Catholic. William Johnson sided with Coleridge, but in January he was reconciled after a fashion to the less controversial selection of Charles Goodford. 'Goodford is honest, righteous, methodical, learned, brave, laconic, prudent, unmeddlesome. He is also acrid, sleepy, weak in health, small, ill-looking, uninfluential, obscure, unpolished. No one loves him, no one admires him – every one respects him. We shall probably be happier under him than under Coleridge.'[3]

Goodford was indeed an unremarkable man, retaining a West Country accent and in every way lacking the sophistication of Hawtrey. He was, however, a good Classic and a more than competent teacher. For Brinsley Richards, a boy in Goodford's time, he was 'an excellent headmaster, not a genius, not a fussy autocrat setting down his foot where a little finger would do, not a stern man delighting in punishment, but equal in his rule and perfectly firm'.[4] His opinions coincided closely with Hawtrey's, and there was to be little pressure for reform. Goodford's decade was to be safe and prosperous for Eton. Numbers continued to rise to over 800 by 1860. Coleridge might have made more changes. In his short memoir of his life he does not even refer to the lost headmastership. Hawtrey was able to secure a majority of the Fellows to offer him a Fellowship, and in 1857, on the second approach, Coleridge accepted, and became easily the best preacher among the Fellows.

Goodford's reforms, such as they were, were all desirable. Sunday Questions, work to be written on Sunday by boys and shown up on Monday, along with Sunday Private, made for a more educational weekend. The Mathematical Masters were treated a little better, being allowed to dress as Assistant Masters.* Some were allowed to board boys – succeeding Dames; but they remained an inferior class, and were seen as such by the boys, which did not make for good discipline. The Mathematical Assistants were generally not Etonians, whereas the Classical Masters all were; however, Goodford was allowed to appoint two former Oppidans, the second of whom, Edmund Warre, was to become a famous Head Master.

There was some increase in the playing of games, towards which Goodford was more sympathetic than Hawtrey had been. Two beagle packs, first for Collegers, and then in 1857 on a grander scale for Oppidans, provided more entertainment in Lent Halves, when football was not played. Exercise for boys, however, remained voluntary. The Captain of the Boats was normally the most prestigious boy in the School, presiding over the internal racing and the two processions held on the Fourth of June and Election Saturday. On these occasions the Captain of the Oppidans organized the fireworks and the meals. Boy officers began to keep account books as records of their stewardship and guides for their successors. Similarly, the Captain of the XI presided over cricket, with the additional stimulus of the important matches against Harrow and Winchester. Until 1854 the three schools played each other during the first week of the summer holidays at Lords. That year

---

* Goodford apparently told them: 'As for [your wearing] the cap and gown, that is for you to decide. As for the boys shirking you, that is for them to decide.'

Winchester withdrew, and thereafter games were played in alternate years at Eton and Winchester. In 1856 and 1857, Goodford barred the Eton team from Lords (though boys in the XI who had left the School could play). The following year Goodford gave way, and two-day matches against Harrow were resumed. Harrow, which had revived strongly under Dr Vaughan as headmaster, were more successful because they played more professionally. There was no Master in charge of cricket, or indeed of any other sport at Eton. Only the swimming test was under Masters' control.

The quality of life for Etonians would seem to have changed. Fights were rarer; boys appear to have become kinder to each other. Swinburne, who left in 1853, had had an easier start than Shelley, but not trouble-free. He spent his time in School Library, acquiring a remarkable knowledge of Jacobean playwrights and writing three such plays himself.* William Johnson in his journal in 1854 noted, 'My chief luxuries were the soft sweetness of one [pupil], and the sweet piquant gaiety of another – two boys so unlike the boys of my time that I think I must have lived into another age.'[5] A certain piety had also taken hold, not from any headmasterly influence as at Rugby, but almost from below. John Coleridge Patteson, a nephew of Edward Coleridge and in his house, who left in 1845, had influenced boys by his example – even threatening to leave the XI unless the other boys improved their language. When Selwyn, Abraham and Patteson were all Bishops striving for Christianity in New Zealand and Polynesia,† some boys were unquestionably impressed, but one should not assume too much: the atmosphere in College Chapel remained lukewarm.

College tended to be a rougher place, even after the reforms, than at least the best Oppidan houses. 'If love be the foundation of morality, morality was entirely absent from our society,' wrote

---

* Swinburne may be best known these days for his obsession with flagellation. He clearly fantasized about it, but it seems very doubtful whether he was ever flogged at Eton. On the other hand he would have seen lower boys flogged, for the Lower Masters flogged boys in public in lower School. So Eton cannot be exempted from its part in the development of his perverted tastes. Possibly his parents recognized this: he left Eton early.

† Coley Patteson learnt Maori on the way to New Zealand, and then many Melanesian dialects. He taught his flocks 'as though they were Eton boys': having been treated as an individual at school, he thought it natural to treat the natives as individuals. He ended his life martyred on the island of Nukapu. The fatal club is preserved at Eton.

Oscar Browning, a Colleger of the 1850s.[6] Unfortunately also, relations between Collegers and Oppidans seem to have deteriorated at this time, although they were by now socially largely undistinguishable. One factor may have been that Collegers no longer needed sick-rooms in Dames' houses, and were less likely to have been Oppidans before they became Collegers. There was something of a tribal attitude, which was seldom broken until older Collegers might become friends of Oppidans, for example when playing games. Some Masters felt that the gowns which Collegers were obliged to wear were seriously regrettable. The gowns, and the white ties (symbols of academia) for all older boys, were the only uniform that the Head Master required. By now, however, boys were dressing in the London fashion approximating to the eventual School dress that became uniform at the end of the century. Small boys would wear short jackets and turned-down collars (but not white ties) until they felt that they had the status to move to more grown up dress.

No attempt was made by Goodford, any more than had been by his predecessors, to rationalize the bounds, or to end the requirement to shirk Masters when boys were theoretically out of bounds. In practice boys remained free to go where they wished, providing they did not get into trouble there. Conflicts with cads in Windsor continued, but were probably fewer than in Keate's time. The civility which boys individually cultivated might drain from them in a group. Boys might make friends with certain shopkeepers or boatmen; they would also be on familiar terms with the various salesmen who provided them with sock, to whom they might well owe money. In short, Etonians were very much a community in themselves which had an enormous impact on the locality, particularly from the money that they brought into it. Nevertheless, they were not in any sense ideal neighbours by present-day standards.

The College did make one neighbourly gesture in giving a site and some money towards the building of a new church for Eton town. There had been a chapel of ease since 1768, paid for by William Hetherington, the only Oppidan Fellow of the eighteenth century, and this was enlarged in 1819.* The new church opened in 1854, but

---

* In the 1980s, the Eton parish church was reconstructed after a period of desolation, to include a new sanatorium, a medical centre for the town, a number of flats, and a new chapel which, by coincidence, has more or less the same capacity as the original chapel of ease.

it was still technically only a chapel of ease served by College Chaplains, and Eton only became a proper parish with its own Vicar in 1875.[7] The neighbourly gesture was in fact a necessity, as the School's growth meant that even College Chapel now became full.

The Antechapel, which was restored in 1852, was soon to acquire stained glass windows commemorating forty-seven Old Etonians killed in the Crimean War – the first war memorial as such, though not quite the first memorial to an Etonian killed in battle, since Trevor Farquhar, who in 1846 charged to his death in India aged only 18, is also commemorated. In 1858, John Wilder extended his generosity, already manifested in College Chapel, to restoring College Hall in the gothic taste, with a higher pitched roof and a new west window.

Some eighty years later, Edward C. Mack – no friend of Eton – wrote:

Eton in the late forties and fifties was in a state of transition between the old system of freedom, idleness, vice and cruelty, and the new system of relative humanitarianism, morality, educational efficiency and conformity. One could, indeed, make out a good case for the fact that Eton in the fifties was in an ideal state. . . . Unfortunately one can reverse the proposition with equal truth. The new evils of standardization, vulgarization, and futile educational efficiency were creeping in, and existed side by side with many of the vices of the old order. Master severity, hostility between master and boy, idleness, bullying, cruel fagging, and snobbery towards Collegers were still in good part the order of the day.[8]

The truth certainly is that Eton was in a state of transition, but this was not seen at the time. As early as 1860, the calm was to be destroyed by a more serious revival of the attacks on the Public Schools, and Eton in particular, which led to the appointment of a Royal Commission. The strengths and weaknesses of Eton, not just in 1860, but seen with a longer perspective, will be reviewed in the final chapter. What can be said is that, judging by its popularity, Eton was a success with its own constituency. It was by now a school more tied to one particular class than at any time in its history, though its expansion meant that its ranks were never closed. As a school for the upper class it was to some extent matched by

Harrow, or, for those of a more earnest disposition, by Rugby; but the many new Public Schools of the time did not prevent Eton's growth. It pleased most Etonians, who led pleasant, perhaps insufficiently demanding, lives. Those few, such as the future Prime Minister, the Marquess of Salisbury, who disliked Eton, might still send their sons. Parents recognized that schooltime contemporaries and companions influence the character, and provide a network of friends. In favouring Eton they were not foolish.

CHAPTER FIFTEEN

Longer Perspectives

IN 1861 A Royal Commission was appointed to look into nine Public Schools,* and Eton clearly emerged as the most important. The term 'Public School' identified an endowed school open to boys from all over the country, and this was undoubtedly a distinctive feature of Eton from its foundation. At first the Collegers had to be from England, but Oppidans could at all times attend the School from all over the realm; and by 1860 they were coming from throughout the United Kingdom, with a few from outside. If there were perhaps disproportionate numbers undertaking the still exhausting and expensive journey from Ireland and Scotland, that was because of the shortage of comparable alternatives in their location. Distinctiveness was always a force: even in the fifteenth century there were local schools throughout England, at which boys could if necessary board, but the few schools that were national were seen to offer something extra – at first to the ambitious hoping for family advancement, and then, from the sixteenth century, even to aristocrats for their eldest sons. Eton retained its dominance except in the later seventeenth century and early eighteenth century, when Westminster was probably ahead in esteem. If the social range from which the boys came narrowed in the nineteenth century, it has certainly widened again since. Today boys come to Eton from all over the world, but are more likely to live in

* The Commission reported on seven schools, Eton, Winchester, Westminster, Charterhouse, Harrow, Rugby and Shrewsbury; they excused St Paul's and Merchant Taylors from their examinations.

the Thames Valley than at any time since the early days, and that is because parents are now less willing to part from their children than was once the case.

The Public Schools also saw themselves as independent. The Crown did have some control at Eton through the appointment of the Provost, but the Eton authorities did not feel it was for the State to intervene in its affairs. The 1818 Brougham enquiry had been resented, and the 1861 Public Schools Commission was similarly unwelcome. It showed Parliament prepared to legislate. Eton was also to find that university requirements were to curb its freedom, and even before 1860 the need for Mathematics at Cambridge had impinged on Eton's total autonomy. Nevertheless Eton still considers itself an independent school, and feels it is important, for example, to be able to offer oriental as well as classical languages. Today, as before 1860, the School can choose its curriculum according to what it believes to be useful and acceptable to parents.

The endowment of Public Schools created their independence, but also made responsible administration essential. The failure to use Henry VI's endowment properly is the greatest fault of pre-1860 Eton, and it also perhaps marks where twenty-first century Eton differs most substantially from its earlier self. In its first century, the uncertainties of its existence excuse shortcomings, but thereafter the stewardship of the College was self-interested. Fellows milked the revenues for themselves and their families, and they made very little attempt to improve conditions for those in their charge, though there were a few small acts of charity and individual cases of generosity.* Witness the sluggish development of Chalcots Farm, one of the two farms in north London which remained with the College after the Hospital of St James was appropriated by Henry VIII.[1] As early as 1796, the College had been told that the estate, 5 miles from London and adjoining a turnpike road, was very eligibly

---

* A number of Fellows of Eton, starting with Provost Bost in 1503, made individual charitable benefactions to Eton town. In the seventeenth century all such endowments connecting the College to Eton were gathered into what is known as the Poor's Estate, which for many years was principally used in supporting apprenticeships for the young; now it supplements old-age pensions. The town also benefits from the Baldwin's Bridge Trust, independent from the College, and from the Porny School and the Porny Trust. In addition the Fellows of Eton were early supporters of the Royal Humane Society and the Incorporated Church Building Society.

situated for building. In 1826 the College's solicitor induced the College to obtain a private estate Act to enable it to grant 99-year building leases on the Chalcots Estate, and to borrow to pay for projects such as roads and drains. Very little, however, happened.

The money raised by new leases, and even possibly by higher ground rents, did not attract the Provost and Fellows, since it would go into the central funds of the College. What the Fellows appreciated was the 7-year renewals of agricultural rents, with their accompanying fines; for example, in 1832 Chalcots contributed £2,500 in fines, to be shared among the Fellows themselves. Some building started about 1840. Yet with Bethell as Bursar, helped by an inconceivably unbusinesslike Registrar, Thomas Bacheldor, little was done until the College fortuitously met up with an energetic developer at the end of the 1840s. Even the building of a church, at that time an essential part of any middle-class development, was only reluctantly and parsimoniously supported by the College.* Chalcots was in due course to provide funds for building at Eton, after the reforms of the 1860s had ensured that any premiums for leases entered the College accounts. Nevertheless the situation in 1860 was that Eton was short of schoolrooms and dependent on private initiatives for any desirable investment. At least something had been done to improve conditions for the Collegers. Quite when they had begun to lag below what were regarded as civilized norms is unsure, certainly from the eighteenth century, when College was no longer full.

The Statutes provided for the appointment of a Bursar from among the Fellows to manage the College properties and to administer the College as originally conceived. When the School grew, the Bursar did not manage its finances; the Dames were responsible for their own businesses, leasing their buildings, furnishing them, feeding their boys, and so on, while the Head Master paid his Assistants. The Bursar's accounts were not adequately audited, as the Statutes required, and when, after reform, they were, his clerk proved to have been making small misappropriations. Now, by contrast, thanks to Parliament, the College is managed by a twelve-strong governing body, of whom ten are unpaid, headed by a Provost and Vice-Provost, who are certainly well housed and who

---

* Such corporate behaviour was general: the Dean and Chapter of Westminster Abbey did no better with their neighbouring estate. By now the College has very little property left at Chalcots.

receive small salaries, but who are expected to put more into Eton than they take from it. The present Bursar who, with his supporting staff, is responsible for the School as well as the College, was trained for the job at Business School. The latest big project of the College (a rowing lake) was assessed with the most sophisticated techniques, and is for the benefit of young people over the south of England, not just Etonians.

Besides the endowments which provided the College income, the College has a very different wealth in its buildings and its collections. Though additions to the buildings were made spasmodically, and generally inadequately, some conservation work was also undertaken, notably in the middle of the nineteenth century. Although the results can be criticized, Eton in 1860 did present itself as a harmonious architectural whole. Notable collections of books, silver and paintings were built up, which owed little to the Fellows. The marvellous College Library was used as a setting for entertaining distinguished visitors, rather than as a resource for the boys or for the interested public, as is now so far as possible the case. The College archives, today available to researchers, were in a terrible state, and many documents were perhaps destroyed by William Roberts, Vice-Provost in Goodall's time, and son of Provost Roberts. At the end of 1859, Hawtrey was lamenting, 'There has been a very general Observance of the System of Higgledy Piggledy which seems to have been – not for years, but for centuries – the Rule with Regard to Papers and Parchments.'[2] It cannot be claimed that the Fellows took seriously their role as responsible trustees for the treasures in their care.

Before 1860 the Fellows were almost entirely conservative; those few, like Sir Henry Savile, who realized that Eton could aspire to greater things, were exceptional. When the link between King's and Eton was strongest, the poverty of new ideas was greatest. In 1857, however, the privileged positions of King's within Cambridge, and of Eton at King's, changed. To the credit of King's, the initiatives came from that College: its members began to participate in University examinations, and it opened its doors to non-Etonians while preserving twenty-four scholarships for Etonians.[3] Okes, the former Lower Master, was the reforming Provost of King's. William Johnson was the leading younger member of the Committee of Seven who brought about the changes. Up to that point King's had only twelve undergraduates a year, but had won more classical prizes than any other College except the vastly larger Trinity – a tribute to the rising standard of College at Eton. With King's taking Mathematics more seriously, Eton had to do so. One hundred years on, however, the scholarships had gone, and it was almost impossible for even the ablest Etonians to get into King's, and they stopped trying. Happily, Etonians once again go to King's, particularly if they are musical. The historic connection is preserved by the automatic appointment of the Provost of King's to be Senior Fellow of Eton.

One manifestation of the King's link was in the closed shop for the recruitment of Eton Masters, but this was slow to develop. Neither the Head Master nor the Usher were automatically from King's until the eighteenth century, and even then Dr Barnard, the outstanding figure, was a notable exception. At times the Fellows set great store upon Henry VI's Statutes, but their observation of them was fitful. Inevitably, a document of the fifteenth century could not remain binding; nevertheless, when it served the Fellows' interests they claimed its authority, but when economic interests worked differently they would change their attitude. By the nineteenth century, Head Masters were rich men; though their stipends remained small, and their expenses, if they were generously minded, could be large, many unauthorized payments had evolved over the years. By 1860 boys were paying 6 guineas p.a. to the Head Master, with an entry fee of 5 guineas, doubled for noblemen, and they were expected to give a leaving present of £10. Collegers would not be made to pay, but could choose to do so. The Head Master's income might amount to over £4,000, approximating to £200,000 p.a. today. (One merit, now fashionable, was that there was an element of payment by results.)

The Lower Master received 4 guineas entry fee and 6 guineas a year from lower boys, again doubled for sons of the titled. Out of his income he had to pay each of the Assistant Masters who taught in the Lower School £30 p.a. The Lower Master took in about £1,000 a year, but he also boarded boys to whom he acted as Tutor; his total income would have varied around £3,000 p.a. Incidentally parents paid less for lower boys than for upper boys, because they did not have Private Business with Tutors, and yet, at 20–1, they had a boy-to-Master ratio in their classes about half what it was in the Upper School.

Assistant Masters were not provided for in the Statutes, and it is uncertain when they appeared at Eton, though they were known to exist by the end of the seventeenth century, their stipends paid by the Head Master. These were quickly supplemented by the fees received for tutoring boys and, by the end of the eighteenth century, income from boarding boys. In 1860 the 42 guineas for teaching was augmented by 10 guineas from each pupil, or 20 guineas if a pupil received Private Business, as most boys did. (Collegers were not charged for Private Business.) Something like £45 p.a. profit could be made for boarding a boy. (Tutors made an all-in charge of £120 for boarding and tuition; Dames were less expensive at £84, but their boys also needed to pay for a Tutor.) Again the Assistant Masters were rewarded according to their success. A popular Tutor might have eighty pupils, but the average in 1860 was nearer forty and, indeed, Dr Goodford was limiting newly appointed Masters to forty pupils. A Classical Master with forty pupils, and boarding thirty boys, would still have an income of £2,000 p.a. Although Masters did not have pensions, the great majority who were in orders could hope to be Fellows or to move to a College living.*

Thus the Masters at Eton had grown to affluence. From the Head Master downwards, their real incomes are today only about half what they were. Inflation has had some effect, but the change in the ratio of boys to each Master is more responsible. Those Masters who were at all conscientious worked extremely hard, even though they did not expect to take any part in out-of-school activities, and their disciplinary duties, outside boys' houses, were limited to Chapel and occasional other policing, for example, at the time of the Windsor Fair. The rewards available explain why appointment to Eton was so attractive to Kingsmen. The Eton authorities defended the closed shop by the argument that only those bred in the system would fully realize the great advantage of combining discipline with as much liberty and independence as possible for the boys. Nevertheless, entry to these coveted academic posts was limited, and the average quality of Masters was inevitably lowered. The School could perfectly well have recruited widely, possibly giving some weight to an Eton background if that was indeed thought to be an advantage. There are now Masters at Eton with

---

* A charity known as the Schoolmasters' Society originated in 1798 at Eton, and it has always been very much supported by Eton Masters. It supplied pensions to less rich schoolmasters and their widows. Today it is more widely based and supports schoolmistresses too.

varied origins, and if anything the number of Old Etonians is inconveniently small.

The shortage of Masters and the nature of the pay encouraged Masters to attach particular importance to their tutorial work. Teaching in class was poorly rewarded, and with such meagre facilities and such large numbers to be taught, the best chances of communicating was in Pupil Room – and that work earned far more income. Some critics argued that tutorial work meant much duplication: why work through construes in Pupil Room and in class? Why have exercises corrected by a Tutor and looked over by the Division Master, the practice introduced by Keate to spur on Bethell and other weak Tutors? Yet the atmosphere in Pupil Room could be very different from that in any large class. Oscar Browning could write of 'the paradise of my tutor's pupil room';[4] he was lucky enough to be with William Johnson. Private Business enabled a Tutor to range outside the narrow syllabus, and sometimes bred a warm relationship between Master and boy which was not always recognized by those outside Eton. Over the years Eton evolved what was for many its principal glory: 'the tutorial system'.* This flourished for another century, but has lately been diminished, as the pressures of exams over widening ranges of subjects have eroded the time for tutorial work, and broken the common basis which was essential to justify Pupil Room as a daily routine. There are still Tutors to provide continuing academic guidance, and they still preside over Private Business, but with other schools imitating some aspects of Etonian practice, the tutorial system is no longer a distinctive feature.

The curriculum was almost exclusively classical over the four hundred years, but the educational role attributed to the Classics changed. At first Latin was studied for utilitarian reasons; it was the language for priests and professional men. At the same time the command of grammar was seen as a training in orderly thought. In the sixteenth century the literary merits of the classical authors was acknowledged, and Greek entered the curriculum alongside Latin. There were probably Masters to the end of our period who regarded classical writing as unsurpassed and they saw Eton as a training ground for good taste. Yet there certainly was an awareness that the best of English literature did indeed measure up to the Classics.

---

* Harrow also had a tutorial system, but it never developed as fully as at Eton.

Perseverance with the Classics was, however, justified because they were difficult, and their study provided a mental discipline which the study of English did not.

The linguistic side of the Classics was given great importance, and analytical skills, which are certainly of immense value, were developed by the emphasis on 'derivations'. It was however, regrettable, that by the nineteenth century the *Eton Latin Grammar* was definitely outdated; Dr Kennedy from Shrewsbury had produced a better Grammar and was training better scholars. On the literary side, critics attacked the small range of authors read by the boys and the emphasis on anthologies rather than on complete works; only the Head Masters' lessons in Greek tragedy for the Sixth Form really aspired high. However, by the end of the period Private Business gave Tutors a chance, for example, to cover whole books of Homer. Again the quantity of Saying Lessons was criticized; learning by heart had been essential before printing and cheaper paper, and there was probably an element of conservatism in the continuation. Such lessons can be most educational if boys learn to speak well and with feeling, but one doubts whether, in the oversized divisions, this could often be achieved; classical tags so acquired could, however, be used in civilized debate, notably in Parliament. Even more harshly criticized was the Eton emphasis on writing Verses. Certainly even the volumes *Musae Etonenses* added little to the world's wealth of literature, let alone the average production in Pupil Room. More significantly, many boys undoubtedly secured help, either legitimately from their Tutor or illegitimately from a brighter student. Yet for those who did at least struggle, fitting words to the necessary scansion was a useful exercise in problem-solving. William Johnson also claimed that it is important to give boys an experience of authorship.

Etonians emerged from their narrowly classical world with some idea of how language works: teachers of modern languages today acknowledge that the study of the European languages, and perhaps others, is facilitated by a classical grounding. Etonians in the eighteenth and nineteenth century also wrote a competent latinate English, to judge from magazines and letters, but perhaps they would have benefited from a bigger injection of the more demotic Authorized Version into their consciousness. Nevertheless, the modern Etonian seldom matches their command and accuracy. His Classics aim more to give a rounded picture of the Greek and

Roman world; Verses and Saying Lessons have died along with those who were educated in the old style, and grammar is acquired more as a precondition to appreciation of literature than as an end in itself.

One should not disregard the minority subjects that came and went, usually as voluntary studies. Henry Tarver, who was teaching French in 1861, having first assisted and then replaced his father, charged 10 guineas a year for his tuition, and the number of boys taking French at the end of our period varied either side of a hundred. His standing in the School was not good, and he famously described himself as an 'objet de luxe'.[5] Generally speaking, the Classical Masters felt that there was insufficient time to teach French in the full curriculum. Edward Coleridge also believed that there was something in the disposition of English boys, especially of Etonians, so utterly repugnant to Frenchmen that French could not be taught in class, and Provost Hawtrey, for all his own familiarity with French and with Frenchmen, sadly agreed.[6] French was, however, the most popular extra subject because it was the most useful of the modern languages.

Mathematics, the basis of so much other learning, and the best training in logical thought, was the most serious curricular omission. Even its introduction under Stephen Hawtrey, as what would now be called an 'independent profit centre', was inadequate. Etonians could be amateurs of Science and surprisingly many were, but they were badly placed to become physicists or chemists, and they were certainly not trained to be entrepreneurs. However, in the first half of the seventeenth century it would seem that some Mathematics was taught to Boyle, and William Oughtred, whose father had taught Etonians writing, became a distinguished mathematician and Fellow of Eton. Medicine was also a fairly common career for early Etonians, but that would have required little basic scientific training. The rejection of Mathematics for so long was partly snobbish; Eton and other Public Schools offered 'a liberal education': that is, not technical nor professional but 'becoming a gentleman' as Johnson's Dictionary put it. This was, indeed, a move away from the objectives of the Founder, for though his 'poor scholars' were not from among the poorest they were certainly to work for their living. In practice most Etonians did need to earn, and both they and the country would have benefited from their acquisition of a wider mental training. Nowadays, of course, all

Etonians expect to work, and are intended by the School to be both numerate and abreast of Information Technology.

It is a pity that Music and Art were not more enthusiastically supported, not least as creative use of boys' leisure. Eton was probably ahead of any other school in offering Art at all, but only about thirty boys would take lessons with William Evans. Music, so dear to the Founder's heart, and so glorious before the Reformation, had sadly declined. From the Commonwealth period the independent Eton Choir gradually withered, and thus even church music was only provided by the St George's Choir (to which, admittedly, the College contributed financially). Boys who wished to learn an instrument needed to make their own arrangements in Windsor. In 1860 Eton music was on the verge of resurrection, but it was the boys themselves rather than the authorities who brought this about.

It is indeed true, as critics of Eton claimed, that in 1860 Etonians lived easy and pleasant lives, and that most were singularly idle. This was apparently not so in the earliest days, when boys were at work very early in the morning and must have gone tired to bed; there was free time, but it was limited. Over the years the hours were relaxed, one suspects as much at the inclination of the Masters as in any search for educational improvement. From the eighteenth century, boys' leisure grew, and with it the possibility of idleness. We should nevertheless remember that there was also the possibility of self-education. One hour spent voluntarily acquiring new knowledge is worth two hours on tested curriculum and three hours on an A-level module. The best Etonians did educate themselves. Interestingly, but perhaps typically and not to be taken too seriously, Edward Coleridge was in 1861 lamenting the declining appetite among Etonians for English literature. In Keate's time the boys used to devour every new poem from Scott, Southey or Byron; there had been a rush to get the first copies of the latter's *Corsair*. Many used to read Dante and other Italian authors, but by 1860 it was doubtful how many of the 800 boys had read the plays of Shakespeare.[7] And by 2000? Time wasted by some is perhaps an inevitable price to pay for time used profitably by others. What is certain is that modern Eton offers a much greater variety of ways to use time to one's advantage.

The nature of boys being what it is, schools should doubtless try to bias them towards virtuous choices; but whether Eton did this effectively must remain highly debatable, particularly as free time expanded. There were too few Masters to be adequate policemen. In the sixteenth century, praepostors may have acted as prefects, and Eton Masters took a prefectorial system with them to other schools, Dr James to eighteenth-century Rugby and a series of Eton Masters to Harrow. But by 1800 the idea that boys should discipline juniors responsibly had died at Eton. Possibly Dr Foster was to blame. The relative wealth of Etonians made a variety of temptations available to them, which were beyond the reach of others. Dr Keate was one of the many schoolmasters to write to parents urging them not to lavish money on their sons.

It is also arguable that the Eton system of punishment was ineffective, indeed wrong. The emphasis on corporal punishment in the old days was natural, given inherited opinion, a feeling that original sin had to be driven out, and the difficulties of alternative sanctions; writing lines was really not an economic possibility, even though, later, writing lines did become standard. Extra Absences, too, were a form of restriction, which might have worked more effectively had the Head Master had an office to which a boy could be obliged to report, for example. Too much reliance by far, however, was placed on flogging. It was wrong not because most boys minded, but because they did not, and because it was less alarming to be flogged for the tenth time than for the first. That said, there was some case for saying it was more forgivable to flog a young aristocrat than any other English boy; his self-esteem might be usefully dented, and the English upper class proved to be less susceptible to feelings of slighted personal honour than European grandees.

The distinction between what was sinful, what was an offence against rules, and what was incompetence was often inadequately drawn. All might be visited by a flogging. At least at Eton not too much weight was attached to sin; if Dr Arnold tended to regard an offence as sin, Dr Keate tended to regard sin as simply an offence, and boys did not for instance, believe that he minded them lying. Perhaps that is the healthier attitude when dealing with the young. Similarly, though Etonians were often punished excessively for unintended inadequacies, for example in preparing work, they did sometimes learn that competence and proper organization are useful, and that, with sufficient care, failures can be reduced.

A school such as Eton is above all a community, and many parents sent sons to Eton just because they felt that the boys would live in a microcosm of the real world with many of its problems. They would have to get along with their fellows, and they would have to cope with difficulties similar to some of those they would meet on a larger scale later. Day boys missed out on full membership of this community. Fitzjames and Leslie Stephen were unhappy at Eton and made few friends because their father took a house in Windsor to permit them to live out; Dr Hawtrey had wrongly advised that there was nothing against this course.[8] Fitzjames Stephen later sent his son J.K. Stephen to College, where he became a schoolboy hero, his memory as a player of the Wall Game revered to this day. Day boys, never numerous, were vanishing by 1860.

The fagging system was in a certain sense the cement of the community, bringing young boys into contact with the old and making the concept of service familiar. One suspects that it probably emerged in College soon after the foundation. The Oppidans lived together in smaller groups, received more attention from their Dames, and in some cases (the Boyles, for example), had servants or personal tutors sent from home. Probably the mid-eighteenth century boom in numbers encouraged fagging. Even in 1860, fagging in College was more arduous than fagging among Oppidans. It was attacked by critics of Eton on three main grounds: it was degrading for boys to do menial service; it was oppressive and cruel to the young; it encouraged the wrong attitudes in the fagmasters. Sir Edward Creasy, who wrote a historical sketch of Eton in 1848, and who had been a Colleger, rightly dismissed the first argument – it could hardly be more desirable that those who were going to employ servants should learn that service need not be degrading if requests are properly made and thanks rendered. He argued that it was not cruel to the fag, and that the fagmaster did offer protection. This was certainly often true, but there always seem to have been ugly exceptions. Creasy was on his weakest ground in arguing that the life of a fagmaster was not corrupting; to be waited on so assiduously so young sapped the will to self-help, and encouraged some abuse of power in requesting the unreasonable (for instance fagging to buy from technically out-of-bounds shops).[9]

Fagging was also associated in the public mind with bullying, and there were occasional bullies among the fagmasters; but bullying was more frequently by boys a year or two older than their victims, or by physically stronger contemporaries. Unfortunately at a certain age boys are apt to think they are almost doing a kindness by punishing someone a little different. One cannot be confident that at any time in Eton's history bullying did not exist, and probably some parents would always say that it was good for their sons to receive some unfair knocks. It is hard to think of anything constructive that arose from bullying, though doubtless there were boys who were suddenly ashamed by the awareness of what they had been doing, and determined to be kinder in future. John Chandos, who has studied the Public Schools in the period 1800–60, thinks that Eton was alone free of what he calls 'quasi official atrocity', a sort of hallowed collective tyranny.[10] The nearest that Eton came to this was perhaps in the habit of hitting boys over the head with books as they went up the stairs to Upper School for the first time on reaching Fourth Form. The number of boys who stayed only a short time at Eton was higher than it would be now.* This was partly the natural consequences of there not being much in the way of an initial selection process, but one guesses that sometimes parents removed sons who just could not cope with the hostility of their fellows.

It would be naive to assume that other forms of sin were absent. Lying and petty theft, for example of school books or hats, were doubtless common. Major theft, on the other hand, such as Hoseason fell into, was not countenanced by School authority or by the boys. Sexual immorality was taken more lightly during the eighteenth century than the nineteenth, and it was not regarded very seriously by Etonian parents until mid-Victorian times. There was certainly no sex education, unless Tutors were enlightened enough to include some words in the course of preparation for Confirmation. The view that young boys learnt from their elders probably has substance – and this was an argument used against fagging, though the logic was less convincing.

By 1860, critics were saying that games played too large a part at Eton. Yet there was an amazing absence of that tyranny of sport

* The school lists with annotations were compiled by Chetwynd Talbot every third year from 1791 to 1859. After each list he names boys who had not arrived at the time of the previous list, but had gone by this one; there might be forty in such an intermediate list. There was certainly far more flexibility about the timing of a school career than there would be now, and some might deliberately spend only two years at Eton before moving on to university, just as others might leave early but honourably for the navy. Nevertheless one suspects that perhaps ten boys a year might leave as misfits, or be expelled.

found in later public school life. Boys could walk and botanize, or they could read. No game was compulsory, and at all times in Eton's history until recently games were always for the boys to organize. Given the difficulties of moving outside Eton, it is natural that Etonians developed a number of games unique to the School. It was also largely inevitable that rowing and cricket, at which boys could be matched with outsiders, acquired a special prestige. If the School is to be criticized for any consistent failure, it was in offering too few games facilities to deter more boys from less legitimate activities. When this situation was reversed, towards the end of the nineteenth century, criticism from the intellectual camp grew even stronger, but could not stand in the way of the ever-growing public obsession with games.

It has to be said that the history of religion at Eton has also followed the tide of public opinion. Henry VI would be more horrified by what took place in Chapel, and indeed by the absence of daily services, than by any other development to his College. Considering that power was almost always in the hands of ordained clergy, such a dismal record might be thought surprising. The Reformation ended Henry's conception of a religious power house and left in its place Waynflete's School. Subsequent religious disputes probably had less effect than the long apathy that followed in the eighteenth century. By 1860, opinion was ripe for revival of daily services and of the Choir; but that was not to last. All that one can say is that Eton today retains more corporate worship than most educational institutions, and that its services seek to be adapted to the young, without descent into populism. As for the boys, Victorian piety is gone and Regency paganism returned; but even today, as two hundred years ago, individual boys still stand out as witnesses to Christianity.

If we seek to estimate the influence of Eton over the centuries, we need to think about Etonians who achieved prominence, and to ask how their education coloured their development. Obviously genetic and social inheritance was vastly significant, and some would argue that, given the class system, any school or no school would have done as well as Eton. Not so; the long succession of political leaders nurtured at Eton owed much to the self-reliance and independence bred at Eton. Variety of opinion was, and is, tolerated. If Etonians were largely Royalist and Tory, they were nevertheless willing to question authority; Gladstone even thought that the boo was valuable – 'it gave us a sense of our national privilege of disagreeing with constituted authority'.[11] Fitzjames and Leslie Stephen praised the absence of religious cant. Given the role that Etonians were to play in the government of India, tolerance and the restraint of missionary zeal can also be seen as useful Eton contributions.* Furthermore, Etonians were never remote from the real world; they were constantly – if technically illegally – in Windsor, and even when trading insults, or exchanging fisticuffs, they learned something of life at large.

What of the lesser Etonians? It would seem that most recognized that they too had learnt something of value. No doubt nostalgia influenced the seventeenth-century gatherings of former Etonians, as it has their successors. The readiness of old boys to yield to uncritical sentiment was often acknowledged by those working at Eton. In the 1850s, old men were shaking their heads because fights had become uncommon; how would Britain fare at a new Waterloo, if there were no longer 'mills' on the playing fields? William Johnson reports old Etonians worried that 'the dear old place' was turning into a 'knowledge-shop', an anxiety that has been expressed many times since. Yet behind the sentiment lies an appreciation of the real benefits which were assimilated almost unconsciously: the beauty of the place, the warmth of lasting friendships, self-awareness. In 1861 *The Times* attributed Eton's success to the training it provided: 'The knowledge of how to give and take, how to bear and forbear, how to keep faith, deal honourably, and act with courage.' It added: 'what the boys learn, they learn mostly from each other'.[12] The wisest Masters recognized this: they too were increasingly often repaid for the care and affection that they devoted to their best pupils by the lasting warmth returned by their charges.

---

* Wellesley, and later Curzon, were perhaps the outstanding Etonian rulers of India, and they displayed what hostile critics regard as Etonian arrogance. Both, however, were notable administrators, who openly acknowledged their debt to Eton. So too did the admirable Metcalfe.

Glossary

Absence   A roll-call, by which boys prove their presence.

The Bill   The list of boys required to see the Head Master. A *complaint* made of a boy by an Assistant Master would lead to a boy being placed *in the Bill*.

Block   Boys to be birched knelt on a wooden block, similar to a mounting block used to get onto a horse.

Brosier   To eat a Dame's larder bare.

Cad   A townsman.

Chambers   The Head Master's Chambers in the corner of School Yard approximated to his office. Masters would meet together there.

Church   The designation of the Chapel before the Commonwealth.

Colleger   A boy on the Foundation, in theory one of seventy.

Con   A best friend.

Conduct   A priest hired to read the services in Chapel.

Construe   A passage set for translation.

Dames   Ladies who kept boarding houses for Oppidans.

Derivations   Description of the grammatical function of a word; identification of the root form from which it comes. Another term for parsing.

Domine   A man who kept a boarding house, possibly a teacher of an extra subject.

Election   The process of choosing boys from College to fill vacancies at King's, and of choosing boys to fill the consequent vacancies in College. Also used to describe the time when this occurred.

Field Game   An eleven-a-side game originating in the open fields around Eton – one of the precursors of Association Football.

First Fault   Boys could ask the Lower Master or Head Master for remission of punishment for a first offence.

The Foundation   Those with a particular position in the Statutes, as opposed to Assistant Masters or Oppidans.

Fourth of June   King George III's birthday, which became a day of celebration.

Half   A term. The word, adopted when there were only two breaks in the school year, was retained when three holiday breaks became the rule.

King's Scholars   Collegers. The identification KS came into use in the reign of George III.

Leave   Permission to be absent from Eton, granted at parents' requests.

Leaving books   Given to friends on leaving, as mementoes.

Leaving money   Given to the Head Master on leaving.

Lock-up   When boys are required to be in their houses, unless they have permission.

Messing   The habit of a few friends eating tea or breakfast together in a boy's room.

Montem   An annual celebration at a hillock in Slough, originally in January. It became an occasion for collecting *salt*, i.e. money used to finance a Colleger at King's. Later it became a triennial festival in early summer.

Mr   Used formally to identify sons of peers.

Oppidan   A boy who is not a Colleger – originally one living in the town.

Passing   The swimming test, introduced in 1840, which had to be passed before a boy was allowed to boat on the river.

Poena   A punishment, generally by writing lines.

Pop   The Eton Society, a debating society.

Praepostors   Boys appointed to carry out a prefectorial role, or such administrative duties as checking absentees from school.

Prayers   The religious assemblies held on Sunday afternoons, known to boys in Keate's time as '*Prose*'; by the middle of the nineteenth century prayers were held in houses to mark the end of the day.

Private Business   Tutorial periods held informally by Tutors in their studies.

Pupil Room   The room in which a Tutor had his pupils working under supervision and hence the activity of working with the Tutor.

Remove   The intermediate block between the Fourth Form and Fifth Form. Boys also spoke of gaining a remove when they were promoted.

Sap   To study industriously.

Saying Lesson   Recitation of a memorized text, normally in Latin.

The Schoolmaster   The original designation of the Head Master.

Schools School periods.

Sent up for Good A boy was sent with outstanding work, normally in Latin verse composition, to the Head Master. The honour three times gained secured a prize.

Sent up for Play As above: the whole School was rewarded by a half-holiday.

Shirking The requirement for a boy in the High Street or Windsor to go through the motions of evading a Master (or member of the Sixth Form).

Sixth Form Once there ceased to be a Seventh Form, this comprised the senior Collegers and Oppidans, eventually ten of each.

Sock Food and drink.

Speeches Recitations by boys in the Sixth Form to the Provost and distinguished guests at Electiontide, and on other occasions.

Staying out Missing school through illness.

Sunday Questions Work on a religious theme to be written on Sunday and shown up on Monday.

Taking leave Bidding a formal farewell to the Head Master.

Torn over Unsatisfactory written work to be repeated by the boy.

Trials The examinations held in the lower parts of the School, by which boys obtained promotion.

Tug A derogatory name for a Colleger, perhaps from *toga*, the Latin for a gown.

Tutor The Master responsible for a boy's work. Parents might send boys with a private tutor, recruited outside Eton, to supervise work and conduct.

Usher A term for an Assistant Master. Originally *The Usher* was the Lower Master in charge of the lowest three forms.

Verses The composition of Latin and Greek verses.

The Visitor The Bishop of Lincoln, ultimately responsible for the observation of the Statutes and the Christian conduct of the School.

Wall Game A game of football originating alongside the wall between College Field and the Slough Road.

Source Notes

Anyone writing about the earlier history of Eton College has the great advantage of building on the work of a number of admirable historians. I have treated as generally reliable first Sir Henry Maxwell-Lyte, and secondly Sir Wasey Sterry and R.A. Austen-Leigh, who have written short biographies of as many Etonians as they could track down; also Austen-Leigh and H.E.C. Stapylton have published school lists from 1678, the date of the earliest-known school list, to the end of the period. It has not seemed useful to provide source notes for each reference, since they are easily checked. College Records, Inventories and Manuscripts are all housed in College Library.

Abbreviations

COLL/INV: College Inventories
ECR: Eton College Records
ETA: *Etoniana*

Notes to Chapter 1

I have relied mainly on *Henry VI* by B.P. Wolffe for the historical setting, and on Nicholas Orme's *English Schools in the Middle Ages* for the educational background. Bishop Radford in the 1930s wrote an *Early History of Eton*, which is printed in *Etoniana*, nos 68–96. The Bishop gives no reference, but does include material not in Maxwell-Lyte.

1. J.R. Lander, quoted in Watts *King Henry VI and the Politics of Kingship* p. 103.
2. ECR 59.
3. ECR 39/78.
4. ECR 39/64.
5. Orme 'Schoolmasters 1307–1509' in *Profession, Vocation and Culture in Later Medieval England* p. 219.

6. ECR 39/3.

7. Birley 'Vostre Royal College' repr. in B. Rees (ed.) *History and Idealism* p. 6.

8. COLL/INV/1 (1445); COLL/INV/4 (1465).

9. Birley op. cit. p. 17.

10. ECR 39/78.

11. Saltmarsh *King's College* p. 6.

12. ECR 60/1/1.

13. Eton MS 300.

14. ETA no. 51.

15. ECR 39/60.

16. Griffiths *The Reign of King Henry VI* p. 492.

17. J. Gairdner (ed.) *Paston Papers* I p. 315.

18. Four collections are deposited in the British Museum.

19. See Watts op. cit. and K.F. Selway The Role of Eton College and King's College, Cambridge in the Polity of the Lancastrian Monarchy.

Notes to Chapter 2

1. ECR 39/124.

2. Birley 'Vostre Royal College' p. 14.

3. Martindale *The Early History of the Choir of Eton College Chapel.*

4. ETA nos. 125, 126 for the story of Jane Shore.

5. Gairdner (ed.) op. cit. III pp. 237–42.

6. ETA no. 39.

Notes to Chapter 3

I have relied on Joan Simon's *Education and Society in Tudor England* for the educational background.

1. Eton MS 178.

2. Williamson The Eton Choir Book: its institutional and historical background.

3. ETA no. 12.

4. ETA no. 9.

5. Orme op. cit. p. 224.

6. Hexter 'The Education of the Aristocracy in the Renaissance' in *Reappraisals in History* pp. 50–5.

7. ECR 62/3.

Notes to Chapter 4

1. Translated in ETA no. 36.
2. ECR 62/4.
3. Eton MS 272a.
4. Maxwell-Lyte *History of Eton College* pp. 156, 157.
5. Birley *The History of College Library* p. 18.

Notes to Chapter 5

1. For Hales, see Birley 'The Ever-Memorable John Hales'.
2. Lambeth MS DCLXIII p. 13, quoted in Maxwell-Lyte op. cit. p. 200.
3. Eton MS 272b, c, d.
4. For Boyle, see Birley 'Robert Boyle at Eton'.
5. Benson *Fasti Etonenses* p. 75.

Notes to Chapter 6

1. Dexter The Provision of Choral Music at St George's Chapel, Windsor Castle and Eton College c1640–1733.
2. Sterry *The Annals of Eton College* pp. 132, 133.

Notes to Chapter 7

1. Rawlinson quoted by Sterry in *The Eton College Register* p. xxiv.
2. Maxwell-Lyte op. cit. p. 263.
3. Pepys *Diary* 26 Feb 1666.
4. ETA no. 31.
5. ETA no. 11.
6. ETA no. 68.
7. ETA no. 46.
8. ETA no. 64.
9. ETA no. 57.
10. ETA no. 14.
11. ETA no. 115.

Notes to Chapter 8

1. ETA no. 124.
2. Maxwell-Lyte op. cit. p. 286.

3. Fielding *Tom Jones*, Introduction to the 13th Book.
4. Dexter op. cit. pp. 67, 152.
5. T. Mowl *Horace Walpole* p. 53.
6. ETA no. 34.
7. W. Cole MS XLVII f. 213.
8. ETA nos. 75–80.
9. ETA no. 31. Hugget, the Conduct, was himself a difficult man.
10. Birley *The History of College Library* p. 40.
11. Ballance *A Town Called Eton* p. 51.

Notes to Chapter 9

1. ETA no. 87. See also ETA nos. 18, 19.
2. ETA no. 109.
3. My thanks to my colleague G. Fussey who brought this to my attention.
4. ETA nos. 7, 8.
5. ETA nos. 4, 10, 14, 111. Eton MS 349.

Notes to Chapter 10

1. ETA nos. 46, 56.
2. COLL/P11/1.
3. ETA no. 22.
4. ETA no. 123.
5. ETA no. 54.
6. ETA no. 91.

Notes to Chapter 11

The Diary of Miss Margaretta Brown is invaluable, also many recollections of Eton at the time and letters printed in ETA. These may not be quoted, but provide a confirmation of events.

1. ETA no. 33.
2. Eton MS 422/6.
3. ETA nos. 83, 84, for example.
4. Collins *Etonians Ancient and Modern* p. 113.
5. ECR ED/165.

6. ECR ED/165/2.
7. ETA no. 29, Maxwell-Lyte op. cit. p. 40.
8. Tucker *Eton of Old; or Eighty Years since 1811–1822* pp. 203, 204.
9. ECR ED/9/1.
10. ECR ED/9/6.
11. Wilkinson *Reminiscences of Eton (in Keate's Time)* pp. 32–40.
12. Letter of 3 Sept 1828. ECR/Keate papers.
13. *Eton Abuses considered in a letter to the author of Some Remarks on the Present Studies and Management of Eton School* (1834).
14. Mack *Public Schools and British Opinion* p. 90.
15. Doyle *Reminiscences and Opinions.* p. 49.

Notes to Chapter 12

1. ETA nos. 117–120.
2. For Milnes Gaskell, see Gaskell *An Eton Boy* or ETA nos. 59–66.
3. ETA no. 29 (Recollection of Lord Monson).
4. Austen-Leigh *Eton College Register* 1753–90 p. xxxix.
5. Gladstone, *Diaries* I 29 January–1 February 1827.
6. Letter to Charles Gordon, 4 August 1805.
7. Eton MS 422.
8. Byrne and Churchill *The Eton Book of the River*; also Selwyn, translated by E. Warre.
9. ETA no. 119.
10. ETA no. 65.
11. Doyle op. cit. p. 50.
12. Collins op. cit. pp. 182–93.
13. Charles Golightly's journal in ETA no. 51.
14. ETA no. 122 has a useful summary of Gladstone in the Eton Society.
15. ETA no. 95.
16. ETA no. 122.
17. ETA no. 18.
18. Disraeli *Coningsby* Book 1. Gladstone thought this the best description of Eton in his time.
19. ETA no. 19.
20. Miss Brown's Diary 9 May 1826.
21. Benson op. cit. p. 503.
22. ETA no. 52.
23. For Hoseason's melancholy career see Miss Brown's Diary vols XXX to XXXIX (ETA nos. 77–85). There are also references in Milnes Gaskell and Bishop Chapman's notes in ETA no. 53.

Notes to Chapter 13

1. F.C. Burnand *My Time, and What I've Done with it*, ch. xx.
2. ETA no. 11.
3. Coleridge *Eton in the Forties by an Old Colleger* p. 6.
4. Brinsley Richards *Seven Years at Eton* pp. 394–5.
5. ETA nos. 37, 67, 101 and 117–19.
6. Oswald Smith *Memoirs*.
7. ECR ED/159.
8. Gambier Parry *Annals of an Eton House* pp. 25–42.
9. Smith op. cit.
10. William Johnson to his brother 15 March 1845.
11. Johnson to his father 20 January 1845.
12. Johnson to his father 30 September 1845.
13. Johnson to his mother 7 May 1846.
14. Miss Brown's Diary 30 September 1834.
15. Maxwell-Lyte op. cit. p. 443.

Notes to Chapter 14

1. Public Schools Report para 3689.
2. ETA no. 81.
3. Johnson to his father 21 January 1853.
4. Brinsley Richards op. cit. pp. 127–8.
5. Johnson Journal.
6. Browning *Memories of Sixty Years at Eton, Cambridge and Elsewhere*, p. 18.
7. Ballance op. cit. pp. 68–9.
8. Mack op. cit. pp. 369–71.

Notes to Chapter 15

1. F.M.L. Thompson *Hampstead, Building a Borough 1650–1964* (1974).
2. ETA no. 122.
3. King's *Report of Committee of Seven* (1857) (KC OB/2/-). Its first recommendation is a well-argued case for ending Eton exclusivity.
4. Browning op. cit. p. 18.
5. Public Schools Report para. 7025.
6. Ibid. para. 3739; paras 3748, 9.
7. Ibid. paras 3748, 9.
8. N. Annan, *Leslie Stephen* (1951) p. 18.

9. Creasy *Some Account of the Foundation of Eton College and of the Past and Present Conditions of the School* pp. 64–9.
10. J. Chandos *Boys Together* p. 83.
11. Benson op. cit. p. 499.
12. 30 April 1861.

Select Bibliography

Unpublished Sources

Eton College Records (ECR)
Letters and Journals of William Johnson (Eton MS 308)
Diary of Miss Margaretta Brown (Eton MS 421)
Memoirs of Oswald Augustus Smith (part transcript)

Printed Sources

Austen-Leigh, R.A. *Eton Guide*, (6th edn, rev. Richard Martineau, 1964)
—— *Eton College Lists 1678–1790.* (1907)
—— *Eton College Register 1698–1752.* (1927)
—— *Eton College Register 1753–1790.* (1921)
Ballance, Selina. *A Town called Eton.* (1982)
Benson, A.C. *Fasti Etonenses.* (1899)
Birley, Sir Robert. *The History of College Library.* (1970)
—— 'Vostre Royal College et Devote Place de Eton', 'The Ever-Memorable John Hales' and 'Robert Boyle at Eton'. (Repr. in B. Rees, ed., *History and Idealism*, 1990)
[Blake, H.J.C.]. *Reminiscences of Eton* by an Etonian. (1831)
Blakman, John. *Henry the Sixth.* (Trans. by M.R. James, 1919)
Brinsley Richards, James. *Seven Years at Eton.* (1883)
Browning, Oscar. *Memories of Sixty Years at Eton, Cambridge and Elsewhere.* (1910)
Byrne, L.S.R. and Churchill E.L. *The Eton Book of the River.* (1935)
Chandos, John. *Boys Together.* (1984)
[Coleridge, A.D.]. *Eton in the Forties by an Old Colleger.* (1898)
[Collins, W.L.]. *Etoniana Ancient and Modern* by WLC. (1865)
Connor, Louisa M. *William Evans of Eton.* (1998)
Creasy, Sir Edward. *Some Account of the Foundation of Eton College and of the Past and Present Condition of the School.* (1848)
Cust, Lionel. *A History of Eton College.* (1899)
Doyle, Sir F.M. *Reminiscences and Opinions.* (1886)

Etoniana. 131 numbers irregularly issued between 1904 and 1975, ed. R.A. Austen-Leigh, R.C. Martineau and T.P. Connor. (ETA)

Firth, J.D'E. *Winchester College.* (1936)

Gambier Parry, Ernest. *Annals of an Eton House.* (1907)

Gaskell, James Milnes. *An Eton Boy.* (Ed. Charles Milnes Gaskell, 1939)

Gladstone, William Ewart. *Diaries,* vol 1. (Ed. M.R.D. Foot, 1968)

Griffiths, R.A. *The Reign of King Henry VI.* (1981)

Hexter, J.N. 'The Education of the Aristocracy in the Renaissance', in *Reappraisals in History.* (1961)

Hollis, Christopher. *Eton.* (1960)

Horman, William. *Vulgaria.* (1530)

Mack, Edward C. *Public Schools and British Opinion 1780–1860.* (1938)

Martindale, A.N.R. *The Early History of the Choir of Eton College Chapel.* (1971)

Maxwell-Lyte, Sir Henry. *History of Eton College.* (4th edn, 1910)

Melvin, John. *Eton Observed.* (1998)

Newsome, David. *Godliness and Good Learning.* (1961)

Ollard, Richard. *An English Education.* (1982)

Orme, N. *English Schools in the Middle Ages* (1989)

—— 'Schoolmasters 1307–1509', in *Profession, Vocation and Culture in Later Medieval England.* (Essays dedicated to A.R. Myers, 1982)

Saltmarsh, John. *King's College.* (1958)

—— *King Henry VI and the Royal Foundations.* (1972)

Sargeaunt, John. *Annals of Westminster School.* (1899)

Simon, Joan. *Education and Society in Tudor England.* (1979)

Stapylton, H.E.C. *Early School Lists (1791–1877).* (1884)

Sterry, Sir Wasey. *Annals of Eton College.* (1898)

—— *The Eton College Register (1441–1698).* (1943)

Thackeray, F. St. J. *Memoir of Dr Hawtrey.* (1896)

[Tucker, W.H.]. *Eton of Old; or Eighty Years Since 1811–1822* by an Old Colleger. (1892)

Tyerman, Christopher. *A History of Harrow School.* (2000)

Watts, John. *King Henry VI and the Politics of Kingship.* (1996)

Wilkinson, C.A. *Reminiscenses of Eton (in Keate's Time).* (1888)

Willis, R. and Clark, J.W. *The Architectural History of the University of Cambridge.* (1886)

Wolffe, B.P. *Henry VI.* (1981)

Ziegler, Philip. *Melbourne: A Biography of William Lamb, Second Viscount Melbourne.* (1976)

Unpublished Secondary Sources

Clark, James G. Eton College MS 300. (2000)

Dexter, Keri. The Provision of Choral Music at St George's Chapel, Windsor Castle and Eton College c1640–1733. (2000)

Selway, K.F. The Role of Eton College and King's College, Cambridge in the Polity of the Lancastrian Monarchy. (1993)

Williamson, M. The Eton Choir Book: its institutional and historical background. (1995)

Index

Index